T0366381

THE FIRE OF THE JAGUAR

HAU
BOOKS

www.haubooks.com

THE FIRE OF THE JAGUAR

Terence Turner

Edited by Jane Fajans

Hau Books
Chicago

Cover, © 1927, A. E. Brehm's *Jagoear (Felix onza)*.

Foreword, © 2017 Hau Books and David Graeber
Introduction, © 2017 Hau Books and Jane Fajans

Cover and layout design: Sheehan Moore

Typesetting: Prepress Plus (www.prepressplus.in)

ISBN: 978-0-9973675-4-6
LCCN: 2017944968

Hau Books
Chicago Distribution Center
11030 S. Langley
Chicago, IL 60628
www.haubooks.com

Hau Books is printed, marketed, and distributed by The University of Chicago Press.
www.press.uchicago.edu

Printed in the United States of America on acid-free paper.

This volume received a Norm and Sibby Whitten SALSA Publication Subvention Award for Anthropological Monographs on Lowland South America as well as a subvention from the Hull Memorial Publication Fund of Cornell University.

Table of Contents

List of figures and tables

Or why myth matters

JANE FAJANS

One of the most influential papers I read in my first year of graduate school in anthropology was Terry Turner's interpretation of the Oedipus Myth (Turner 1969). It was a masterful reanalysis of what was already an iconic subject in the structural analysis of myth (cf. Levi-Strauss 1963: 206–231). Shortly after that academic introduction, I met Terry at a conference on Symbolic Anthropology at Stanford University. I could say that it was love at first sight and that "the rest was history," but life sometimes takes a bit longer to acknowledge its inevitabilities. What I can say is that my meeting with him inspired me to get to know his broader work, and I vividly remember reading his papers "The Fire of the Jaguar" (see Part I, this volume) and "Transformation, Hierarchy, and Transcendence in Ritual" (Turner 1977) (which was initially entitled "Groping for the Elephant"). Although the latter, like many of Terry's other papers, was eventually published, "The Fire of the Jaguar" languished on his desk, unpublished. Yet, in spite of existing only in mimeographed form (remember those?), it became widely circulated among his students and colleagues. These informal distribution networks steadily expanded, but Terry was never ready to let go of this work or acknowledge it as final. Originally intended as a book, he continued to tinker with it intermittently over the course of the next forty-five years. This is not the only manuscript he neglected to publish; his file cabinet sits full of them. In fact, I've been known to say that Terry only relinquished his texts when he had an editor badgering him to meet a deadline. Nonetheless, he did manage to publish a large number of articles in a far wider array of publication venues than most anthropologists publish in, including not just peer-reviewed anthropology journals and edited volumes, but also forums for the general public. A partial list of his publications appeared in 2006 (Turner 2006), and some other works are included here (see "Referenced cited"), but Terry never did pull all of his works together into a single bibliography. Many other articles, however, remained in draft form, often virtually ready for publication. Such was the fate of some of the previously unpublished papers in this volume. Since Terry is no longer around to continue his tinkering or otherwise hinder their publication, I have embarked on the task of ensuring that many of these papers move from mimeo to published form, in no small part due to the badgering of HAU editor, Giovanni da Col, for which I'm immensely grateful.

In my mind, "The Fire of the Jaguar: The Origin of Cooking Fire" always topped the list of Terry's works to publish. In this volume, we have paired this essay with several other analyses of Kayapo ritual, social life, cosmology, and socialization practices that combine to give a rich picture of Kayapo life. In Terry's analytical perspective, ritual, social organization, politics, and personhood were all intricately intertwined with daily life and social continuity. These papers illustrate how the essence of personhood is produced through kinship relations, ritual attributes, and the embodiment of cosmological principles. They endeavor to show how the activities of daily and ritual life are intrinsically intertwined and how the different aspects of these processes play out in individual and communal practices. The different foci of the articles look at these processes through the lens of particular contexts and events, but each necessarily refers to descriptions and analyses presented elsewhere throughout the book. Cumulatively, these descriptions illustrate the layers of embeddedness that build persons and community, culture and history within these particular contexts and, in Terry's view, well beyond.

Terry recorded the myth recounted in "The Fire of the Jaguar" while living among the Kayapo, a tribe scattered across a large territory in the states of Pará and northern Mato Grosso in the Brazilian Amazon. He began his field work with this group in 1962 and continued to return almost annually over the next fifty-two years and visiting most, if not all, of their communities. He heard and documented the fire myth in many of the villages he visited over several decades,

told mostly around the household fire as a bedtime story. Its popular evening re-
tellings persisted, even as significant social and cultural changes triggered by the
arrival of boom boxes, videos, and television transformed traditional routines.
Over the decades that Terry continued to return to these villages, he was able
to experience and document many such changes and continuities in Kayapo life
using written, audio, and visual mediums. He served as the anthropological con-
sultant for six British documentary films about the Kayapo, but a turning point
came when he set up the Kayapo Video Project in 1990, providing significant
guidance, financial support, and travel opportunities for the Kayapo to make
their own films to document their culture and experiences on their own terms.
He was intrigued by what he learned by observing and discussing the Kayapo
filmmakers' documentary approaches, and he studied everything from their subject selection to their filming methods and editing styles (Turner 1991b, 1992).
Video became an important part of the way that the Kayapo produced, documented, and defended their lifestyle and territory, both for internal community
use as well as for external communications to broadcast their struggles to the
international community.

Terry did all he could to facilitate this work and took great joy from the
Kayapo's savvy emergence as powerful ambassadors for indigenous and environmental causes on the international stage. This was one way in which he became
increasingly involved with the Kayapo's ongoing struggle to defend their territory, and thereby their communities, from incursions by gold miners, loggers,
cattle ranchers, soy farmers, and unsustainable infrastructure projects like mega-
dams on the Xingu River. As part of this work, he also encouraged, collaborated
with, and wrote about the Kayapo's younger generation as it prepared to step
into new leadership roles at pivotal moments in the tribe's history. He supported the Kayapo's own nongovernmental organization, the *Instituto Raoni*,[1] and
worked with other organizations that stepped in to help indigenous struggles in
the Amazon and elsewhere.

Although Terry visited many Kayapo villages multiple times, he formed a
deep and lasting relationship with the community of Mentuktire, the home
of Chief Ropni. Terry and Ropni's relationship spanned decades; they became
acquainted as young men in their midtwenties and grew old together. During

---

1. Chief Ropni is commonly known as Chief Raoni, the name he has come to use in
   international circles. Terry continued to call and refer to him as Ropni, given it is
   the name he uses in his village. For that reason, I refer to him as Ropni here.

Terry's last trip to Mentuktire in 2014, he and Ropni spent many quiet moments reflecting on the time they had spent together, the changes they had
witnessed, and the continuities that nevertheless persisted.

I accompanied Terry to Mentuktire on his last trip, which coincided with a
multiday, village-wide performance of the Kayapo's *Ta Kut* naming ceremony.
As an anthropologist who does not work in Amazonia or speak Kayapo but has
read what Terry has written about them, I felt a strange familiarity with the *Ta
Kut* rituals being performed in front of me and appreciated the significance of
the relationships and values it created. Believing that this might be Terry's last
trip to the field (it was), our group included family members, a journalist and
former student of Terry's, a photographer and videographer, and select friends.[2]
However, we were not the only spectators of this ritual: in addition, several other non-Kayapo had been invited by the world-traveling Ropni to witness this
ceremony. None of these other guests had had the benefit of access to Terry's
teaching or writings. I felt sorry for them, as I would not have come close to
understanding the ritual without the context that Terry's insights—his life's
work—provided. Just witnessing the ceremony was not sufficient to understand
it, given how embedded its structure is in the way the Kayapo perceive and value
their social relations, as well as their relationship to the natural environment.
The ritual is not an enactment of a myth or story, but its meaning is imbued
with Kayapo notions of the world they inhabit. It references myth, social ties,
status, and values in ways not explicitly articulated, yet implicitly understood by
its participants.

As I've edited the papers in this volume, I've frequently thought about how
these papers would have benefited the outside spectators at the *Ta Kut* event.
The ceremony involves the confrontation of young children with dancers be-
decked as jaguars. The children, adorned with beads and feathers, are expected
to face the menacing approach of the jaguar-men with stoicism; they are subsequently honored for their bravery with the bestowal of "beautiful" names by
specific categories of kin, the significance of which is further explained by the
writings in this volume. Although these articles bring together Terry's many
insights on the ways that social life and ritual practices are embedded in the
Kayapo's daily routines, each one examines these topics through a different lens.
The first article focuses on a particular myth but draws on kinship, initiation,
and communal organization to explicate the myth. Another paper starts with

---

2.   The trip was generously funded by the Avatar Alliance Foundation.

cosmology but melds into a discussion of body decoration and kinship. A third article explains how asocial behavior gets interpreted through social connections built up through ritual performance. A fourth one shows how Kayapo notions of social bodiliness challenge certain poststructuralist theoretical models proposed in Amazonian analyses. Together these papers emphasize the importance of the dialectical relationships that social, cultural, and ideological beliefs play, and how each practice or belief takes on meaning in relation to the community's set of beliefs and practices while consequently shaping and evolving those encompassing beliefs. This emphasis on dialectical relations was deeply instilled in Terry's thinking about important subjects across the board from his teaching to his politics to his family engagements. In the larger corpus of his work, this same attention to the imbrication of belief and activity is a focal aspect of his analyses.

As you will read in the different articles of this volume, Terry's dedication to interpreting the beliefs and practices of the Kayapo goes beyond a commanding understanding of the stories and performances that characterize social life. He seeks to show how these activities are the fundamental building blocks of that life. Consciousness is a product of action, and action is a result of goals, desires, and beliefs. For Terry, this matrix was best embodied in Marx's notion of praxis. This perspective is why Terry spent so much time appreciating and trying to understand the Kayapo's continued valuation, performance, and perpetuation of the activities that actively constructed their unique cosmology and perspective on the world.

The example of the *Ta Kuk* event, as with so many other examples in the life we built together, highlights how Terry's observations, analyses, and insights enhanced and enriched not only my intellectual understanding of an anthropological experience but also my profound appreciation of our collective human experiment to produce—and re-produce—ourselves, our communities, and our world. The editing and publication of this book is an attempt to amplify and more broadly share some small part of those insights while providing a foundation that emanates outward into his wide range of social and cultural analyses. I believe this volume will revitalize certain anthropological perspectives and values in contemporary debates with ramifications well beyond the specific case study of the Kayapo. In addition, I hope this book, like my in-person introduction to Terry, will lead you, its readers, to seek out his writings beyond these. And if you've already read them all, then stay tuned: I intend to continue editing and publishing his archive of work that still resides in those mimeo-filled file drawers.

I have been helped in what for me has been an emotional but also ca-
thartic process of preparing these papers for publication, by many friends and
colleagues. In particular, I want to thank my (our) daughters, Vanessa Fajans-
Turner and Allison Fajans-Turner. In addition, I want to thank Catherine
Howard who was a student of Terry's and a long time reader of his work. In
addition, Catherine (Carine to her family and friends) is an Amazonianist who
has visited the Kayapó on several occasions. She has done a thoughtful and
thorough job of editing these papers and articles and they are much stronger for
her keen eye. Thank you!

At long last

David Graeber

For anyone in the Chicago anthropology department in the 1970s, '80s, and '90s, *The fire of the jaguar* holds a legendary status. I mean this in the almost literal sense: it was wondrous; it had strange and awesome powers; no one was entirely sure if it really existed. Terry refused to publish it. Or even to show it around. Yet the very fact of its hiddenness made it a kind of talisman of secret potency.

Terry had a peculiar aversion to publishing. There were rumored to be anywhere between three and half a dozen brilliant monographs in his closet, all of them effectively finished, all in a kind of permanent state of final revision.[1] There were many stories as to where this aversion to publishing came from. At Cornell—again, I am repeating the legend here—he had been a close personal friend of his namesake Victor Turner, even though in many ways the two could hardly be more different theoretically, and they had a kind of understanding that they wouldn't stray too far from one another. When the University of Chicago offered Terry a job as assistant professor in 1968, he said he'd only

---

1. I know three definitely existed: the *The fire of the jaguar*, a collection called *Critique of pure culture* contracted to Berg but endlessly delayed, and *The Kayapó of eastern Para*, a manuscript prepared for "Cedi, Povos Indigenas do Brasil, Volume VIII" of which I still have a copy of the first 56 pages—I can't for the life of me figure out what happened to the rest of it. Other rumored volumes may or may not be mythical.

come if Victor accepted his offer too; they both arrived, and Terry quickly won tenure there on the basis of what was to be his first monograph, hailed by his colleagues as a brilliant work which proposed an entirely new approach to structuralism and the interpretation of myth. This was *The fire of the jaguar*, and the book had already been accepted and existed in galley form when he submitted it to tenure review. The moment he actually received tenure, he withdrew it from publication. Ever since, the story went, he had been tinkering away at perfecting it, along with anywhere from three to half a dozen other books (it varied with the narrator) he was rumored to have somewhere in his closet, all of them not quite ready for publication.

People used to beg him to just release the books. He always found some reason not to.

Terry's lectures were mesmerizing. He appeared to have an absolute mastery of social theory, to have read everything there was to read, and—almost uniquely among those with that kind of comprehensive knowledge—whatever the topic, also had something startling and creative to say about it. He had an uncanny ability to listen to another anthropologist deliver a ninety-minute paper, then stand up afterward and say, "That's an interesting interpretation. But you know, you could equally well see that material from another point of view . . ." and then proceed to take every single ethnographic detail the paper contained and reorganize it into a grand synthesis that seemed—and I'm pretty sure in most cases usually was—ten times more theoretically sophisticated than the presenter's own.

Needless to say, a lot of people hated him.

He was also notoriously contentious.

* * *

I used to say it sometimes seemed as if Terry had spent twenty years coming up with a theoretical synthesis that resolved all outstanding problems in social theory, and now he was going to have to spend another twenty years trying to figure out how to explain it to anyone else. At least, how to explain it in writing. I remember being quite impressed (in a horrified sort of way) when I first encountered two of his essays as an undergraduate. There were plenty of anthropologists who could write sentences I didn't understand a word of; I knew of a few who could write incomprehensible paragraphs; but here, uniquely, was one who could write entire pages where I simply had no idea what was going on at any point. Therefore, it was all the more startling when I met the man, began taking his classes, and found in person he had a remarkable ability to make the exact same (still extremely complicated) ideas sound like matter-of-fact common sense, and even to render them fairly straightforward. It was putting it on the page that seemed to be an issue. I well remember one seminar when he was explaining an idea—I think it was about polyphony—and a student asked if there was anything more on the subject she could read. "Well, I wrote a paper a few years ago," Terry said, "but to be honest, it's a little rough going. I was looking over it the other day and even I couldn't figure out half of what I was saying." Terry was occasionally accused of being "Parsonian." This is a slander: really he took only one idea from Talcott Parsons, that of a generalized symbolic medium; in almost every other respect his approach was the exact opposite. However, he does seem to have absorbed something of Parsons' impenetrable prose style.

He tried to fight it. These essays, largely unpublished in his lifetime, might be seen as the products of a struggle to render his ideas transparent. He reworked some of them again and again. He did publish quite a number of essays, some for edited volumes, others when friends took over journals and compelled him, but mainly when he felt it would make a political difference, either in Brazil, or, particularly, for the Kayapó. (Thus, from the '90s onwards, he was much better known as a writer on indigenous video activism than as a social theorist.) The majority of his most important theoretical essays were never published, but only shared with friends, students, and colleagues—including a few which acquired a legendary status in their own right, like his magnificent 1984 essay, "Value, production, and exploitation in noncapitalist societies"—and floated about, sometimes in multiple versions. At the time, it was possible to place unpublished papers on reserve as course readings at the Regenstein Library at Chicago, and there they'd remain afterward in special file cabinets until the professor found out and usually had them instantly removed and destroyed.[2] Some of us would copy them at the time; others such as myself worked in the library and knew about the file cabinets. As a result, different versions of some of Terry's unpublished theoretical interventions would sometimes circulate, often in copy-of-a-copy-of-a-copy form, invariably with handwritten headers by the author saying

---

2.   I once got my hands briefly on a draft of Marshall Sahlins' "Peloponnesian and Polynesian Wars" book this way, but the manuscript was so enormous that my library wages were not adequate for me to be able to afford the costs of photocopying it all. I was already living on ramen noodles at the time there were no more corners to be cut.

things like "DRAFT: FOR GOD'S SAKE DO NOT QUOTE." Later they were pdf'd and exchanged by email. Everyone had their own collection.

These essays did have an impact on the discipline. I am speaking not just of my own work. My first published monograph (the second one I actually wrote), *Toward an anthropological theory of value*, was largely inspired by Terry's ideas and, I will now admit, was written with half an eye to coaxing him out—I thought if he saw his theories expressed in another anthropologist's words, he would immediately say something to the effect of "the fool, the fool, he got it all wrong!" and, as a result, some of the unpublished texts would actually see the light of day.

It didn't work.

His lectures and published and unpublished essays did, certainly, have a profound effect on anthropologists of many generations—one thinks here of anyone from Dominic Boyer to Michael Cepek, Jane Fajans, Jonathan Hill, David Holmberg, Nancy Munn, Fred Myers, Sasha Newell, Suzanne Oakdale, Stuart Rockefeller, Stephen Sangren, or Hylton White. (Some of them, of course, were just as much an influence on him.) But at the same time, the core concepts have really not become the common coin of the realm in the way many of us felt they should; the overwhelming majority of anthropological theorists active today, in fact, have barely heard of Terry.

* * *

The fire of the jaguar is Terry's most sustained attempt to carry out the structural analysis of a single myth. It may well be the most sustained and detailed analysis of a single myth that any anthropologist has ever carried out. Obviously, any anthropologist dealing with Amazonian mythology must be at least in tacit dialogue with the work of Claude Lévi-Strauss, and, for Terry, this was very explicitly the case. To put it bluntly, Terry felt that Lévi-Strauss had set off from a brilliant set of insights on a project that could hardly be more important for social theory and then went completely off the rails.

What follows is my own take on the matter, but very much inspired by Terry's (I was, after all, his student.)

* * *

Much of Lévi-Strauss' later work can be seen as a cautionary tale of the effects of extreme hierarchical social arrangements on human thought. The French academy is structured in such a way that there is typically one man (at least, it is almost always a man) on top of the field in any given discipline. Lévi-Strauss became the king of the anthropologists[3] and, while of a modest and unassuming character personally, was entirely comfortable with this role.[4] As a result, in the second part of his career, he remained largely unchallenged by alternative perspectives, which allowed a brilliant creative mind to devote most of its intellectual life to working out the equivalent of crossword puzzles. Contrast here the startling insight of his early essays with the four massive volumes of *Mythologiques*. While the latter has proved a delight to fellow Amazonianists, other scholars have labored in vain to find a point in them. By detaching myths from social life and rendering them into a series of formal elements, he could rearrange those elements in an endless variety of fascinating patterns, but did anyone learn a single thing of interest to humanity by the process of doing so? Mainly we learned that there was a very powerful French professor who claimed to despise the cult of individualism and creativity, but demanded an individual monopoly of all creative production so he could indulge the fantasy of being engaged in an ongoing dialogue with primitive philosophers on topics of interest largely to himself.

The result of this massive intellectual self-indulgence was predictable: a frenzied cult of personality and attempts to decipher the true meanings of the master's oracular pronouncements, along with the usual arguments abroad about who was the truest disciple, followed by the inevitable ritual abjuration. The entire project of structuralism was tossed out the window except insofar, of course, as its replacement ("poststructuralism") was in most important ways exactly the same thing.

I know I am being unnecessarily harsh: Lévi-Strauss was kind and encouraging to his students and can hardly be held personally responsible for either the structure of French academia, or the fate of a movement that included everyone from Jacques Lacan to Pierre Vernant or Edmund Leach. It is, rather, written out of a sense of frustration with what might have been. Terry represented an

---

3. This is why Pierre Bourdieu had to move from anthropology to sociology, as there was basically no room for another theorist, and anyway, Lévi-Strauss did not approve of the theoretical direction he was taking.

4. Terry insisted to me he'd once heard Lévi-Strauss actually say that he was entirely comfortable with an arrangement where other French anthropologists would work primarily to gather and organize data, and he would interpret it. I'm just reporting. Terry's memories were not always entirely accurate, but sometimes they were.

unrealized alternative form of anthropological structuralism that never quite
came into being. Like Lévi-Strauss an Amazonianist, he made himself in many
ways his exact structural inversion. Perhaps we can best see this by using a classic Rodney Needham-style binary table:

Claude Lévi-Strauss	Terry Turner
painfully effete	gleefully embraces manners of common man
delicate	athletic
politically conservative	politically radical
static models	dynamic models
academically all-powerful	academically marginal
endlessly prolific	never published a book

The power of the structuralist approach is that it provides a uniform set of tools
that can allow one to at least begin to put apparently disparate aspects of human
culture—kinship and social organization, myths and rituals, economics, poetics,
and so forth—on the same conceptual table, as it were, so that each can provide
insight into the other. This holism was always part of the special promise of
anthropology, and it cannot be denied that its loss would empty the discipline
of much of its raison d'être. If we *can't* say that it's impossible to understand
forms of musical improvisation on a Greek island without also understanding
the structure of their cheese making, courtship rituals, or knife fights, then we
might as well throw in the towel and just become sociologists. Since poststructuralism, as I note, actually is a form of structuralism, this has not been entirely
lost—but it has certainly been endangered in some quarters, and there has been
a noticeable tendency within the discipline to fragment back into subfields.

* * *

Lévi-Straussian structuralism never quite answered this promise—or not in the
hands of the Master himself. Lévi-Strauss did not, in fact, end up using his
techniques to compare different domains of the same social or cultural orders, to
come up with the kind of holistic analysis the Boasians, for instance, had always
dreamed of but never figured out quite how to produce—or at least he never
did so systematically. His interests lay elsewhere. Partly as a result, the structuralist project largely fizzled out, only to be replaced by a poststructuralism
that, rather than resolving any of these dilemmas, effectively abandoned them.

Poststructuralism, as the discipline knows it now, largely through the works of Deleuze and Foucault, took aim largely at the very ability to render elements comparable, to put them on the same table—or even, really, to say there was a table in the first place. To put the matter bluntly, while Deleuze, its main theoretical avatar, rejected the static models typical of classical structuralism and insisted that he was working in the dynamic, Heraclitean ontological tradition rather than the static, Parmenidean one favored by almost all analytic and most Continental philosophers, his primary philosophical project appears to have been to preserve its core insight (that objects are processes, that individuals are sets of relations . . .) while absolutely rejecting every aspect of the work of the one man most identified with it—Hegel. In the context of the French intellectual left of the late '60s, it's easy to see why Hegel would become the particular object of ire and disdain. At the time, it seemed as if all radical thought was trapped between Kojève-inspired master–slave dialectics (whether in its Lacanian or existentialist variety) or some form of slightly more or slightly less dogmatic Marxism. This had become depressing fare. And the political implications were dire.

Deleuze worked his way through almost every available alternative Heraclitean tradition, from Spinoza and Nietzsche to Bergson and (at least tacitly) Whitehead, in order to create his own anti-Hegelian synthesis. It is not at all clear, however, that he succeeded. Obviously he succeeded magnificently in setting the intellectual agenda for fellow academics in the years to come, at least in anglophone countries—most "social theorists" in the United States or the United Kingdom, for example, are familiar with the ideas of European philosophers like Spinoza, Leibniz, Bergson, and many others almost exclusively through Deleuze, and many seem unaware that Deleuze did not invent them. In fact, his political success within academia is so complete that I rather feel like writing what I am about write counts as minor heresy. But let me say it anyway.

The key objection to Hegelian dialectics in Deleuze, but increasingly on the part of almost all French thinkers who came to be identified with "'68 thought," was twofold. First of all, Hegel's emphasis on negation, or, in structuralist terms, binary opposition, was seen as denying the real complexity of the play of positive forces that constitutes natural, social, or human life. We are not really talking about subject/object, self/other, nature/culture, and so on—all this is reductionism; we are talking about degrees of pressure, gravitational fields, converging and contradictory flows of matter and energy. Second of all, the notion of subsumption, of the maintenance of the dynamic tension between any such opposition (subject/object, self/other, nature/culture, etc.) as the subordinate moment in a higher synthesis, which could then be part of a further opposition and further synthesis, was denounced as leading inexorably to authoritarian outcomes. Again, it's not surprising that, in the context of the '60s Left Bank, radical theorists should have thought this. Subsumption is a hierarchical notion, and it had been put to hierarchical uses: whether by Hegel, to posit the nation as a higher subject encompassing the various contradictions of the classes and factions that make it up, or by various communist parties, to pose themselves as the revolutionary subject. However, the question was how to ditch all this baggage and still retain the key insight, which is that subjects, or objects, are in no sense fixed substances but are really just particular perspectives on processes of action.

I know I'll likely lose some friends by saying this, but, honestly, I don't think Deleuze really pulls it off. The advantage of a dialectical approach is that it not only allows one to see what seem to be objects ("forms") as being composed, on another level, of elements in dynamic tension with one another (their "content"), but it also allows us to realize that, on a different level, those forms are themselves the dynamic content of some higher level of organization or form, and so on. We are all made up of atoms that have a constant patterned motion we know as "matter" (form), but, on another level, we are all ourselves atoms that have dynamic relations with each other that make up something even more concrete—say, a social system. And so forth.

The problem, of course, is that the result is a series of hierarchical layers, with higher and higher forms, where all contradictions would appear to be eventually subsumed and overcome. This not only has disturbing political implications, but it doesn't correspond to what life is actually like. Contradictions and tensions are not really overcome. To the contrary, the world seems rather a mess. Obviously you can look at the degree to which they do seem to be overcome and say, "Well, that's the structure," but then the word "structure" no longer tells you very much—it just means "that tiny portion of reality that seems to make some sort of sense." Alternately, you can say matters are still in the process of working themselves out. To put this in more formal language: you can posit the results as a formal logical system, but, in that case, there is some ultimate equilibrium where everything is coordinated by the highest level, which is a very conservative perspective with little explanatory power. Or you can, like Hegel in the *Phenomenology*, or Marx, see the dialectic as a historical progression, with a resolution perhaps to come in some redemptive future. Both have unfortunate political histories, and it's not surprising that, after May '68, intellectual rebels were beginning to think about how to move away from them.

Still, it seems to me, all the poststructural rejection of this logic of subsumption really ends up doing, in most cases, is to divide the static forms and the dynamic content into two camps and set them at war with one another. Myself, I just can't see this is an improvement. Certainly, in the hands of masters like Deleuze and Guattari, the results are always provocative and extremely sophisticated—so much so it allows professional academics in 2017 to propound on concepts that have been circulating for half a century and still feel they're doing something vaguely naughty. But in the final analysis, it always comes down to the same thing: whether it's the juxtaposition of open-ended, free-flowing, polymorphous "desire" versus the fixed form of the Oedipal triangle, the dynamic "war machine" versus the bureaucratic state, or rhizomes versus trees, its end result is a rather New-Agey opposition between (good) dynamic energy and (bad) constraining structures. Foucault (who disliked the way Deleuze and Guattari framed desire in *Anti-Oedipus* for this reason) tried to overcome the tendency to dichotomization by declaring that everything was power and hence dynamic, but this didn't really solve the problem, since it left him no cogent way to say power was objectionable, and anyway, the bad constraining forms still lingered in his analyses, just pushed into the background, like all those walls and guns and truncheons keeping the prisoners from fleeing the Panopticon.

* * *

Terry Turner's theoretical corpus can be read as an attempt to overcome such predicaments. To do so, he looked to a different, dialectical variation of structuralism for a way to think his way out of this dilemma. We see it as received wisdom now that structuralism means privileging the synchronic "code" over diachronic process. It resembles dialectical thought in that it sees relations as intrinsic and constituting—it's not as if there are already-existing objects that then come into relationship in one way and not another; these objects *are* the relations they have with one another—but structuralism departs from it in that it does not see the play of those relations as a dynamic process with the potential of generating higher totalities that can then themselves enter into relations with one another, and so forth. It is, as Bruno Latour (2007) was later to put it in an only slightly different context, a "flat ontology."

For a Hegelian, this would have meant structuralism was, quite literally, meaningless. Hegel once remarked that reducing everything to equations essentially means reducing everything to tautologies, since all equations can be ultimately reduced to a simple statement that $A = A$. We already know that $A = A$. If you want to say something you don't already know—that is, if you want to begin to *think*—you have to look at the degree to which terms are not self-identical and thus break out of the level where $A = A$ and generate a higher one. And Turner would entirely agree that structuralism is, in that Hegelian sense, meaningless. In fact, Lévi-Strauss would occasionally admit this too: he was not interested, he said, in questions of meaning, in the classic hermeneutic sense, where meaning is the message that some author or speaker is *trying* to convey, the intention lying behind a statement. He was interested in *langue*, not *parole*; language, not speech; and intentionality, therefore meaning, fell into the latter category. His work was to look at the elements that made meaning possible. Other people could worry themselves with trying to figure out what a given author or text was trying to say.

* * *

So Turner's project was first of all to reinsert meaning—intentional action—into the equation. Which meant to go beyond just equations. He tried to create a different structuralism, which fused together the German tradition, wherein the basic units of analysis are actions, and the insights of classical French structuralism, about working out the possible formal permutations of a set of logical terms (raw/cooked, left/right, matrilateral/patrilateral, etc.). In order to do this, he traced a different theoretical genealogy, originating in Hegel's *Logic* (rather than his *Phenomenology*), proceeding through Marx's *Capital* (more than, say, his historical or ethnographic works), and culminating in Jean Piaget's *Genetic epistemology*.

* * *

Now, the importance of Piaget here cannot be understated, so it's worthwhile to dwell on it a moment, since his presence might otherwise seem odd. Nowadays, Piaget is remembered as a theorist of child development and one who, however significant his ideas to mid–twentieth-century thought, is now considered somewhat passé, since he tended to downplay both the existence of innate structures of the mind and cultural variation. As a result, he might seem an unlikely savior for anthropological theory. For Turner, though, what was important about Piaget's work was much less the particular stages of moral or intellectual development he came up with but, rather, the way he went about it and what he thought those stages and structures in general ultimately *were*. In a way, Hegel's *Logic* and Piaget's *Genetic epistemology* are very similar books: they are both meant to demonstrate how, even if one starts from nothing else, no presuppositions whatsoever other than an acting subject confronting the universe, it would still be possible to generate all the most sophisticated categories of human thought simply by their interaction. Abstractions arise from the way that we are forced to reflect on the process of our interactions; these allow more sophisticated interactions; those more sophisticated interactions, in turn, allow more sophisticated reflections, and so forth. In the course of describing the process, Piaget manages to develop a genuinely dynamic version of structuralism. This is the model Turner adopts.

* * *

What makes Piaget's structuralism so different from the Lévi-Straussian variety is that the elements that are organized into more and more complex structures, the "content," as it were, are not ideas or objects but *actions*. We may imagine that we start with an abstract set of numerals, 1, 2, 3, and so on, and then start adding and subtracting them, but, in reality, numbers do not exist outside the process of counting, adding, subtracting, and so on. Just as no action can take place without thought, all thought is an element in some schema of action. So the materials being organized in a structure are always "operations," conscious or potentially conscious attempts to transform the world in some way. So whereas in classical structuralism, everything ultimately comes down to a tautological equation, in dynamic structuralism, even equations are really actions. A "structure," it follows, is a way a particular group of actions coordinate with one another. Hence, structures are forms of "self-regulation" or "self-organization." Nowadays, most social theorists seem to think the latter term is derived mainly from complexity and chaos theory, but, in fact, in the '60s, when Piaget was writing, it had already emerged from cybernetics, and while the principle was only beginning to be applied in the natural sciences, it was already the object of experimental applications by social scientists with training in the natural sciences, such as Gregory Bateson or Piaget himself.

Few of these experiments ended up leading to full-blown social theories, because, by the time ideas like self-organization did become dominant in the natural sciences—and they only really began to take off in the '70s—the most creative branches of anglophone social science, at least, had largely abandoned the idea that they were engaged in science of any kind at all. Social scientists had already begun to redub themselves "social theorists," drawing largely on Continental philosophers for inspiration and ignoring developments in science (which they increasingly characterized as if it were still stuck in nineteenth-century positivism, so as better to dismiss it.)

So the potential opening of the '60s was not pursued.

* * *

Self-organization sounds like the sort of notion that would be embraced enthu-siastically by radical social theorists, and there are occasional, if usually rather wistful, calls to do so. But nothing much ever seems to come of it. The main reason, I suspect, is that the notion of self-organization is inextricably bound up with notions of totality as well as of hierarchy. Both terms immediately raise the suspicions of anyone with antiauthoritarian instincts—who are, of course, pre-cisely those who would otherwise be most attracted to the notion that structures can regulate themselves.

A self-organizing structure has to be a totality with respect to its own self-organization. There may be all sorts of overlapping and contrasting totalities operative in different situations or even in the same one, but to understand something as a structure means to understand it as a whole that is larger than the sum of its parts. You can't have self-regulation without a self. But that also means a hierarchy between a higher level of "invariants" that coordinate the transformations and a lower level of the transformations themselves. Usually, it means a hierarchy of a whole series of levels in which that invariant structure becomes a mere dynamic element ("abstract content") in a larger structure, and so forth. The existence of logical hierarchies of this sort in no sense implies the existence of social hierarchies; but one reason I think left-wing scholars have avoided this kind of thinking is the assumption that on some level, one must imply the other. This idea is promulgated on the right, where conserva-tives like Louis Dumont have had remarkable success in convincing their fellow anthropologists that all conceptual systems imply the superiority of some terms (and hence some people) over others, and on the left, where "hierarchies" of any sort are often treated as equally objectionable. The two positions play off one another, with the typical result (I've seen this) a veering back and forth from a kind of extreme poststructural rejection even of spontaneous self-regulating order and a resigned acceptance that even social hierarchies (say, the elaborate administrative chains of command in contemporary universities) are probably inevitable after all.

* * *

Piaget agreed with Lévi-Strauss (who, at least in the early part of his career, also drew on scientific models) in seeing structures as, to quote Turner, "groups of transformations bounded by invariant constraints" (p. 209, this volume)—the invariants being the rules that govern the arrangement and rearrangement of the elements. But where Lévi-Strauss was content to see those rules as givens, part of the elementary structures of the human mind, Piaget, who started from action, could not. As a result, as he put it, "the idea of *structure* as a system of transformations becomes continuous with that of *construction* as continual formation" (Piaget 1970: 34, original emphasis)—the structure is always building itself, and, as soon as it seems to have reached the top, it always must necessarily create an even higher degree of coordination of which the actors cannot be entirely conscious, because it is the self-regulating mechanism that's making it possible for them to think about such questions in the first place:

> Gödel showed that the construction of a demonstrably consistent relatively rich theory requires not simply an "analysis" of its "presuppositions," but the construction of the next "higher" theory! . . . The pyramid of knowledge no longer rests on foundations but hangs by its vertex, an ideal point never reached and, more curious, constantly rising! In short, rather than envisaging human knowledge as a pyramid or building of some sort, we should think of it as a spiral the radius of whose turns increases as the spiral rises. (Piaget 1970: 34)

This is why we're not dealing with some kind of authoritarian, closed system here. Structures are always open. But critically, they are always open at the top. Even those who think they're operating at the very top of a conceptual (or social) system cannot, by definition, completely understand what they're really up to. Turner supplemented Piaget's insights in this regard with those of Soviet developmental psychologist and educational theorist Lev Vygotsky's notion of "proximal level of development"—that is, that all of us are always necessary operating on one level of sophistication higher than we can consciously explain. This is why, for instance, it is possible to speak in grammatical English sentences even if one is completely incapable of explaining the difference between a past participle and a gerund, or even never actually heard that past participles or gerunds are things that are supposed to exist. It's obvious why such approaches should be of interest to anthropologists, because, in a way, this is the key question in any cultural analysis. How do people operate with tacit codes of which they are not consciously aware? Structuralism just makes this problem explicit. Even if we are able to demonstrate that a Greek musical performance or courtship ritual is really an exact inversion of the symbolic code on display in a typical knife fight, one still has to eventually get to the question of where this code actually resides. Is it somewhere in the actors' heads, some unconscious level of the mind? Would that be an individual or collective unconscious? Is it inscribed in the architecture, as it were, so that people absorb the tacit categories and associations by which they live—hot/cold, wet/dry, high/low, male/female—simply by moving about in culturally appropriate ways through the physical environment? Or is it somehow implicit in their language?

The solution proposed in "The fire of the jaguar"—and the other essays collected in this book—is not just to see structure as emergent from action, as the forms in which action self-organizes, but to see what we call "mythic thought" as the way that the highest level of self-organization appears, as it were, from below. A very simple example might suffice. The moment one does the same thing twice—say, gives food to a child—that is, the moment one not only performs a specific action again, but does so with the understanding that it is "the same" action as one has performed before, one generates, through the repetition (of an action that, like any, has both material and mental dimensions), a kind of hierarchy, since there is a more abstract level at which those actions are both tokens of the same type. But the moment one says a different kind of repeated action is not the same—say, giving food to husband or to a rival at a competitive feast—one is generating a third level, where different types are being compared. At the same time, by defining certain types of action in this way, one is typically generating certain identities (child, husband, rival), kinds of person who typically perform or are the objects of such actions (a nurse and patient, a dishwasher, a heavy drinker, a student, and so forth). This isn't just a matter of abstract reflection, it's practical. There has to be a way of arguing about who is a heavy drinker and who isn't; who's a real husband or a real child; there have to be ceremonies for matriculation as a student or qualification as a nurse. This brings us into the domain of ritual, since, at least for the really important categories, this is how such transitions are effected. But as anthropologists have long noted, rites of passage, where one passes from one status to another ("status" here defined as a person seen as typically performing or who is allowed to perform certain kinds of action), have a peculiar quality: even if they mark the transitioning from child to adult, there is always a stage in between, where all the usual distinctions (boy/man, girl/woman, alive/dead, inside/outside, freedom/authority) seem to be thrown into complete disarray, all social rules suspended . . . For Victor Turner, this was a moment of "antistructure." For Terry Turner, in contrast, it is "metastructure"—this is simply what the proximal level of development, that level which we can never completely understand (at least, without creating a new level which we also won't be able to completely understand), will always look like. The effect is the same as it would be if two-dimensional creatures were staring at a three-dimensional object; some aspects will simply not make sense. But in this case, even if they could enter into a 3D world, they would be immediately confronted by the fourth-dimensional objects that had allowed them to do so, and so on . . .

This is exactly why myths (such as the fire of the jaguar) so often deal with origins of social institutions. It is easy to understand arranging a marriage or conducting a wedding ceremony as simply something people do. These are human actions that the people involved chose to do the way they did and could have decided to do otherwise. But in arranging marriages in the same way over and over, those same people are also continually re-creating the *institution* of marriage—which, after all, only really exists as the form of those actions' self-regulation. Yet once again, it is almost impossible to keep track of this level of social reality—and, of course, the authoritative effect of the ritual largely depends on the fact that we generally don't. This is why institutions like marriage, chiefship, or the culinary arts are typically said to originate from creative acts not now, but in a one-time mythic past, what Mircea Eliade referred to as the *illo tempore*, a time of creation characterized by an apparently random kaleidoscopic collection of subject/object inversions, talking animals, and strange powers, in which the social and natural laws we know today appear to have been almost entirely suspended. This is, again, what the ever-disappearing top of the pyramid looks like from below.

* * *

The essays collected here are all in one way or another about myth, and one can see them as Turner's unique effort to come up with a radical—in the sense of politically left-wing—theory of mythology. It is interesting to reflect on the fact that, as academic subjects go, the study of myth has been overwhelmingly dominated by conservatives. The great triumvirate that dominated theory about myth in the mid– to late–twentieth century, C. G. Jung, Mircea Eliade, and Joseph Campbell, all considered themselves right of center in one way or another: Jung was a Burkean; Campbell considered himself a free-market libertarian; and about Eliade, who was a member of the Iron Guard in his youth, probably the less said the better. Georges Dumézil was close to the Nazi party, and the only left-wing theorist who fully embraced the power of myth as a means of revolutionary struggle, Georges Sorel, ended his life an admirer of Mussolini. Lévi-Strauss was an "apolitical" conservative pessimist. There are a handful of exceptions, from feminists like Jane Harrison, to antifascists like Karl Kerenyi, to leftist structuralists like Jean-Pierre Vernant and Pierre Vidal-Naquet, but, from the days of William Blake and Percy Bysshe and Mary Shelley to those of Robert Graves, left-wingers entranced by the power of myth have been far more likely to put their hands to creating new myths than interpreting old ones.

I suspect there are good reasons for this. If left-wing thought, whether in its romantic or Marxist variants, has always been a celebration of creativity, then myth poses it a problem. Mythic thought is endlessly creative. The corpus of world mythology is essentially a vast compendium of human creativity. Yet most myth consists of elaborate arguments why we latter-day humans can no longer be genuinely creative. The great foundational gestures were all performed in the misty past; in these lesser days, we are no longer capable of anything truly new. Myth, then, is creativity turned against itself. To celebrate myth as the deep structure of human society or human thought is to say that all the important things have already been established: all heroic narratives, all ways of conceiving gender relations, all conceptions of authority, all are already given, and even history, as Eliade so famously argued, should be conceived as an eternal return of the same archetypal gestures and characters. Obviously it's possible to avoid this conclusion: to see myth instead as, for instance, ideology, or, in a more positive light, as a well of self-denying creativity that can and should be drawn on to

continually revolutionize society. But it's unsurprising that few of those drawn
to dedicate their lives to the study of myth have embraced such an approach.

* * *

Terry Turner's basic question, then, with regard to myth was: Why have so many
human societies embraced such conservative conclusions? Certainly this was
true of the Kayapó. As Turner writes in "The fire of the jaguar":

> The question becomes this: why should the Kayapó regard the very power to cre-
> ate and maintain their social order . . . as itself, in origin and essence, an asocial
> ("natural") power? The answer is that they do not regard the structure of society
> itself as within their power to change, or, therefore, within their power to create.
> It follows that the basic forms, that is, the basic transformative mechanisms upon
> which their society rests, must derive from an extrasocial source. (p. 30, this volume)

Hence his embrace of Marx and the fundamental insight—one seen nowadays
as so intrinsically suspicious by poststructuralists—that there is a necessary link
between humans' misunderstanding of the process of their own creativity and
forms of authority and exploitation.

The great moral danger of any such approach is (as Bruno Latour, for instance,
emphasized) condescension: Are we really prepared to say that the people we
study are fundamentally wrong about the workings of their society and that we
know better? This sounds like a very serious charge until we consider that, by doing so, we are really just reducing the Kayapó (or whatever group we are analyzing)
to the same status as our professional colleagues, whom we accuse of being fundamentally wrong about the workings of society all the time. Turner would no
doubt add: while Kayapó folk understandings of their own society are in many
ways more sophisticated than those of most social scientists (certainly, than most
structuralists), they're not social scientists, have no interest in becoming social scientists, and Kayapó social order is in no sense an attempt to resolve intellectual
problems. (As Terry notes, when he attempted to outline some of the interpretations developed in this book to Kayapó friends, their main reaction was not disagreement, but indifference. They simply didn't find such questions interesting.)

Finally, there is a degree—already noted—to which such questions can never really be answered anyway.

* * *

This might seem somewhat contradictory: How can one both say that myth is the product of an intellectual puzzle and, simultaneously, that it is not an attempt to solve that puzzle? What, for Turner, are myths actually about? Here, at least, he is considerate enough to spell the matter out:

> ... the basic notion of the function of myth put forward in this study [is] that of directly connecting the "subjectivity" of the social actor with the objective structure of the socioeconomic system to which he or she belongs. (p. 146, this volume)

"Subjectivity" here is meant in the literal sense: it is about the formation of the subject, as an entity disposed to act and capable of acting in a certain way. Myths provide those who hear, learn, and retell them not only with tacit models for how to act but, even more, with a tacit guide to how to feel about the process by which we do so, with all its attendant dilemmas, tensions, and contradictions, what it is justifiable to fear and to desire.

This focus not just on the intellectual but also on the "affective" dimension, on "patterns of feeling and motivation," is, of course, extremely unusual for the structural analysis of myth. Most of those who study myths would never be able to attempt such an analysis, except perhaps speculatively, since they deal with stories told long ago or far away, often in languages no one has spoken for centuries. We would have little way of knowing if there were certain incidents in the story of Inanna and Dumuzi, or the Labors of Hercules, that Babylonian or Greek audiences considered particularly amusing or terrifying. The response is to create forms of mythic analysis where such questions don't really matter. Terry's many decades of fieldwork, in contrast, meant that he had heard the same stories over and over from different narrators and, as a result, knew exactly what parts were supposed to be funny, which scary, as well as what was idiosyncratic in any given performance and what essential to the narrative itself. This in turns allows him to read myths in their social context as oriented to shaping desires and sensibilities in a way that more intellectualist readings simply can't.

Here, too, Terry saw himself as positioning himself in much the same way as did Marx: as synthesizing the best of the French and German traditions. Marx admired French Enlightenment thinkers because they understood one had to see humans as existing in the material world and meeting material challenges; however, since they started by basically plunking down a collection of purposeless humans fully grown into a world of objects, they ended up seeing them as simply reacting, Marvin Harris-like, to material conditions. German Hegelian philosophy started from action and therefore understood humans as creating themselves through their projects: objects were by definition objects *of* action, even when that action was mere contemplation. This was much better, Marx believed. The problem is that German philosophers tended to forget there even was a material universe. Terry entirely agreed with this assessment. He just carried the same work of synthesis over into the analysis of myth, where his project was to combine a static French theory of signification (Lévi-Straussian structuralism), which admitted it had nothing to say about meaning, with a dynamic German theory of meaning (Schleiermachian hermeneutics), which saw texts as intentional forms of action. In the latter, the meaning of a text was what an author was *trying* to say.

For this reason, the analysis of "The fire of the jaguar" proceeds on two levels simultaneously: it deals first with structure, the "formal aspects of the logical relations among [a myth's] symbolic elements"—the level with which all structural analysis necessarily deals—and second, with its subjective meaning to the actors, "the type of message it conveys" (p. 4, this volume). On the one hand, a myth "lay[s] down a pattern of action." On the other, it is about "knowing and experiencing and deeply feeling that structure of social relations" (p. 146, this volume), which said pattern of action creates. The power of myth, however, does not lie in either one of these two levels. The power of myth lies in the implicit proposition that they are both the same. Ultimately, the meaning *is* the structure. The structure is the meaning. The inevitable becomes desirable. Hence inevitable.

* * *

To demonstrate how this can be the case and what it means in practice, Terry develops his own unique theory of narrative. It bears little resemblance to narratology as it currently exists and, to my mind at least, is far more promising than anything the semiologists have yet managed to come up with. His approach was first outlined in a piece in the classical journal *Arethusa*, published in 1977, called "Narrative structure and mythopoesis," which argues that the plots of stories can themselves be seen as self-organizing structures. Ostensibly, it does so through a reanalysis of the Oedipus myth. Unfortunately, the piece is so long and presented in such an obscure style that it seems to have left most classical scholars scratching their heads, was missed completely by anthropologists, and nowadays has been almost completely forgotten.

Still, it's an important essay, if only for the reason that it introduces Terry's notion of the minimal episodic unit. This notion of an elementary structural unit actually is key to Turnerian structuralism (if we can call it that) more generally. To understand any structure, Terry held—whether a poem or story, or a social system—one must first identify what he sometimes called, in typically ungainly fashion, its "minimal modular unit" of structure, the smallest unit that nonetheless contained within itself all the key relations operative within the larger whole. In the case of a narrative, mythic or otherwise, this minimal unit is the episode. Each episode that makes up a story is organized around an action or set of actions. A plot is, after all, as Aristotle insisted, "an imitation of action," the episodes that make up a plot, its minimal units, are each in each case acts in which characters change something (the world, themselves, their social relations with other characters—usually all three at the same time). It's only over the course of the story that it becomes clear that each episode shares a common structure, which also becomes the principle that regulates the relation of the episodes to each other.

To illustrate, Terry took the Oedipus story, so famously reinterpreted by Lévi-Strauss as a meditation on the relations of eyes and feet, and applied a model of triangular structures inspired by Roman Jakobson's phonemics, defined by reciprocal transformations of its elements. (This is the same triangular model that reappears in this book.) There are always two key axes, and in every case, one change along one of them will trigger a complementary transformation of some kind: that is, the old king dies, his warrior usurps the throne. With the first episode, the key relevant features (foreign/indigenous, loyalty/ ambition, etc.) might not be entirely apparent, but the moment there is a second episode and other transformations along the same axes recur, then the very comparison that allows them to be seen as similar necessarily generates a higher level of structure, which becomes a "general principle or force responsible for creating the common pattern it manifests" (1977: 142). To put it more simply, each episode marks an action that changes the overall situation, but, as the story continues, a common pattern in those changes emerges, and that emergent pattern becomes the governing principle—or, as Terry once puts it, "cosmic demiurge"—that generates the plot as a whole. So, just as each episode contains a complementary transformation, so does the story as a whole: that is, the narrative begins with Oedipus as an infant, having pins stuck through his feet, and ends with him as an old man, sticking pins in his own eyes. It is similar, in a way, to the hermeneutic circle, where one reads each episode in a work of fiction as a way of understanding how they together form an overall totality, that totality being seen as identical with the intention of the author—the meaning of *Hamlet*, that which binds all the episodes together, is assumed to be what Shakespeare is "trying" to say. ("Shakespeare," in this sort of analysis, is not even really a person, but also a demiurge; the author is just conceived as that unifying intentionality.) In a myth, however, there is no single author, even as an abstraction. The story writes itself.

True, the audience doesn't typically notice this, instead following the apparent back and forth of episodes with apparently contradictory messages as the plot weaves between them, but it's the emergence of this "demiurgic" power of self-regulation that allows the reader to feel that a satisfying story has been told. And doing so allows the audience to not just think through, but feel through, the quandaries and contradictions of family life—in each case (the fire of jaguar, the Oedipus myth) in a way sufficiently compelling that the story has been repeated for thousands of years.

* * *

Some stories endure. Most theories tend to be a lot more ephemeral. I hope this book will prove an exception.

The fire of the jaguar should, in my opinion, be considered one of the great achievements of anthropological theory. It deserves a place among the classics. It was a book that had the potential of opening doors that no one has been able to walk through, since the doors were dangled in front of us only *in potentia*, like the kind of shimmering dimensional doors one might see in a science-fiction story, always lingering ghost-like above our heads. One such door has now materialized. Will anyone now choose to pass through it? Has it materialized too late? Does anyone even now care about the possibility of a truly dynamic structuralism?

Well, pendulums do swing. It's possible that the current adamant hostility to the Lévi-Straussian project, the rejection of any dream of reconciling advances in scientific understanding with social understanding, might be showing signs of giving way. Perhaps the belated appearance of *The fire of the jaguar* will encourage anthropologists to think about such big questions once again.

REFERENCES CITED

Latour, Bruno. 2007. *Reassembling the social*. Oxford: Clarendon.

Piaget, Jean. 1970. *Structuralism*. Translated and edited by Chaninah Maschler. New York: Basic Books.

Turner, Terence S. 1977. "Narrative structure and mythopoiesis: A critique and reformulation of structuralist concepts of myth narrative and poetics." *Arethusa* 10 (11): 103–64.

PART ONE

The fire of the jaguar
The Kayapo myth of the origin of cooking fire

CHAPTER ONE

General problems and methodological issues

SOME GENERAL PROBLEMS OF THE STRUCTURALIST APPROACH

Over fifty years ago, Claude Lévi-Strauss revived interest in myth analysis and other symbolic phenomena such as ritual and cosmological systems in his four-volume opus, *Mythologiques*. Among the more general and important of these questions are:

1. What are the formal properties of the structure of myth?
2. What kinds of meanings do myths encode, and precisely how do they convey them?
3. What relations exist between the structure and message of myth, on the one hand, and, on the other, the social and cultural milieu within which the myths are created and told?

In the following pages, I try to suggest some new answers to these general questions through an intensive structural analysis of a single myth, together with a thorough examination of the pertinent aspects of its social and cultural context. Briefly, I attempt to develop a new conception of myth structure as a hierarchically organized system of transformations of a single set of symbolic oppositions that recurs as the basis for each successive episode of the narrative. This model, as I will show, is able to give an account of the narrative or temporal dimension of myth and the type of message it conveys, as well as giving proper weight to the nontemporal, paradigmatic aspects of myth structure, as stressed by Lévi-Strauss and many other structuralist analysts. The following analysis is not merely a formal structural analysis, since it takes into account relevant aspects of the culture and social system of the tribe from which the myth is taken. Cumulatively, these analyses show that the generative structure of the myth revealed by my analysis is isomorphic and homologous with certain key generative processes in the social and cultural domains to which the myth symbolically refers. The emphasis of my analysis in this respect is that the structures of myths as wholes are metaphors and thus have a referential aspect. Myths, in other words, are not context-free at the level of structure, nor are they attached to their sociocultural and environmental settings only at the level of the content of their elements, as Lévi-Strauss seems to suggest at many points in the *Mythologiques* (Lévi-Strauss 1969b, 1973, 1979, 1981).

As structures that generate meaning across a range of levels, myths are modeled on and, in turn, reproduce these social, cultural, and ecological patterns. Myths reflect, in other words, not only static aspects of the social and cultural world (e.g., classifications, moiety systems, and so on) but the processes through which these aspects are produced or maintained (or, as the case may be, transformed or destroyed).

As a corollary, this hypothesis has an important point concerning the nature of the meaning or "message" of myths. As models of generative social or cultural processes, myths in a sense "reflect" certain objective aspects of society and culture. They only do so, however, from the perspective defined by the social and cultural rules for generating or reproducing those aspects. This perspective is also, of necessity, that of the category or categories of social actors, that is, collectively defined "subjects," who carry out the productive processes to which the rules apply. This study therefore does not offer a detached bird's-eye view of the social and lived patterns. The most significant way in which it differs from a structural analysis is that it will show how the myth operates on two levels. On the first level, the myth describes the origin of fire and thus of society, as it is known by the tellers. On the second, it describes the cultural patterns of subjectivity—the standardized orientations of categories of social actors—as well as the objective aspects of the social and material environment. These two levels of meaning are, in fact, inseparable in myth: each is stated through, and as the implicit corollary of, the other. Although myths invariably encode both of these levels as the structural corollaries of one another, structuralist analysis, up to now, has dealt almost exclusively with the former and ignored the latter. One result of this is that it has failed to develop a satisfactory interpretation of the cultural meanings of myths—that is, of the meanings myths have to those who actually tell and listen to them. Another result is that it has failed to develop an adequate concept of structure. This paper represents an attempt to redress this imbalance.

Having said this, I should like to declare what would in any case swiftly become clear: my great debt to Lévi-Strauss. The analysis I shall present differs sharply, both on points of concrete detail and on questions of a general theoretical nature, from Lévi-Strauss' own. It should be emphasized, nevertheless, that my analysis bears out Lévi-Strauss on several important points. Most importantly, I should never have conceived this study, nor carried it out in the same way, had it not been for Lévi-Strauss' work on the structure of myth and what he playfully called "savage" thinking.

METHODOLOGICAL ISSUES

The structuralist analysis of myth has increasingly come to be identified with the proposition that the structure of a myth can only be understood by treating it in relation to a group of related myths, of which it can be considered a variant or permutation. It seems to me, however, that this approach to myth has suffered from its failure to push the analysis of individual myths to the point where it could provide a comprehensive account of their structurally and semantically significant features. Because of this failure, it has continued to deal with structures that can be found *in* myths rather than, strictly speaking, the structures *of* myths: the two things are not necessarily the same or indeed even closely related.

By declining to accept the constraint of providing a comprehensive account of its own subject matter and, in fact, by ignoring significant aspects of both structure and content (notably, the narrative or temporal dimension of structure and many other symbolic elements of myth texts), structuralist analysis has, in effect, shirked the task of developing a satisfactory model of myth structure, either at the level of the structure of particular myths or the general level of the common properties of myth structure.

It goes without saying that, until more adequate models of myth structure can be developed, the comparative structural analysis of myth, especially on the grand scale of *Mythologiques*, suggestive and illuminating as it unquestionably is, must prove far less fruitful than it might otherwise be. Comparative analysis, especially the controlled comparison of variants of the same myth from a closely related group of societies can, to be sure, serve as an invaluable concomitant to the analysis of the structure and meaning of an individual myth variant. Detailed comparisons make it possible to distinguish between various levels of common and idiosyncratic features, which can then potentially be associated with correspondingly common or unique features of the social, cultural, or environmental context of the myth. The analysis I present in this paper makes use of other Gê and Bororo variants of the same story as a controlled comparative context of reference. I do not, in short, mean to belittle the value, much less the validity, of comparative analysis; I simply question an approach that substitutes it for, or regards it as prior to, the comprehensive analysis of the structures of individual myths and their relations to their particular social and cultural contexts of reference.

The analysis that follows represents an attempt at such a comprehensive structural analysis of an individual myth or, more precisely, a single variant of the myth, which represents the standardized version of the story as it is told in a particular tribe, the Kayapo, a Gê-speaking group of central Brazil. By "comprehensive structural analysis," I mean specifically the analysis of all relevant aspects of a myth's structure (i.e., the formal aspects of the logical relations among its symbolic elements), the message or meaning it conveys to Kayapo listeners, and its references to its social, cultural, and environmental context, and approaching all three analytical domains at the levels of both content and form.

It would be appropriate to begin by setting out in programmatic fashion my conception of what a comprehensive analysis of a myth should include. Ideally, such an analysis should comprise the following steps:

1. Examining a sufficient number of narrations of the myth to ascertain whether there exists a consensus within the relevant cultural or social unit as to a "correct" or "standard" version of the story, what (if any) variation is accepted, and at what points; this allows us to select a standard version or range of variants of the myth to be used in the analysis;

2. Observing the myth being told in its normal setting by the usual tellers to the usual audience, in (it should go without saying) the original language,

noting all expressive features (tone, gesture, paralinguistic sounds, etc.) used by both those who tell the myth and those who listen to it;

3. Eliciting the culturally established purposes for telling myths and the culture's roles or categories for the tellers and audience of myths;

4. Providing ethnographic documentation of all relevant cultural meanings of items or relations referred to in the myth, including relevant aspects of social structure, linguistic tropes such as puns and double meanings, references to specific places or species of plants and animals, etc.;

5. Documenting the use of elements or episodes from the myth in other contexts (for instance, rituals, shamanism, subsistence practices) and considering the light these activities throw on the significance of these elements within the myth;

6. Eliciting native commentaries and exegesis on the myth, including both the explanation to the outside investigator of allusions normally taken for granted among members of the culture and therefore not included or explicated in the text of the myth as normally told, as well as any esoteric or alternate interpretations of the myth on the part of specialists, exceptional individuals, shamans, etc.;

7. Determining the myth's place in a connected cycle of myths, if such exists; if possible, collecting the culture's entire corpus of myths and assessing the relation of the myth in question and its thematic content to this corpus;

8. Analyzing the pattern of relations among the symbolic elements of the myth within the clusters, levels, and situational contexts in which they are presented in the myth as a "text" (e.g., if the myth is divided into episodes, each episode should be separately analyzed, their structures should then be analyzed in relation to each other, and so on);

9. Comparing and integrating the structure of the text of the myth (revealed by step 8) with the social, cultural, and environmental structures comprising its referential context (revealed by step 4);

10. If possible, conducting a controlled comparison of the structures of variants of the myth from related societies, considering them in relation to the analogous social, cultural, and environmental features, to determine if the sort of covariation that would be expected from the analysis of the original variant and its relations to its sociocultural context in fact occur (ideally, this comparative study should be made not after, but during and in intimate relation with the analysis of the original variant).

Although I collected in the field what I believe to be a virtually complete corpus of Kayapo myths, I have not had the opportunity to study them systematically, so I am in no position to make more than intuitive, superficial judgments as to the relation of the myth of fire to the corpus of Kayapo myth as a whole, other than to affirm that it does not form part of any cycle or connected set of myths. Nor have I conducted a controlled comparison of the Kayapo version of the myth with those told in other Gê societies or elsewhere in Amazonia. With these exceptions, I followed all of the steps listed above in the course of the present analysis.

CHAPTER TWO

The myth of the origin of cooking fire

The myth of the origin of cooking fire holds a place of unique importance in the culture of the Kayapo, a Northern Gê tribe among whom I carried out multiple stints of field research from 1962 to 2014. It is probably the most widely known and certainly one of the most commonly told of all Kayapo myths. It is also perhaps the most widespread Gê myth: it is the only myth that has variants reported from every Gê tribe so far studied. For these reasons, I collected several versions of it on my first field trip to the Kayapo (1962–1963). Lévi-Strauss' study of the myth in *The raw and the cooked* (1969b) appeared before my subsequent trips to the field, so I had numerous opportunities to check certain problematic points in his interpretation of the Kayapo variant of the myth, on which he bases much of his argument in the book. I also collected two more versions of the story during these later trips and recorded narrations of the myth on tape and video.

In all, I have collected more than a half dozen complete versions and another partial one from three different Kayapo villages. The villages in question had been separated from one another for sixty and thirty years, respectively, at the time I tape-recorded them. I was able to cross-check my recordings of the versions collected in one village by playing them for informants in the other two villages. I found that there was general consensus among all three villages as to which features were essential to the "correct" telling of the story, which features on the tapes were considered "errors," and which represented nonessential but permissible variations. A number of versions of the story have been published by other investigators in various European languages, abridged and rewritten to varying degrees (Banner 1957; Cowell 1961; Metraux 1967; Nimuendajú n.d.; Wilbert 1978; Wilbert and Simoneau 1984). The best is that collected by Nimuendajú and published in a French translation by Metraux (1967), unfortunately without crediting Nimuendajú, whose unpublished manuscript I managed to obtain (Nimuendajú, n.d.).

The Kayapo do not differentiate genres of oral narrative. The myth of the origin of cooking fire, like all their other myths, is treated by the Kayapo themselves as a story to be told to children. The most frequent setting for the telling of myths is at bedtime, when a father or older man takes it upon himself to regale some child (and, incidentally, everyone else who is trying to fall asleep in the large extended-family household) with myths and songs. That myths are primarily told to children does not imply that the Kayapo do not take them seriously. On the contrary, traditional stories form, along with ceremonies, an essential part of the collective "knowledge" (*kukrà-djà*) that Kayapo feel should be learned by every child. For the Kayapo, the telling of myths to children is, in short, a significant part of their education, that is, of their formation as fully socialized members of Kayapo society.

I attempted to elicit exegeses or interpretations of the fire myth from my informants. As in virtually every other case in which I made such attempts, this was a total failure. The very idea of "symbols," and therefore of exegesis or interpretation as well, is alien to Kayapo culture. On several trips to the field, I tried out a preliminary version of the analysis offered in this paper on a few of my best informants. I think they understood perfectly well what I was saying. They did not disagree, but neither did they agree nor did they show the slightest interest. I must therefore serve notice that the analysis I am about to present failed to cause that shock of recognition I hoped to elicit from the Kayapo or, for that matter, any other reaction beyond boredom faintly relieved by politeness.

THE MYTH ITSELF

Let me now turn to the narrative of the myth of the origin of cooking fire. For convenience of reference, I have divided the myth into sections corresponding to the major episodes. I should emphasize that this is my own division and is not based on any overt clues or other features of the story as it is ordinarily told. I have also indicated points at which tellers typically insert expressive cries and gestures.

Introduction: the initial situation

Long ago, people did not have fire; they did not cook their food. They ate honey, hearts of palm, rotten or wet wood, caterpillars, and fungi. When they killed game, they cut the meat in small pieces and set it out on rocks to warm in the sun.

The macaw episode

One day, a man was walking in the forest and saw two macaws fly out of a hole high in a rocky cliff (or in some versions, heard the chirping of young macaw chicks). He told his wife, "I will take your brother to fetch down the young macaws." The next day, the man and his wife's brother (WB) went to the nest, which was situated in the forest some distance from the village. The sister's husband (ZH) cut down a tree with his stone ax and notched it to make a ladder. He then leaned it against the cliff for his WB to climb up to the nest. The WB, meanwhile, had secretly found a stone, which he took with him on his climb up to the nest. Although there were fledgling macaws in the nest, the WB called down to his ZH, "There are only eggs in the nest." "Throw them down," commanded the ZH. The WB threw down the stone he had carried up to the nest, pretending it was an egg. The ZH attempted to catch it, but the stone broke his hand. He cried out in pain, "Ay! Ay!" grimacing and clutching his hand (the teller mimics these acts). He became furious and pulled down the ladder, marooning the WB in the nest. The WB, alarmed, cried out, "Sister's husband, there are young birds in the nest!" to no avail (the teller mimics the youth's panicked tone, terrified at the prospect of being stranded in the macaws' nest). But the ZH returned home, leaving his WB marooned in the nest.

Several days passed, and the young WB almost died of hunger and thirst. He was reduced to eating his own feces and drinking his own urine.

The jaguar episode, part one

When the WB (henceforth referred to as the "the boy") was almost dead, a jaguar passed by at the foot of the cliff. He was carrying a bow and arrows (which were unknown to humans at that time) and, on his back, a collared peccary (the smaller species of wild pig) that he had killed. The boy leaned out of the nest to get a better look at him, causing his shadow (*karon*) to fall across the jaguar's path. The jaguar pounced upon it with bestial grunts and cries (mimicked by the teller), mistaking it for a real boy. When he found nothing in his claws, he looked up and saw the boy. He retracted his claws and covered his fangs with his paw and asked, "What are you doing up there?" The boy replied, "My sister's husband took me to fetch some macaws, but I threw down a stone and broke his hand, so he got angry and threw down the ladder and left me here! I am eating my own feces and drinking my own urine!" The jaguar then asked, "Are there macaws in the nest?" "Yes" replied the boy. "Then throw them down," ordered the jaguar. The boy complied and the jaguar pounced upon the fledglings with ferocious roars and grunts (mimicked by the teller), which terrified the boy.

When he had devoured the fledglings, the jaguar again looked up, covering his teeth with his paw. "Where did your ZH throw the ladder?" he asked the boy. "Over there!" The jaguar fetched it and leaned it up against the tree again. "Climb down, I'll take you home and find you something to eat!" he cried. The boy climbed part way down, but, overcome by his terror of the jaguar, he went back up the ladder to the nest, crying out "*Hiayy! Hiayy*" (mimicked by the teller). The jaguar reassured the boy, "My son, I like you! Don't be afraid! Climb down! Climb down, and I will give you food so you can grow up big and strong and be my hunting companion." The boy, reassured, mastered his fear and climbed down and sat on the jaguar's neck. (In one of the versions I collected and in Nimuendajú's variant, the jaguar threw the collared peccary over his shoulders so the boy could sit on it rather than directly on his neck.)

The jaguar episode, part two

The jaguar carried the boy home on his back. When he arrived at his house in the forest, his jaguar wife was spinning cotton thread. When she saw them, she cried angrily, "*H! kra pram-ti-re!*" ("You, with an inordinately great desire for children!"). "Why have you brought home this ugly and thin child of someone else (*me'onlfil kra*)?" The male jaguar responded, "I always have to hunt alone, so I have brought home *a-kamrere* (the term normally used by a man to his wife to refer to their son) with me to become my hunting companion!"

In the jaguars' house, the boy ate roast meat, which the jaguar's wife cooked in earth ovens or roasted on grills above the fire (these are the ordinary methods of cooking meat among the contemporary Kayapo). The fire itself consisted of a single huge jatoba log that was kept blazing at one end.

The boy lived with the jaguars, ate much roast meat, and became strong and robust.

Before dawn one morning, the jaguar "father" left to hunt, instructing the female jaguar, "Give *kamere* (our son) meat to eat if he grows hungry." The boy, in due course, became hungry and asked the female jaguar to allow him to take some tapir meat from the *ki* (earth oven). The jaguar "mother" ordered him to take venison rather than tapir.

The boy took the tapir meat anyway and went to the far corner of the house to sit and eat it. The jaguar "mother" growled at him in a menacing tone, "*Heeeya!*" When the boy looked up at her, she glared at him, bared her fangs, and extended her claws toward him, hissing in a hoarse whisper, "*Ma ketere!*" (literally, "Do not fear!" but which the teller mimics in a terrifying tone of voice, together with the accompanying gestures and facial expression). The boy, terrified, fled from the house, crying with fear as he ran, "*Hiayy! Hiayy!*" (again mimicked by the teller). After he had run some distance from the house, he climbed a tree.

The male jaguar found him in the tree on his way home from hunting and asked him what he was doing there. The boy told him what had happened. The jaguar told him to climb down and carried him home again on his back. He remonstrated with his wife and ordered her not to repeat the incident: "Do not behave thus toward your son!" The next time the jaguar went hunting, however, the same events recurred. After bringing the boy back again to the house, the male jaguar took him outside again to the river bank to bathe. When they were well clear of the house, he told the boy, "Don't be afraid of my wife. I will make a bow and arrow for you. If my wife threatens you again, kill her with them. Shoot her right through the nipple. If you do this, we will separate. You go in that direction (pointing toward the village) and I will go in the opposite direction." In one version, the jaguar then warned his wife about the bow that he was making for the boy and the consequences of her displaying hostile behavior again.

Soon the male jaguar went hunting again, telling his wife as usual to give the boy whatever he wanted to eat if he grew hungry. Once again, the female jaguar threatened the youth when he took one kind of meat from the *ki* after she had ordered him to take another kind.

As she menacingly approached, the boy took up his bow and arrows and placed an arrow on the string. The jaguar mother screamed in terror, "Wait, don't!" but the boy shot her dead with an arrow, right through the nipple. He then shot his other arrow through her other breast.

The hero heaped the roast meat from the *ki* into a basket, grabbed the bow and arrows, some cotton spun into string, and an ember from the jatoba log and fled the house.

The return to the village

In one of the versions of the myth I collected, the boy met the male jaguar on his way back to the village. The jaguar showed him the way to his village, saying "Your people's place is over there. Don't wait around here! Go on!" In Banner's (1957) version, the boy arrived at the village after dark and could only find his mother's house with difficulty; once inside, he managed to locate his mother and sister by touch. In other versions, the boy first met his sister, who broke into passionate wailing, the kind that Kayapo use to greet kin returning from a long journey. The boy, however, found himself unable to respond to her greeting in the same vein, as would be called for by etiquette. He then sent his sister to fetch their mother. After first refusing to believe her daughter, the mother went to see her returned son. Recognizing him, she broke into the wailing salutation. However, the boy found it even more difficult this time to reciprocate in the normal fashion. All then returned to the mother's and sister's house. In Nimuendajú's (n.d.) version, the boy then showed his mother and sister all the treasures he brought from the jaguars' house (this detail was omitted from all the versions I collected).

Concluding episode

The men of the village assembled in the central plaza and called the returned youth to join them (in several versions, they sent a younger boy to his mother's house to summon him). They asked the boy to lead them back to the jaguars' hut so they could bring the fire back to the village. For this purpose, they all changed into animals when they entered the forest. In different versions, two of them, a tapir and a large deer of the savanna (*mo-ti*), were designated as the animals that ran ahead of all the others that were carrying the burning log. Other men changed into a collared peccary and a varying number of other species. Nimuendajú's version has the strongest man transforming himself into a tapir and carrying the burning log; another man became a collared peccary and carried off the cotton string; and a third changed into a deer and took the basket of roast meat. Several real animals—particular species of toad and of two types of small game birds, the guan and the tinamou—ran along swallowing all the sparks that fell from the log, thus acquiring their red throats. When the men arrived back in the village, they turned back into humans. They took the log to the men's house in the center of the plaza, where they chopped it into pieces with a stone ax. They then distributed bits of the fire to the women of all the households (in one variant, the women came with tinder to light with the fire from the log and then carried it back to their houses).

Ending: the present situation

Since that day, people have had fire for cooking. They no longer have to cut up meat into tiny pieces in order to get it barely warmed by the sun. They no longer eat foul things like fungus, rotten wood, or caterpillars. They eat cooked meat.

VARIANTS OF THE MYTH

There are some disputed points concerning Kayapo variants of this myth, which should be considered.

The summary of the myth given here conflicts in certain ways with the versions given by Cowell (1961), Banner (1957), and Nimuendajú (n.d.), one of which is crucial to Lévi-Strauss' (1969b) interpretation of the myth in *The raw and the cooked*.

Cowell refers to the roles of the two actors in the macaw episode as son-in-law and father-in-law instead of wife's brother and sister's husband. This is an error that probably resulted from the pidgin-Portuguese of Cowell's informants or, perhaps, from the close resemblance of the Kayapo terms for wife's brother (*umrê*) and wife's father (*umrê-ngêt*), and the use of the same term (*'ud juò*) for both sister's husband and daughter's husband.

Cowell presents his variant of the myth as his informant's explanation of "why the jaguar is angry," and Banner makes the anger of the jaguar at the theft of the fire and at his son's ingratitude the subject of the finale of his rendering of the myth. On the basis of the versions I collected, as well as of Nimuendajú's version, I believe that the "anger of the jaguar" theme is not an integral part of the story, although it is probably an original feature, optionally added by some tellers and not by others, rather than a point added for the benefit of European listeners. I certainly never heard the jaguar's anger mentioned as part of the myth. In Nimuendajú's and my versions, the jaguar maintains his friendly attitude toward the boy throughout the myth, assisting him to find his way home after the boy has killed the jaguar's wife and taken the meat, cotton, and fire from his house.

My versions differ from Nimuendajú's with respect to certain details of the stone-throwing incident in the macaw episode. In Nimuendajú's version, the boy finds "only round stones" (i.e., no fledgling macaws) in the nest, and these stones are what he throws down to his ZH. In my versions, the boy carries a stone with him on his climb up to the nest, which he then throws down to his ZH. Both Cowell's and my versions mention the presence of young macaws in the nest, which the boy later throws down to the jaguar. From my informants' statements, I believe that the presence of the macaw fledglings is an essential feature of the story, which was misinterpreted and erroneously omitted by the informant who was the source of Nimuendajú's variant.

Lévi-Strauss (1969b:66–67) rests his interpretation of the Gê fire myths as a group on the notion that the wife of the jaguar is a human female, given by men to the jaguar in reciprocal exchange for the fire. He bases this interpretation exclusively on Banner's version of the Kayapo variant of the myth, in which the jaguar's wife is at one point referred to as an *índia* (the Portuguese term for Indian woman). Banner's version is written in rather flowery literary Portuguese, obviously extensively rewritten from the original form in which it must have been told to him. Banner does not indicate the language of his informant or even whether the versions of the myths he presents are a single informant's version or a composite version he composed from many versions of the story. Banner's text seems, however, internally inconsistent on this point. He recounts, for example, how the female jaguar *arranhava* (Portuguese for "clawed" or "scratched" out) the eyebrows and eyelashes of the boy while threatening him. The verb seems more compatible with the behavior of a jaguar than a human female, who would have *arrancava* (yanked or plucked out) the eyelashes, which Kayapo mothers customarily do with their children (since the plucking of all facial hair is a standard part of the toilette of both sexes). Ambiguous as Banner's version may be, the more detailed versions, such as my own and Nimuendajú's, in which the jaguar wife bares her fangs and extends her claws, leave no doubt that the jaguar's wife is herself a jaguar. In all the other Gê variants reviewed by Lévi-Strauss, the female jaguar performs unambiguously jaguar-like acts, such as roaring, extending her claws, baring her fangs, growling, and the like. On textual evidence alone, therefore, it is clear that Banner's version of the story is in error on this point. It is worth noting that R. and L. Makarius (1968) reached this conclusion exclusively on the basis of a careful reading of the texts presented by Lévi-Strauss (1969b) in *The raw and the cooked*, with no additional evidence or background.

Textual evidence aside, the Kayapo themselves are quite unambiguous on the point of the jaguar identity of the jaguar's wife. I have heard the story told spontaneously and have recorded it from informants in all three of the villages in which I worked. All of the times I saw and heard the story told, the wife of the jaguar was unambiguously treated as a female jaguar. This does not ordinarily have to be specifically pointed out in the text of the story as it is told because everyone already knows it; in any case, it is made unmistakably clear by her terrifying gestures of extending her claws, baring her teeth, and growling as she threatens the boy, all of which are acted out by whomever is telling the story. The informants whom I explicitly questioned on the point uniformly insisted that the jaguar's wife is indeed a jaguar; no one had ever heard of a variant interpretation of the story in which she is a human woman.

CHAPTER THREE

The social setting of the myth

Let us first consider Kayapo social organization and how it illuminates the myth of the origin of cooking fire. The myth consists, on the face of it, of two distinct but intertwined stories. One is the story of the boy who is the hero of the myth: how he is stranded in a macaws' nest by his sister's husband, how he is rescued and nurtured by jaguars, and how he finally returns to his village as a robust young man, capable of taking his place in the mature men's association. The other is the story of the fire itself: how it was at first known only in the form of the sun in the sky, how it was discovered by the boy in the house of the jaguars, and how it was finally stolen and brought back to the village by the adult men of the community. The acquisition of fire by human society is presented as a decisive step in the differentiation of human society from "nature," inasmuch as human beings ceased eating animals' foods when they became able to cook. The boy's passage through a series of animal-like stages in which he lives with macaws and jaguars before he is effectively transformed into a man (at which point he decisively repudiates his animal attributes) seems to reflect the same notion of differentiation from a "natural" state.

The myth seems, in other words, to be pointing toward a connection between the development of the boy into a man and that of society as a whole into their present fully human condition through the acquisition of fire. More specifically, it seems to be saying that men make society by the same process through which they make themselves and that these two aspects of the process are not only causally linked but formally parallel. A fundamental feature of this process is the transformation from a relatively "natural" or animal-like state to a series of relatively more "socialized" ones. For the boy, this involves the transition from living in a macaws' nest in the forest to joining a jaguars' household (which bears many resemblances to a Kayapo family household) and, from there, joining the men's collective group in a village complete with multiple households. For the fire, the transformation involves the transition from a distant sun in the sky to a single burning log in the jaguars' house and, thereafter, being carried to the human village, where it is broken up into pieces and distributed to the various households.

Even obvious and superficial observations such as these are enough to bring home the value of grasping the nature of Kayapo family structure and village organization, as well as Kayapo notions of "nature" and "society," in order to understand the myth. In the following sections, I shall try to give a brief account of the relevant aspects of these subjects.

VILLAGE ORGANIZATION AND ECONOMY

The Kayapo are organized in relatively large, autonomous villages, with populations that currently average between 150 and 400 people. The villages are located at a considerable distance from one another (the average distance between the existing villages is well over one hundred miles). The region is rich in both agricultural and wild floral and faunal resources. The community subsists for part of the year in the permanent base village, supporting itself predominantly on the basis of swidden agriculture, supplemented by hunting, fishing, and gathering. For part of the year, however, it divides into trekking groups, which subsist primarily on the basis of hunting and gathering, supplemented by agricultural produce brought from the gardens. The social basis of these trekking groups rests on the moieties.

The bimodal economy of the Kayapo, with its alternating forms of social organization, presents both a challenge and a positive catalyst for the integration of Kayapo communities. In one sense, the two modes of production and their associated social forms, based as they are on opposite organizational principles (the concentration of the entire community in a single village, on the one hand, and its dispersion into autonomous trekking camps, on the other), are at structural cross-purposes. Opportunities for trekking are not seasonally limited, so it is possible for a community to break up into trekking groups or for any subgroup to leave the main village by itself and go off on a trek at any time of the year. In the presence of large stretches of uninhabited land, this means there is a high fissive potential in the community and a weak basis for the imposition of any form of corporate or binding structure at the level of the village as a whole. Nevertheless, the coexistence of the two modes of production and social organization within a single society may also serve as a catalyst for developing communal institutions powerful enough to coordinate and integrate both modes within the same society, as if in defiance of the fissive tendencies that permeate it.

Kayapo social structure does include, at any rate, a strongly developed system of communal institutions that serve to coordinate and integrate the disparate forms of social organization associated with the two modes of production. This is not, however, their only function: they are organized with an equal functional emphasis upon coordinating and integrating the families and households that form the lower level of the community structure. The two sets of problems are inseparable in practice, since the monogamous conjugal family unit is at once the basic unit of production of both modes of production as well as the basic unit of household and kinship structure.

The communal institutions of the Kayapo village can be seen as a "model of" the basic pattern of relations within and between families, which serves as the framework of household and kinship structure. At the same time, they constitute a template or "model for" the process of dispersing the village into hunting-and-gathering trekking bands and reintegrating them into a single village community (Geertz 1973).

At the communal level, Kayapo social structure consists of two sets of moieties, each including both sexes, which are then divided into subsections according to age and gender. Men are recruited to the junior level of each moiety through adoption by a ceremonial "substitute father," who may not be a relative of any kind, either consanguineal or affinal. They graduate to the next set when they become fathers in their own right. Similarly, women are recruited to the junior set by "substitute mothers," but they do not pass into the senior women's set until after they have ceased bearing children. These moiety associations do not, however, define groups that marry out or set up marital alliances with each other, as in some other societies studied by anthropologists.

The other level of social organization consists of the extended-family household and the bilateral kindred. These are radially focused around the conjugal or nuclear family. Residence in these households is matri-uxorilocal: that is, a man goes to live with his wife in her mother's house upon consummating his marriage with her when he fathers a child by her.

The life cycles of individual men and women as they move through successive stages of family and household relations are tightly correlated with the structure of the communal moiety institutions. Males leave their maternal homes and take up residence in the men's house upon joining the junior level of either moiety, which is called "the young men's set," at about the age of eight. They move from the men's house into their wife's house upon joining the second set (when they consummate their marriages by becoming fathers). Men of the senior set of moieties (called "fathers"), however, continue to belong to collective associations that meet in the men's houses (traditionally there were two, one associated with each moiety), but they no longer sleep in the men's house. The men's senior age set is subdivided into "fathers of few children" and "fathers of many children," while the women's senior age set is made up of "women of many children." These collective associations are the effective jural-political corporate groups of the community and, as noted above, form the basis of the trekking groups into which the village divides at least once a year. Traditionally, there were two men's houses located in the center of each Kayapo village, one for each moiety. Nowadays, there is only a single men's house, which is used by both moieties.

The moiety system thus provides an effective framework of community structure for integrating both forms of social organization associated with the two modes of production. Since the moieties themselves, or subdivisions of them, form the basis of the trekking groups, the latter become defined not as mutually autonomous and structurally equivalent segments but, rather, as components that combine to make up the social totality of the agriculture-based village.

At the same time, the moiety system regulates the dynamic process of dissolving and reconstituting families and households. It thus generates the pattern of family ties within and among households that form the level of social organization below the overarching moiety structure. The determining feature of this pattern is the relative weighting of natal ties against marital family ties: that is, how much a man's ties to his natal household and family will be severed in favor of his ties to the household and family of his wife. This general feature, however, breaks down into distinct problems of weighting specific relationships. Some of these relations relevant to the patterning of family relations in the myth will be discussed in the latter part of this section. For the moment, it may simply be asserted that the patterns by which the key family relationships are weighted for each sex are precisely reflected in the criteria used for moiety recruitment and the other concomitants of moiety membership.

The prerogative and obligations of membership in the communal men's and women's associations are adjusted so they not only replicate but also engender the pattern of the family and household cycles, including the individual life cycle insofar as it is patterned in terms of successive configurations of family relations. Taken together as a system, the communal moiety groups function as a "template" for the process of constituting and dispersing families among households. The moieties do so by virtue of their power to regulate residence and communal status in relation to particular transformations of family relations. For example, a boy's relations with his true father are severed through the "substitute" father institution, removing him from his natal family to join the men's house, then allowing him to move into his wife's household when he matriculates to the "fathers" set in the moiety.

Kayapo society is, in sum, organized as a hierarchically stratified system, which, to borrow from cybernetics, could be described as a self-regulating feedback system: the upper level, comprising the communal moiety institutions, serves as a model of, and a template for, the reproduction of the pattern of family and household structure at the lower level of community organization. This template also enables the dispersal of the community into hunting-and-gathering trekking groups (which also comprise, in relation to the village as a whole, a lower level of social organization). The relations between the levels of the system, then, are both metaphorical and dynamic: the formal parallelism between them is both an expression and a precondition of their functional (causal) relationship. This functional interrelationship takes the concrete form of transformations of family structure, transformations that become the means not only of dissolving old families and forming new ones in the normative pattern but also of recruiting and thus continually recreating the communal institutions that guide and coordinate the process.

The central emphasis of Kayapo social organization as described here, then, is not based upon static formal patterns of relations per se but, rather, upon the dynamic processes by which these forms are reproduced. The major processes involved are, moreover, intimately interconnected in a causal sense and, to a large degree, are homologous in a formal sense. The distinguishing characteristic of the Kayapo social system as a whole is that these various processes—the process of forming and dispersing the family in the course of the family cycle, the process of forming and dispersing the village in the course of the annual cycle of ecological adaptation, and the process of forming or socializing the individual through the social patterning of his or her life cycle—are dynamically interrelated and formally parallel in certain key respects. Both the functional interrelationship and the formal homology among them are derived from the fact that they are all regulated by the same set of communal institutions, each of which helps in a different way to reproduce and maintain these processes. There is thus a solid sociological basis for the myth's presentation of events—the transformation of an individual boy into a mature youth, the accompanying dispersion of his family, the departure of the men of the village as a collective trekking group to steal the jaguars' fire, their subsequent reintegration into the village, and the creation of society itself in its fully "socialized" form—as causally interlinked and formally parallel processes.

"NATURE" AND "SOCIETY"

In terms of the analytical sketch of Kayapo social organization that has just been presented, the family, as the basic unit of production, and the moiety system, as the means by which the two primary modes of production are coordinated and integrated at the communal level, represent the lower and upper frontiers of human "society" in relation to "nature" defined as the external, economically exploitable environment.

The family and the system of communal institutions also constitute the basic parameters—the upper and lower limiting terms, as it were—of society considered as a hierarchical structure of levels of organization. What they share, in an organizational sense, is viewed as "social." What lies outside of them, whether beyond, below, or above, is therefore "asocial" and in some sense "natural." Although we in Western society may have no trouble understanding that the Kayapo consider what lies "beyond" society as being "natural" (the natural world, the environment, and so on), it is more difficult for us to grasp their notion that what lies "below" or "above" the social level is also "natural." The Kayapo, however, see the three as closely related and, in fact, as aspects of the same thing. Before analyzing the myth, it is essential to come an understanding of these variant meanings of the "natural" and their relationship to the "social" in Kayapo thinking.

Let us first come to terms with the meaning of the "natural" as in some sense lying "below" the social. The means to understand this requires unraveling what may perhaps be characterized as the central paradox of Kayapo social thought. We might suppose that, for them, the family (or, more precisely, the consanguineal relations of filiation and siblingship that arise within the individual family) and the set of generalized transformations of family structure would be considered as the epitomes of "social" being. However, they are, in fact, regarded by the Kayapo as nothing of the sort. Each is regarded as either intrinsically or originally "natural." Human society, for the Kayapo, may be said to consist essentially of the operations required to "socialize" both the individual family and the transformations of family strucure, the "natural" structural bases of the social system.

Siblings, parents, and children, but not spouses (that is, close kin whose relationship arises from membership in single family), are regarded as linked to one another by bonds of physical essence of an infrasocial character. This shared essence means that physical actions by one family member, such as hard exertion or, above all, the eating of "strong" foods like meat, are thought to adversely affect the physical condition of other family members who share this essence. It is especially problematic if they are already weakened by illness. No concrete medium, such as physical contact, is necessary for the effect to be transmitted. This belief implies the proposition that intrafamily relations are basically infrasocial, based on "natural," physical connections, and that such social character as they possess is a relatively superficial and fragile veneer that is easily destroyed by overly obtrusive "natural" behavior on the part of the other family members. No relatives outside the nuclear family are thought to stand in such relations with one another.

It is significant, in view of this unbreakable bond, that personal names and other significant aspects of community status and social identity cannot be bestowed by such intimate relatives. Names, status, and social valuables can only be given by kin at least one link removed. Such kin include, in ascending generations, maternal uncles, paternal aunts, and grandparents. Each of these relations is not only a generation removed but is also sexually bifurcated (for example, mother's brother, father's sister, etc.). For a child's own parents or older siblings to confer names upon him or her would be unthinkable. Informants insisted that, in such a case, the named child would never survive to the age for beginning the initiation process, when he or she would have begun the process of leaving the natal family and passing into the public, social sphere.

The implications of these practices and beliefs are clear: intrafamily relations are essentially "natural"; by contrast, "social" relations per se begin at the frontiers of the natal family and therefore consist, minimally, of interfamily relations. This much is consistent, in a way, with our previous analysis. If the structure of society is built up out of transformations of family relations (which are invariably the products or concomitants of interfamily relations), it makes a certain sense that relations originating within a single family, being untransformed, should therefore be considered unsocialized or infrasocial. They are, in a sense, prior to society, at least in terms of their biological, sexual, and psychological foundations. These relations are the raw material, as it were, out of which society is created; on this basis, they are distinguished from society as a more integrated, finished product.

The major transformations of an individual person's social identity from child to adult are synchronized with the transformations of family structure through which families are dispersed and formed. Indeed, it would be accurate to speak of the two sets of transformations (individual and family) as different aspects or levels of the same process. It is therefore not surprising to find that the notion of the family as a "natural" group, which derives its "social" characteristics only from relations outside itself with other families or communal groups, is closely reflected in the notion of the characteristics of the individual person.

The Kayapo think of the individual human being as beginning life as a mere biological appendage of its parents, without any independent social identity of its own. The progressive stages of socialization are conceived in terms of parallel series of transformations of the "social" and "natural" aspects of the person. The "social" level of the process is conceived in terms of the inception of relationships with kinsmen, ceremonial sponsors, and collective groups representing increasingly higher levels of social complexity and, by the same token, increasing independence from the natal family. At the "natural" level, the earlier steps in the process are associated with rites stressing the progressive attenuation of the child's biological ties with its parents. The later stages are accompanied by ritual recognition of the individual's own developing biological (sexual, reproductive) powers and by the assertion of collective control over them. The progressive development of the social aspects of the person, in sum, is correlated with a parallel series of transformations of the "natural" core of the person. The two series are not only formally parallel but causally interdependent. The natural transformations uniformly have a dual character: a negative, socially regressive or disruptive aspect (e.g., the child's biological connection with its parents, concretely continued through nursing and coresidence, or the potentially uncontrolled and promiscuous character of developing sexuality) is attenuated or suppressed; correlatively, the energy associated with it is redirected into a new, more generalized, positively valued social identity or status attribute, implicitly associated with a new moral attitude or level of self-control.

It should be emphasized, nevertheless, that the person's "natural" inner core is never transformed into a "social" entity (see Turner 1980). It remains the source of his or her energy and vitality, essential for the assumption and performance of social roles, although it also remains, under some circumstances, a potential threat to them. As a source of vitality, it is variously channeled, blocked, or encouraged by social forms designed to harness it to social roles. In itself, however, such energy is beyond the power of society to create or to possess in any total sense. The person thus remains a dual being, part "natural" and part "social." In operational terms, an individual's social personality is essentially a framework for integrating the social and natural parts of the person without altering the essential characteristics of either.

Under some circumstances, the suppressed aspects of the natural core of the person can burst out and threaten the entire structure of social relations. The Kayapo spectrum of behaviors includes, for example, a form of going temporarily berserk (*aybanh*). This involves running amok with whatever weapons are at hand, attacking anyone at random, losing the power of speech (or at least coherent speech), and finally lapsing into a coma. The disorder is likened to reverting to an animal-like state and is normally said to be caused by the entrance of the hair or substance of certain animals (notably the jaguar) into the body. This etiology is typical of Kayapo notions of disease, which is frequently diagnosed as being caused by the entrance of some animal or plant substance or essence into the body. The resulting illness is conceived not merely as a physical disorder but as a partly desocialized condition. Death, the ultimate desocialization, is ritually referred to by the euphemism "to become an animal." The ghosts of the dead are said to form close liaisons with living animals in the forest and to take revenge upon hunters who kill them. (These issues are discussed in detail in "Beauty and the beast," this volume.)

I draw attention to Kayapo notions of "berserkness," disease, and death because they reveal the close relationship that exists in Kayapo thought between the inner psychobiological core of the individual person and the outer natural environment surrounding the village. Berserkness, disease, and death are defined as socially disruptive natural phenomena because they invert the normal order of relations between the "social" and the "natural." This is what is implied by the notion that all three are typically caused by some element of external nature (the environment or animals) making direct contact with the internal natural core of the person. The result is, as it were, a short circuit between the two natural poles that are normally prevented from coming into contact with each other by a double layer of social insulation: on the one hand, the structure of society, which keeps external nature "outside," and, on the other hand, the structure of the person, which keeps internal nature "inside," that is, contained and channeled within a framework of sociality.

The notion that sick people must not eat meat (which the Kayapo regard as the strongest form of "natural" food substances) is consistent with this interpretation. The idea behind the dietary prohibition is that, since the social framework of the person has already been breached by the disease, he or she is rendered more than usually vulnerable to disruptive natural influences. Any potential vehicle of such influences must therefore be avoided. Within the framework of this notion, family members of the patient must also observe the same taboos, lest they serve as natural conduits of the effects of whatever strong food they eat themselves.

These data demonstrate that the Kayapo regard the "natural" character of family relations, of the inner psychobiological core of the person, and of the external animal and plant world as essentially homogeneous and, for some purposes, directly continuous. This continuity, if allowed to manifest itself, is thought to be profoundly threatening to society and the socialized person. The data show, in other words, that the relationship between the natural and cultural domains is not conceived in static terms, as a metaphorical relationship between parallel, separate orders, but as a constant process of accommodation and attrition. In these terms, "society" strives to capture, canalize, and assimilate energy sources and raw materials of various sorts from "nature," while "nature," conceived as a category of potentially autonomous forces and entities not inherently subject to human social control, constantly threatens to encroach upon, disrupt, or evade "society" and its efforts at control.

This dynamic relationship is essentially the same form on all three of the levels that we have so far considered: the economic, the sociological, and the individual. In each case, the basic unit of production (which, for all of them, is the same, namely, the conjugal family) or, more precisely, the pattern of relations that constitute it, is transformed into a generalized and socially standardized framework of relations that becomes the means of integrating its products into society. In each case, the productive process in question (the production of the material means of subsistence, the renewal of social units such as families and households, and the socialization of individual persons) is thought of as organized on two levels. The lower level consists of direct transformations of nature, which, by virtue of its direct involvement with the "natural" substratum in question, is considered to take on some of the autonomy of natural phenomena in relation to the rest of society. The higher level consists of generalized social relationships (especially those in the communal institutions) that integrate the basic relations at the lower level into the social community through deliberate processes (such as the various rituals) that harness, channel, and coordinate them toward "social" ends.

The relationship between "nature" and "society" is thus not primarily defined in terms of the opposition between human society taken as a whole, on the one hand, and, on the other, the natural world, defined as a totally asocial environment, but in terms of a fundamental relationship *within* society itself: between the aspect or level of social organization (including the structure of the person) that is directly involved with "nature," and the aspect or level that is concerned with integrating those natural relations into communal society as a whole. The relationship between these two levels of social organization is one of reciprocal tension, accommodation, and interdependence. This intrasocial relationship, then, is the true paradigm for the relationship between nature and culture or society. The nature–society relationship is, in other words, not dyadic but essentially triadic: its three basic terms are nature itself; the quasi-natural, quasi-social level of society comprising the basic relations of material, social and psychosocial production; and the fully social superstructure of interrelations that are coordinated and integrated into collective society.

This brings us to the heart of the paradox to which I alluded earlier. The reader will doubtless have noticed that I have thus far avoided giving a positive general definition of either "nature" or "society" in Kayapo terms. It might be supposed, on the basis of the evidence that has been presented, that the essence of the natural for the Kayapo is that it is confined to the extrasocial (the surrounding world of flora, fauna, elements, etc.) and the infrasocial, below the level of the relatively complex systems of generalized transformational relations that make up the essence of the social system. Despite this apparently reasonable and straightforward conception, however, there is another category of "natural" phenomena that I have not so far discussed: the domain that lies "above" society, as it were. This consists of the ceremonies that transform the key aspects of family relationships within the larger pattern of Kayapo communal institutions and which recruit new members into those institutions themselves. These ceremonies constitute the actual transformational mechanisms of Kayapo society and, as such, form part of the highest level of the social system: precisely the level, in short, which one might have thought would be regarded by the Kayapo as the quintessence of the "social." Nonetheless, the "natural" character of these ceremonies consists in their having been originally bestowed on humans by natural beings (animals, birds, fish, ghosts, or, in certain cases, heavenly bodies). The Kayapo believe, in fact, that human (social) beings are not capable of creating songs or ceremonies. These are invariably thought to be derived from natural beings of one sort or another. They are "socialized" through being detached from their original "natural" sources and generalized in the pragmatic sense of being transformed into collective, repetitive performances. The replicated collective performances of a ceremony signify, for the Kayapo, a transformation from "nature" to "society" of the same logical order as the harvesting and cooking of food, the transformations of the family cycle, the socialization of individuals, and the recruitment of communal groups.

The question becomes this: why should the Kayapo regard the very power to create and maintain their social order (for the collective ceremonies represent nothing less than this) as itself, in origin and essence, an asocial ("natural") power? The answer is that they do not regard the structure of society itself as within their power to change or, therefore, within their power to create. It follows that the basic forms, that is, the basic transformative mechanisms upon which their society rests, must derive from an extrasocial source. This source, then, has in common with the other categories of natural phenomena that have already been discussed that it is outside of human (social) power to create or alter in any fundamental way. It must be taken, in other words, as having existed prior to the advent of human beings in their fully socialized form. It cannot have been produced by humans but only appropriated and transformed by them in certain ways. "Society," in other words, is what can be recreated or transformed by human beings; in the Kayapo view, human creative powers are limited to the transformation of some classes of natural phenomena by means of other natural phenomena. The latter consist of natural transformational processes appropriated and modified for human use. The distinctive features of this social modification consist first, of coordinated processes of detachment or differentiation from the original natural source, and second, of generalization, which results from the transposition of the transformational mechanisms (tools, rituals, songs, etc.) or processes from a lower (family or personal) to a higher (collective) level of social organization.

It will not have escaped notice that this account of Kayapo notions of "nature" and "society" exactly parallels the account of fire, how human beings come to possess it, and what they did with it presented in the myth. The implications of this parallelism will be one of the principal themes of the following analysis.

SPECIFIC KINSHIP RELATIONSHIPS IN THE MYTH

Kayapo society has thus far been discussed only in general terms. The myth, however, is concerned not only with society in the general sense but with several particular relationships in the sphere of consanguineal and affinal relations. To understand the significance of these relationships in the myth, it is necessary to present next a more detailed account of certain aspects of Kayapo family and kinship structure.

Sister's husband and wife's brother: marriage, affinal relations, and uxorilocal residence

The rule of postmarital residence in the natal household of the wife, which is the basis of Kayapo extended-family household structure, has several consequences for the form of family and kinship relations that are directly relevant to the myth. One of these is the social form of the male life cycle. The uxorilocal residence rule means that, to make the transition from child to adult, a boy must leave the household of his mother and sister and eventually move into that of his wife. By contrast, a girl continues to remain in her natal home as she becomes a woman.

For a man, then, marriage connotes displacement from the household of his birth. The figure of the sister's husband is an especially apt symbol for the structural connotations of marriage in this respect, since he not only directly displaces a wife's brother from his sister's household, taking his place as the resident male of the household of his own generation, but he also represents what wife's brother must himself become in another household, that of his wife. As a symbol, in other words, the sister's husband points to the future as well as the present implications of marriage for the domestic situation of an immature youth. It is thus appropriate that the process of displacement and transference

from the mother's and sister's household to the wife's is a gradual process, usually stretching over more than ten years. It begins long before marriage, starting
when a boy is taken from his maternal household to reside in one of the men's
houses in the center of the village plaza. This happens when the boy is about
eight years of age. The boy remains domiciled in the men's house until he consummates a marriage by fathering a child, whereupon he moves to the household of his wife, that is, his child's mother.

Initiation, which usually occurs in a boy's midteens, stresses the attenuation and redefinition of his ties to his natal family and household. His relations
with his father, mother, and sisters are especially singled out for symbolic attenuation. Initiation also takes the form of a ritual marriage. This is a symbolic
dramatization of the boy's ability to assume affinal ties rather than a socially
binding union. No young man is considered socially qualified to begin conducting the sexual liaisons that lead to marriage until he has passed through this
rite. Although, in structural terms, marriage constitutes both the cause and the
culmination of a youth's displacement from his natal to his affinal household, it
must wait upon the transformation of a boy's natal family relationships, which
are prior from the standpoint of the individual life cycle.

Father and son: the uxorilocal dilemma

The Kayapo emphasis on marriage and procreation as a criterion of mature
male status, along with the stress on the displacement of boys' social attachments from their natal households, first to the men's house and then to the
wife's household, reinforce one another in contributing to the predominance of
the role of father-husband as the primary component of the social identity of
the adult Kayapo male. The emphasis on the father-husband role is a striking
feature of all levels of Kayapo social organization, from family structure to the
communal system of moieties and men's houses.

The emphasis on the father-husband role, however, gives rise to a latent
structural contradiction that I have elsewhere called the "uxorilocal dilemma"
(Turner 2012). The difficulty is that the more the new role of father is stressed
as the concomitant of the displacement of a young male from his maternal
household, the more the tie between father and son is reinforced. This renders
the displacement of his son all the more difficult when it comes time for him to
leave his natal family, which is necessary if the same process is to be repeated in
the next revolution of the family cycle.

The Kayapo have resolved this problem through an ingenious device, the institution of "substitute" parents. When a boy comes of age to be inducted into the men's house, the rite of induction is performed by a "substitute father," a nonrelative specifically recruited for the purpose. As a part of this rite, the boy's actual father and other kin loudly mourn "for dead fathers," thus underscoring the demise, for all public social purposes, of the tie between the father and his son. The boy joins the moiety of his "substitute father," who also presides over the definitive attenuation of his natal family ties at his initiation some years later. The substitute father continues to serve as the boy's mentor for collective ritual purposes until the youth consummates his marriage by becoming a father in his own right. At that point, he passes into the senior age grade and moiety set of mature men (significantly called in Kayapo *me kra-re*, literally, "people with children," thus "fathers") and simultaneously moves out of the men's house into his wife's household. With these two transitions, the youth's transformation into an adult man is essentially complete. The relationship between the father and son can thus be considered as a structural "pivot" of the youth's transitions from boy to man and from natal to affinal household. The transformational process of which both of these transitions are staged involves a polarization of the two complementary aspects of the father–son relationship: the relationship of the boy as a son to his father, on the one hand, and, on the other, that of the man as a father to his children. The transformation occurs through the negation of the former relationship and the affirmation of the latter, in that sequence. The recruitment criteria of the two moiety subsets (the "boys" and "fathers") are the means by which these two aspects of the father–son relationship are respectively negated and reinforced. The two moiety subsets and the institution of the men's house with which both are associated thus serve, in a sense, as the institutional pivot of the father role itself. By the same token, they also form the pivot between the two consecutive families and households to which a male belongs in the course of his life cycle.

The role of the substitute father, in light of these considerations, takes on attributes that are both retrospective (in a negative sense) and prospective (in a positive sense). On the one hand, the "substitute" attribute of the substitute father clearly symbolizes the severance, for public social purposes, of the son's ties to his own "real" father. On the other hand, as a symbolic tutelary figure, the substitute father represents the role itself of "father" as the criterion of adult male status, which the boy must aspire to attain for himself. The social reality of this prospective function is demonstrated by the fact that the youth passes out of symbolic tutelage to the substitute father upon becoming a "real" father in his own right, thereby joining the age grade and moiety set of "fathers."

This analysis of the pivotal role of the status of father in Kayapo society provides the necessary basis for understanding why the pivotal symbolic figure in the myth, the jaguar, takes on the role of a "father" toward the boy. It also clarifies the significance of the jaguar's ambivalent behavior toward the boy, which, as we shall see, has the effect of polarizing aspects of their relationship in such a way as to negate some aspects and reinforce others. A full discussion of these matters must be postponed, however, until the analysis of the myth itself.

That the jaguar figure might be a symbol for the pivotal male role is confirmed by a comparative survey of other Gê societies and their variants of the fire myth: in every society with a single identifiable pivotal status, the jaguar assumes that status toward the boy. In the one society where no one status seems to play such a pivotal role (the Akwe-Sherente, among whom this function seems to be divided among the father and mother's brother), the jaguar assumes no specific status at all.

At first glance, it might seem reasonable to suggest that the jaguar who adopts the boy as his son in the Kayapo variant of the myth is a symbolic stand-in for the Kayapo substitute father. This interpretation, however, may be somewhat simplistic if considered at the comparative level. All the Gê variants have jaguars who adopt the hero, but only the Kayapo and Apinaye have the institution of the "substitute father." These are also the only two Gê societies in which the father is the pivotal male role and in which the jaguar assumes the role of father in the myth. It would therefore be more accurate to say that both the substitute father role in the social organization and the jaguar in the myth are, each in his own domain, symbolic representations of the pivotal adult male status in the society, rather than to consider one as directly symbolizing the other.

The essence of the structural ambivalence attaching to the pivotal male status is that a boy must, in the course of his life cycle, sever or attenuate his connection with the adult male member of his natal household who plays that role toward him in order to free himself to play the same role in adult life. This ambivalence is, as we shall see, well conveyed by the intensely ambivalent symbol of the jaguar, which is a focus of emulation and fear, admiration and repulsion, and is specifically thought to embody the most desirable as well as the most threatening, dangerous, and therefore undesirable qualities of adult manhood.

It should perhaps be explicitly pointed out that there is very little tension of an Oedipal sort in the relations between Kayapo fathers and sons. Fathers are generally regarded, both before and after the separation of their sons from the household, as benignly supportive, permissive, and patient to a fault.

On the rare occasions when a young child of either sex is physically punished or even spoken to sharply, it is always the mother who is the agent of the discipline. The father, by contrast, regularly acts as intercessor for the child. The father's role in the family is conditioned by the fact that his primary social involvements lie outside the household, in the mature men's societies. He has less social stake in the affairs of his family and household, which are regarded as the proper domain of female interests and concerns.

The father's semidetachment from the day-to-day problems of his family makes him an ideal tutelary and exemplary figure for his son, whose future social development is associated with his physical and social detachment from the family household. In the same way, the detachment of a son from his father through the substitute father relationship is not fraught with emotional tension or conflict between the father and his son; it might even be said to forestall such tensions. The incompatibility of father and son in relation to the latter's natal household, as expressed in the ritual of adoption by the substitute father, thus arises within a framework of family structure that provides little ground for psychological tensions or Oedipal rivalries between fathers and sons. On the contrary, a boy's emotional conflicts associated with growing up and leaving the household tend to be focused on the mother rather than the father. The Kayapo situation is thus close to the inverse of the classical Oedipal pattern. This is faithfully reflected by the myth in its account of the boy's conflict with his jaguar "mother," who consistently acts menacingly toward the boy and who is eventually killed by the boy upon the advice of his jaguar "father."

Sister and mother: cross-sex ties and the structure of interfamily relations

The bilateral nuclear family constitutes the fundamental unit of Kayapo kinship and household structure; there are no exogamous corporate groups capable of subordinating or reducing the structure of the family to relations of wife-exchange. This means that the transformation of a boy's family relations as he passes from boyhood to manhood must take both sides of the family—the mother and sister as well as the father—into account.

The boy's removal to the men's house under the aegis of his substitute father, besides entailing a major transformation of his ties to his real father, also constitutes a decisive attenuation of his childhood relation to his mother, which had been based on constant contact and nurturance in the residential setting of the maternal household. Both qualitatively and quantitatively speaking, the boy's removal to the men's house means that his relations with his female nuclear family relatives are much reduced, and the sort of relationship to them he had as a child is definitively terminated. The wife of the substitute father assumes the role of "substitute mother" and brings the boy his first meal and load of firewood in the men's house. The boy's relationship to his mother is thus symbolically attenuated in the same terms as his relation to his father.

There is, however, an important sense in which relations with the sister and, to a lesser extent, the mother, are continued, albeit in a transformed and indirect sense. This continuation takes the form of a close relationship between a man's sister and his wife. His mother also participates in this relationship, although less intensely. After a young man consummates his marriage by founding a family of procreation and moving in with his wife and her parents, his mother and especially his sister become constant visitors in his wife's house. Sisters-in-law, in effect, have a formal "friendship" relation. This stands in sharp contrast to the relation between brothers-in-law: the wife's brother is supposed not to visit his sister or even enter her house if her husband is present, and the two men generally try to have as little as possible to do with each other.

The brother–sister relation is thus transformed and skewed to conform to the patrilateral bias of the Kayapo marriage pattern. Relations between a man and his sister's husband and children are, respectively, relatively more inhibited and less emphasized than those between a woman and her brother's wife and children. This pattern is a corollary, at the interfamily level, of the internal structure of the Kayapo nuclear family itself, with its emphasis on the role of the father and husband and the definition of the husband's role in terms of the production of children of either sex.

The cross-sex sibling relation of brother to sister and, to a lesser extent, mother to son, thus constitutes the axis of continuity between a man's natal and affinal households, and therefore also, in a structural sense, between the two discontinuous aspects of his own pivotal status (as son and father, respectively). In other words, the mother and sister form the principal link between the key transformational status of father, with its structural focus on the isolated nuclear family, and the wider social network of interfamily and household relations. It is therefore appropriate that, in the fire myth, the sister and then the mother are the agents through whom the hero is reincorporated into human society upon his return to the village after his transformative encounter with his jaguar father.

CHAPTER FOUR

An ethnography of symbols

The previous chapter considered the myth in the context of Kayapo social relations. Here, I wish to explore some of the cultural associations of the symbolic elements of the myth.

SPACE AND TIME

The episodes or clusters that form the structural units of the myth have, as we shall see, a common basic structure. In the broadest terms, this consists of a dimension of action resulting in dynamic transformation. This aspect is juxtaposed against a dimension of classificatory contrast or differentiation created as a result of such actions. These two dimensions are represented in the myth by different modes of space (with two significant exceptions, to be discussed later). These differing forms of space are, in turn, associated with distinct modes of time.

Neither the dimension of dynamic transformation and action (which I shall call, for the sake of brevity, the 'y' axis) nor that of classification of the modes and results of action (which I shall call the 'x' axis), however, are uniformly associated throughout every episode of the myth with the same concrete form of space or mode of time. The shifts from episode to episode in the spatial and temporal forms assumed by the two constant axial parameters form a pattern of great significance for the structure of the myth. This pattern will be analyzed in detail in the following chapter. The present chapter is devoted to noting the general ethnographic associations of symbolic elements of the myth, such as modalities of spacetime, in Kayapo culture. These general cultural associations will serve as invaluable guides to the interpretation of the function and meaning of these elements in the structure of the myth itself.

At the beginning of the last section, I noted that the myth ostensibly seems to be concerned with two distinct though related stories: that of the growth and socialization of the individual boy who is the hero of the myth, and that of society as a whole and its acquisition of the fire. This observation might be reformulated as the proposition that the myth is concerned with two distinct modes or levels of process: the psychological and physical growth of the boy from the helpless child of the first episodes to the competent and self-sufficient youth of the final episodes; and the socialization of the boy, the fire, and ultimately of society itself.

These two modes of process form the primary concern of different sections of the story. The boy's psychophysical development is the focus of the earlier episodes through the end of the boy's stay with the jaguars, while socialization per se is the principal theme of the final two episodes. Each of these two groups of episodes and the process with which each is primarily preoccupied are identified with a distinct mode of spacetime.

These two modes may be called, for the sake of convenience, vertical space associated with linear, nonreversible time, and concentric space associated with cyclical, repetitive time. Vertical, linear spacetime, which entails the process of individual psychophysical growth, is presented as taking place within the boundaries of a minimal social unit (a conjugal family). Concentric, cyclical spacetime, by contrast, is the modality of processes that cross the boundaries of discrete social groups and levels of organization and which combine them in a systematic way. The two modes of spacetime and the processes with which they are identified are thus treated as phenomena of distinct structural levels: the intrafamilial level (a relatively "natural" domain); and the interfamilial or communal level of relations (the preeminently "social" domain). The problematics of the myth might be defined as the attainment of coordination and integration between these two social levels, types of processes, and modalities of spacetime.

For the coordination of two such disparate and distinct levels of phenomena, however, a mediating process, some means of bridging the gap between the levels, is required. We should therefore expect (if the above assessment of the structural and meaningful coordinates of the two modes of spacetime is correct) a third, intermediate form of spacetime that functions in the myth as a mediator between the other two. This is precisely what we find: the contrast between inside and outside the family household, which comes into prominence in the episodes of the boy's stay among the jaguars and his return to the village, can be shown to play this mediating role. On the one hand, it can be described as "proto-concentric" in spatial terms, since the contrast between inside and outside the house is formally analogous to the contrast between the center and periphery of the village, which forms the paradigm of concentric space. On the other hand, it links the intrafamily domain, associated with vertical spatial transitions, with the crossing of thresholds or boundaries between social units, which is the chief feature of concentric space. As a modality of time, it may have either reversible linear connotations (such as everyday exits and entrances) or irreversible ones (such as leaving the maternal home for good, as all Kayapo boys must eventually do).

What I want to do here is simply to note the relevant Kayapo cultural associations with the three modalities of spacetime that I was able to record in the field, plus a few speculations of my own on the subject of vertical space.

Vertical space, as noted earlier, is preeminently associated with psychobiological developmental transitions. These are basically natural in character, even though they have social results. Concentric space, on the other hand, is organized on the basis of the distinction between human society, which, in the form of the village community, serves as its central reference point, and asocial nature, represented by the peripheral forest and savanna surrounding the village on all sides. Vertical transitions, whether from "down to up" or "up to down," occur only in the peripheral (natural) zone of concentric space.

That vertical spatial movement is associated with natural developmental transformations in the myth of cooking fire, as well as in other Kayapo myths and symbolic contexts, may ultimately be explained by the fact that the lower orders of developmental transformations or irreversible processes in nature tend to take vertical form: plants grow upward, inert matter and meteorological phenomena flow or fall downward, the sun rises and sets. The vertical spatial continuum within which these developments occur is, moreover, essentially homogeneous between its upper and lower extremities. Only human beings and animals have the capacity for horizontal locomotion, which is associated with purposive (social) movement or transitions between spatial points or zones of contrasting qualities.

The Kayapo recognize two modes of vertical spacetime: up-to-down and down-to-up. Both of them are associated with unidirectional time flow (i.e., time that is linear and irreversible), which, in both cases, is expressed as a movement between points in vertical space. One difference between the two modes is that the directions of the temporal associations of their upper and lower poles are reversed. In what I have called the "up-to-down" mode, the upper level or pole (usually the sky) represents the beginning of a process or transformation, while the lower level (usually the earth) represents the end. In the "down-to-up" mode, the lower extremity (usually referred to in Kayapo as the "root" or "base") is taken as the beginning, while the upper extremity (the tip or "end") is seen as the later or final phase. The most striking difference between the two modes is, however, the association of the "down-to-up" mode with continuing or un-finished processes, while the "up-to-down" mode is associated with completed events that do not continue. This contrast follows directly from the concept of time as a function of a dynamic transition between upper and lower levels or extremities. In the down-to-up mode, time is thought of as passing in an upward direction: the latest stage of the process is also the highest, so the basic vertical temporal field is preserved and time can continue. In the up-to-down mode, by contrast, the end of the process (e.g., the descent from sky to earth, the chopping down of a tree) usually corresponds to the annihilation of the vertical spatial field that made the transition and the passage of time possible in the first place. Time, as it were, can no longer happen. The result is therefore perma-nent and irreversible. The up-to-down mode is therefore the temporal mode in which the Kayapo think of the past, in the sense of events that occurred long enough ago to be regarded as complete and remote, without continuing effects or direct repercussions in the present. This is, at least, implied by their otherwise enigmatic expression for relatively remote (mythical or postmythical) times: "*a taytch*," literally, "on firm ground."

The up-to-down mode of vertical spacetime is the mode employed in the myth. It is obviously appropriate for myths that purport to explain how things come to be just so, once and for all. It is equally appropriate for the description of irreversible developmental processes, such as the development of a boy into a man.

There is ample evidence that the Kayapo conceive of the vertical spatiotem-poral contrast of the up-to-down mode as a dimension of linear, nonrepetitive time, in which the contrast between up and down represents the relationship between the initial and final stages of an irreversible transformation. There are other Kayapo myths in which vertical spatial contrast in the up-to-down mode is directly linked to irreversible temporal processes and events. The irreversibility of the temporal mode of the events recounted in these myths is usually expressed by the severance of the original vertical link between the upper and lower poles (such as sky and earth) of spacetime. In some stories, this is accompanied by the overt negation of the cyclical, repetitive mode of time. In one of them, defining the dimensions of human space, humans engage in the cutting down of enormously tall trees that originally reached to the sky. This activity only becomes successful when the work is continued both night and day, thus obliterating (temporarily) the primary form of cyclical, repetitive time, the diurnal cycle. In one version, the result of trees falling is that the sky, which had been supported by the trees, collapses so that it comes to rest directly on the earth, thus irreversibly establishing the limits of space. To the Kayapo, the known world is a circle under a dome of sky that touches the ground at the periphery (see "Cosmology, objectification, and animism in indigenous Amazonia," this volume). In the other version, the result is the equally irreversible dispersion of the peoples of the earth, all speaking different languages.

Still another Kayapo myth that employs downward movement from sky to earth as an index of irreversible, developmental change is the tale of how the first people came to the earth. The story recounts how, at one time, the earth was uninhabited, since all people lived in the sky. One day, an old man digging out an armadillo burrow broke through the underside of the sky and saw the earth far below. He summoned his fellow villagers, who made a long rope of vines and lowered it through the hole to the earth. Half of them, led by a daring youth called "son of the people," climbed down the rope. The other half, including the old man, stayed in the sky after the rope was cut. In this story, the vertical opposition between earth and sky is identified with the succession of generations, epitomized by the contrast between the youth, specifically identified as a son, and the old man. Both the advent of human beings on the earth and the sequence of generations are irreversible events or processes, an aspect fittingly represented by the cutting of the rope between earth and sky. This severance has the effect of rendering irrevocable the vertical separation between the two levels, while preserving the structure of the spatiotemporal (and social) field within which it is defined.

The up-to-down mode of vertical spacetime, as the time of finished, noncontinuing processes and nonrepetitive events, is easily the most restricted and least-used mode of time in Kayapo culture: it is utilized almost exclusively for referring to long-past historical and mythical events. In contrast to this, the other modes of spacetime that play important roles in the myth, such as the contrast between the inside and outside of the house or the concentric opposition of a "social" center and the "natural" periphery, are prominent features of everyday Kayapo experience, serving as referential frameworks for many of the spatial terms and concepts in daily life.

Concentric spacetime is undoubtedly the most complex mode of temporal and spatial organization in Kayapo culture. It is articulated at two levels: the structure of the village itself, which may be designated concentric microspace; and the structure of the socionatural cosmos, or concentric macrospace. Both of these levels of concentric space play significant roles in the myth of the origin of cooking fire.

The basic paradigm of concentric space is the structure of the traditional Kayapo village, which is built in the form of one or more circles of extended-family households arranged around an open central plaza. In the center of the plaza stands the men's house of the two moieties (formerly, two men's houses, one for each moiety). The communal ceremonies are celebrated in the plaza center, which is thus the focus of the highest expression of society as a collective entity. By contrast, the peripheral ring of households (the households themselves and the area of the plaza immediately in front of them, called *kikre kabem*, "in front of the house") is a zone associated with segmentary and particularistic social groups, the nuclear and extended families. The area immediately behind the houses (*kikre bu'a*, "in back of the house") is associated with illicit, clandestine, or infrasocial activities, such as sexual liaisons, urination, and defecation. Whereas the family houses themselves are a relatively "natural" zone in contrast to the center of the plaza, they are still relatively "social" in contrast to the zone lying immediately behind them.

The concentric contrast between the plaza and households has, as I have just noted, a gendered dimension. The households of the village periphery are considered to be preeminently the domain of women (and children) and the uxorilocal extended family, which occupies a single long house; even more concretely, the household is the domain of the individual conjugal family, which maintains its own social and spatial identity within the larger household. The collective groupings of the central plaza are predominantly associated with men. Women, because of their association with particular households and, above all, with the relatively "natural" domain of intrafamily relations, are considered to be less "social," more "natural" beings than mature men, who are accepted as the epitomes of human sociality.

The outside of the house, in the central space of the village onto which the doors of Kayapo houses open, is, by contrast, primarily associated with initiated youths and men. The men's house in the center is the meeting space of the collective men's associations, which constitute the expression of the unity of the community per se. The contrast between inside and outside the house, in these terms, has connotations of the contrast between "nature" and "society," which link it to the more powerful and comprehensive concentric mode of spacetime. The space inside the house is relatively natural and is implicitly associated with the village periphery, along which the family dwellings of the village are arranged. The space outside is, by contrast, a relatively social, masculine sphere, associated with the central village plaza.

At the macrospatial level, the circular village as a whole serves as the central reference point for the spatial organization of the world, which is conceived as a round, flat disc. Surrounding the village is a zone of finite depth, usually extending outward for one or two hundred yards, called *a-tuk* (*a* = "earth," "ground"; *tuk* = "black," "dead," "transitional, liminal condition"). The *a-tuk* zone is a transitional region, outside the village but still relatively heavily involved in ordinary social activities, and thus not completely "natural" like the forest and savanna beyond. Rituals involving transitional states or mediation between society and asocial or "natural" conditions, beings, or forces are ordinarily celebrated in the *a-tuk* zone, such as the boy's jaguar feasts (described later), the seclusion of initiands, and mortuary rituals. Beyond the *a-tuk* lie the forest and savanna, the domain of wholly "natural" beings like wild animals and ghosts.

Concentric space, at both levels, thus serves as a system of categories for classifying relatively "social" and "natural" phenomena. It should be noted that, at both levels, the set of categories generated along the concentric dimension is triadic rather than simply dyadic in character. Between the natural and social extremes there is always a middle term, which partakes of the characteristics of both without being wholly either. Concentric space, however, is not merely a mode of classification: it also serves as a frame of reference for dynamic processes of transformation from "natural" to "social" (as when hunters bring the animals they have slain in the forest back to the village to be cooked, or when participants in a rite de passage are brought back to the central plaza from their seclusion camp in the *a-tuk* zone) and in the opposite direction (as when corpses are borne out of the village to be buried in *a-tuk*). It is, in other words, a dimension of time as well as of space.

The time expressed by concentric spatial transition is, however, different, both in form and content, from the vertical mode of spacetime discussed above. Concentric time consists of transformations from relatively natural to relatively social states or vice versa. In either case, the nature of the temporal transition in question consists in the crossing of the boundaries between distinct social groups or spatial zones, whereas the vertical mode of time, as we have seen, consists of transitions that take place within the bounds of a single group or zone. The second major difference between concentric and vertical time is that, whereas the latter is linear and irreversible, the former is reversible and thus potentially cyclical. Concentric temporal transitions can occur in either a natural or a social direction, and, once made, they can be repeated. Examples of both kinds occur in the myth of fire.

ANIMALS, COOKING, AND FIRE

"Nature," for the Kayapo, is primarily a category of animate forces. Animals, in this sense, are the prototypical "natural" beings, yet they are at the same time the natural beings that most closely resemble human ("social") beings (as contrasted to plants or stones, for instance). It is presumably for these reasons that the Kayapo define the various modalities of the distinction between "nature" and "society" in terms of a transformation into animal form, vulnerability to animal influence, or the reverse transformation from animal into social form.

The cooking of meat is the most prominent instance of the latter type of transformation, both in terms of everyday experience and symbolic expression. The Kayapo regard direct contact with uncooked meat, especially with raw blood, as dangerous, since such substances, retaining their natural form, can serve as vehicles for natural forces that are inherently destructive to socialized human beings. A certain amount of contact with raw blood and meat cannot, of course, be avoided. This is not particularly dangerous in itself if quickly followed by washing. But to eat raw or inadequately cooked meat, to eat meat without carefully washing all traces of raw blood or other animal substances from one's hands, or even to allow dried blood or offal from butchering to remain on the body for long without washing is to invite disease or going berserk (*aybanh*).

Cooking for the Kayapo is thus far more than a mere method of making food more palatable or digestible: it is an indispensable technique for insulating society against the disruptive and antisocial influence of raw animal meat and blood by transforming these substances from their "natural" state into a "social" form. It is consistent with this symbolic significance of cooking to find that the term for "cooking" (or, to be precise, baking or roasting) is also the most commonly used generic term for collective social groups. The term for "community," or, more generally, any institutionalized collective social unit, such as an age grade or men's society, is *tchêt*, which means "baked," "roasted," or "burned." The Kayapo, incidentally, cannot themselves explain why the same word should be used for both meanings; for them, it is simply a homonym.

The fire of the jaguar and the connotations of the jatoba wood

The fire the boy finds burning in the jaguars' house is a most peculiar fire by ordinary Kayapo standards. For one thing, instead of the normal fire made from a number of small pieces of wood, it consists of a single huge log. For another thing, it consists of a specific kind of log. There is consensus on this point among tellers of the myth in widely separated Kayapo villages and insistence that the detail is an integral part of the story. This again makes the jaguars' fire a different proposition from the ordinary Indian fire, which may make use of many different kinds of wood. Jatoba, the species used by the jaguars, incidentally, is not much used for firewood by the Kayapo because its toughness makes it difficult to split into convenient pieces.

The log burning in the jaguars' house is of jatoba (*Hymenea courbaril*, Kayapo *moytch*). It is a hardwood distinguished by the deep red color of its wood and especially by its resinous sap, which is blood red in color. This sap is used by the Kayapo to decorate the points of their hunting arrows in imitation of the animal blood they are intended to draw.

Another peculiar characteristic of the jaguars' fire is its shape. The myth states quite precisely that the fire consists of only one end of the thick, round log. In form, then, the jaguars' fire is not unlike the sun, the round form in which the fire first appears in the story. This suggests that the fire of the jaguars is in some essential respect intermediate between the totally natural fire represented by the sun and the totally socialized fire of human society.

This interpretation is consistent with the other unusual properties of the jaguars' fire. The fact that the fire is all of a piece, for instance, indicates that it is not replicable or generalizable, as are ordinary human fires. Like all of the jaguars' cultural possessions, such as the bow and arrow or the cotton string, it is one of a kind. When the men take the fire, the jaguar couple cannot make another. This is in keeping with another peculiar characteristic of the jaguars' quasi-social way of life: there is no jaguar society, no village, not even any children. The jaguar culture consists of only a single household, which is not even a complete family. The lack of children (that is, jaguar cubs) suggests that jaguar society lacks the capacity to replicate itself. Jaguar culture, in short, lacks a decisive feature of human culture: generalized processes and techniques. This generalized property of cultural phenomena depends, in turn, upon the detachability of transformational processes (i.e., the process of production or reproduction) from the particular objects and situations with which they are associated in any particular instance. These two properties together make possible the truly distinctive features of human society, as defined in the myth: the infinite replicability of cultural artifacts and social forms.

If the transformational processes on which human culture is based are generalized processes, it follows that the essential transformation from nature to culture must involve generalization. It has already been documented that the Kayapo regard cooking as the prototypical example of a cultural transformational process and, consequently, they equate rawness with the "natural state" and cooked-ness with the transformed "social state." In thus using cooking fire as a symbol of cultural transformation, the Kayapo are referring to their own fire, that is, fire that is already fully generalized and transformed into a cultural tool or, in concrete terms, lit from another (human) fire. What, then, from the point of view of contemporary, fully developed human (i.e., Kayapo) society, is to be made of a fire that cooks but is not itself culturally generalized, one that is not made from a generalized, detached, socially controlled fire, and therefore (to pursue the Kayapo symbolic idiom to its logical conclusion) is not itself cooked? The answer is encoded, with relentless consistency, in the blood-red sap of the jatoba log: the jaguar's fire is raw.

The macaws

The feathers of the scarlet macaw (*màn*), the species that figures in the fire myth, are more highly prized by the Kayapo than those of any other bird for the manufacture of ceremonial ornaments. For this reason, macaws are the most sought-after birds as household pets. The tame birds are a perennial source of plumes and are periodically plucked by their owners. My Kayapo informants unanimously affirmed that the motive of the sister's husband in the macaw episode of the myth (like that of any Kayapo under the same circumstances) was to make pets of the macaws in order to use the feathers rather than to eat them (cf. Lévi-Strauss' [1969b] description of the macaw hunters as "eaters of macaws").

The birds are tamed by being taken from the nest while still too young to fly and nursed by the women of the household, who masticate food and feed the young birds directly from mouth to mouth in the manner of the parent macaws. The owners of the birds continually pluck their feathers so that they never become able to fly. They become, in effect, permanent fledglings and, as such, apt symbols for the prevention of the normal transformation from child to adult.

To be captured and kept alive, macaws must be of a certain age. It is virtually impossible to capture adult birds (those that have already learned to fly) without fatally injuring them. Eggs or even freshly-hatched chicks are too difficult to raise. The macaws should, in short, be fledglings on the point of learning to fly, about to leave the maternal nest, and become adults. They should be, in other words, of exactly the same stage in their life cycles as the boy in the myth. The macaw chicks in the myth are said to be fledglings of this age (*no turu*). Their medial position on the vertical dimension of space (their nest in the high cliff is poised, in effect, halfway between earth and sky) reinforces the parallel between their stage of life and that of the boy, who is also poised at the structural midpoint of his development from a totally natural neonate to a totally socialized adult.

The macaw fledglings, in sum, symbolically condense the key aspects of the structural position of the boy who comes to capture them. The boy's success in his mission would mean for them a life of permanent fledglinghood, but it would have the same implications for the boy. If he were to throw down the fledglings as his sister's husband asks, he does what no boy of his age can do in Kayapo society, namely, to return to his sister's household, the household of his childhood, rather than leave it for the men's house, and to continue living there together with his sister's husband. It is thus not merely the physical and spatial attributes of the young macaws but the fate intended for them by their human hunters that make them powerful symbols of one of the alternative solutions (both in hypothetical structural terms and in subjective psychological terms) to the problem of a boy growing up in his sister's household: to wit, that of remaining in the household and never growing up. This metaphorical correspondence between the plight of the boy and the macaws clarifies why in none of the Gê or Bororo variants of the myth can the boy ever fulfill his sister's husband's demands to throw down the macaws. To do so would be to symbolically condemn himself to a social situation of artificially prolonged childhood, analogous to the artificially perpetuated fledglinghood that would be in store for the macaws. Sociologically, there can be only one outcome of his situation: he can never go home again.

Stone, egg, and hand

In the macaw episode, the wife's brother tricks his sister's husband by throwing down a stone instead of the macaw fledglings, using the pretense that it is a macaw egg. The stone breaks the sister's husband's hand and, by extension, the wife's brother's link with his sister's household, since doing so prompts the sister's husband to take down the ladder and return home without the boy.

We have given an answer in the last section to the overriding question: why does the wife's brother not throw down the macaw fledglings? Let us now take up the more specific questions. Why does he throw down a stone? Why does he claim it is an egg? What is the significance of its breaking the hand of the sister's husband, and why is this made the immediate pretext for the break with the sister's husband and the household he represents?

Let us begin with the question of the egg. An egg represents the previous phase in the life cycle of the macaw chicks that are actually in the nest: the phase of full infantile dependency on, and thus membership in, the natal family, to adopt human social terms. The boy's assertion that there are only eggs in the nest may be taken as an assertion that only eggs belong in the nest. This fits with the interpretation given earlier of the circumstances in which the assertion is made, that is, that the boy is thereby saving the macaw fledglings from an unnatural return to a permanent childlike condition in the sister's household. Having claimed that there are only eggs in the nest, the boy's next act is to throw the stone "egg" from the nest. This amounts, in symbolic terms, to a rejection by the boy of the childhood tie to the "nest" and his affirmation of the necessary separation of child from natal household. The substitution of the stone, a lifeless object, for the living egg symbolically asserts that the childhood connection to the natal family has now reached the end of its term. In other words, it has become an unviable attribute of an outworn identity, a lifeless husk, as it were, which must now be discarded like a cast-off chrysalis—or the shell of an egg that has hatched.

That the falling stone breaks the outstretched hand of the sister's husband continues the theme of breaking the childhood tie to the household. It is almost certainly significant in this connection that the Kayapo term for "hand" *(-ikra)* is a homonym of the first-person possessive form of the kinship term for one's own offspring, "my child" (in Kayapo, *i-kra*). The sister's husband's hand is, of course, extended to catch the supposed egg (i.e., in terms of our interpretation, to confirm the infantile connection of the boy to the sister's household) at the moment it is broken. Both situationally and in terms of its homonymous associations, therefore, the breaking of sister's husband's hand by the stone completes the symbolic statement of the rupture of the childhood ties of the wife's brother to his natal household. These are, of course, the ties that form the basis of the relationship of sister's husband and wife's brother. Sister's husband's action of pulling down the ladder thus only confirms, in straightforward operational terms, what has already been accomplished at a higher level of symbolic condensation by the stone in its guise as a hand-breaking egg.

The jaguar

In the Kayapo scheme of the world, in which animals and human beings have relatively clearly defined places in relation to each other, the larger predators (e.g., anacondas, caimans, giant otters, felines) play an anomalous role. They are not human, but their relationship as predatory carnivores to other animals is similar to that of humans. Some are even able to reverse the semantic field, as it were, by assuming the role of predator toward humans. Such carnivores are in some respects the equals and competitors of human beings, while in other respects they are the quintessential embodiments of the wild, threatening, asocial, and inhuman characteristics of animals that set them apart from human society. Carnivores, in short, are medial, monstrous creatures with respect to the human–animal, social–asocial continuum. The Kayapo (with one exception we are about to consider) maintain a strict taboo against eating the flesh of any carnivore. Perhaps this is because the idea seems to them to involve a confusion of categories, an intolerable blurring of the human–animal distinction, similar in some ways to that involved in cannibalism.

Of all the carnivores, the jaguar is regarded as the most potent and fearsome. The eyes of the jaguar are thought of as glowing with a sort of inner fire: when flashlights were introduced, the Kayapo christened them "jaguar eyes." The hair of the jaguar, upon entering the body, is believed to be more potent as the cause of going berserk, *aybanh*, than that of any other animal.

The unique position of the jaguar in Kayapo myth and ritual is doubtless in part the result of its status as the most powerful and fearsome terrestrial carnivore, and thus the prototypical exemplar of the ambiguous animal–human properties of predators as a class. This cognitive, classificatory ambiguity of the jaguar is, however, linked to another type of ambiguity in Kayapo attitudes toward jaguars. This is a powerful affective ambivalence between terror and admiration, the recognition of the jaguar as at once the most threatening and potent antisocial being in the "natural" world and, at the same time, the most potent exemplar of the qualities of strength, aggressiveness, and courage, which are the most valued qualities of the properly socialized Kayapo male. The combination of these two types of ambiguity—the predator's blurring of the cognitive boundary between the natural and the human, and the jaguar's juxtaposition of terrifying antisocial and emulative social qualities—renders the jaguar a uniquely powerful symbol of the terrors and transformations of male socialization. This role is epitomized by the ritual of the boy's jaguar feast, which I shall now briefly describe.

It may be suggested that the unique combination of qualities of the jaguar is what makes boys able to absorb with profit this animal's characteristics. Eating jaguar meat is destructive for an initiated man because the jaguar, besides its admirable "manly" qualities, has many qualities that go well beyond, even against, the social limits of human masculine behavior. These would be destructive in one who has already become defined in terms of these limitations. Boys of the appropriate jaguar-eating age, however, have not yet done this. Their "polymorphousness," the expression of the marginality of their structural position, makes them able to absorb the total spectrum of jaguar traits, antisocial as well as social, without derangement. Their relative weakness and lack of development ensures that the symbolic ingestion of antisocial traits will lead to no harmful social effects. At the same time, their plasticity guarantees that ritual direction by initiated youths and men can lend the proper emphasis to the socially emulative manly traits they are absorbing.

The boys' jaguar feast illuminates the symbolic appropriateness of the role of the jaguar in the fire myth as the mediator of adult male qualities and attributes for the boy. Certain obvious differences between the symbolic role of the jaguar in the myth and in the ritual feast, however, should be emphasized. In the myth, the jaguar not only mediates positive social attributes for the boy (the father role, the bow and arrow, the fire, the cooked meat, etc.), but the predator's negative, antisocial attributes also play a role. These negative qualities, as we shall see below, erupt during the boy's first encounter with the male jaguar, when the latter scarfs up the macaw fledglings, sharply contrasting with the jaguar's positive attributes in its friendly attitude toward the boy. Later in the myth, the negative and positive attributes are again polarized in the contrast between the female jaguar's menacing gestures toward the boy and the male jaguar's continued support and encouragement toward him. Furthermore, by the end of the myth, the boy not only acquires manly social attributes from the jaguar for himself but also the fire as well, the means by which society acquires the ability to transform the natural into the social state.

The shadow

The jaguar episode begins when the hunting jaguar catches sight of the boy's shadow projected before him on the ground. Taking it for a real boy, he pounces upon it as if to kill it, as he might act toward a game animal. It is significant that the jaguar acts at this point in a completely animal or natural fashion toward the boy, in spite of the fact that he is equipped with a bow and arrows, that is, a social means of hunting. It is only after he realizes that the "boy" is only a shadow, that is, a separated projection of the real boy, that he becomes friendly toward the real boy, adopting a social attitude toward him by retracting his claws and covering his fangs, both being natural predatory attributes, when he talks to him. The question therefore arises, what is there about the shadow that should lead the jaguar to change his attitude toward the boy?

In terms of its functions and associations within the myth itself, the casting of the shadow serves as the opening move in the boy's relation with the jaguar and thus (to get ahead of the analysis for the moment) in his positive transformation into an adult man. The shadow has several qualities that are admirably suited to encode the related aspects of the beginnings of this crucial transformation.

In the first place, the shadow is a quasi-distinct, partially detached aspect of the boy: a projection of his person yet different from it, in one sense his double, in another sense his opposite. As such, the shadow, as a physical phenomenon in space, stands in the same relation to the boy that his future status as mature man stands to him in time. This analogy takes on intensified force from the connotations of certain other qualities of the shadow.

The most significant of these are the characteristics and direction of the shadow's spatial manifestation. It is projected vertically downward onto the ground, in other words, in the direction that the boy must travel, practically as well as symbolically, in order to survive and grow into a man. It is, as it were, only a projection of the actual physical presence of the boy himself, a promise not yet fulfilled, of where the real boy will eventually be. In this respect, it is significant that the boy casts his shadow as a result of his act of leaning out from the nest to look at the jaguar on the ground. The shadow is thus the manifestation of the boy's first movement (however feeble and tentative) toward separation from the macaws' nest in the direction of the ground and the jaguar.

The structural role of the shadow is that of making contact between the boy and the jaguar and, in the process, of conveying to the jaguar the vital information that the process of separating the boy's physical and social person from his childish condition has already begun. This implication of the shadow is confirmed by the first verbal exchange between the boy and the jaguar, in which the boy reports to the jaguar his conflict with his sister's husband and the circumstances leading to his becoming stranded in the macaws' nest. This information, following the jaguar's discovery that the "boy" upon whom he pounces is actually a shadow, produces the transformation of the jaguar's attitude from one of feral hostility to one of social solicitude. What the jaguar learns from the shadow and the verbal exchange that follows is that the boy is no longer merely a boy but a being in transition between two aspects or phases of himself. He sees that the boy, by the very act of leaning out of the macaws' nest to look down at him, has managed to generate a secondary, quasi-distinct aspect of himself, which is contrasted to his as-yet primary childish aspect in the next. His maturation begins as he assumes a vertically elevated position in the macaws' nest and projects his shadow downward and toward the jaguar.

These connotations of the shadow take on resonance from the more general symbolic associations of shadows for the Kayapo. The Kayapo term for shadow, *karon*, also means "image," "ghost," and "soul." Like many other cultural groups, the Kayapo conceive of death, illness, and liminal phases of ritual passage in terms of the separation of the soul from the body. The separation of the boy's shadow from his body is thus suggestive of both his separation from society (his liminal status midway in the passage between child and adult) and his physical travail (being near death from thirst and starvation). The latter is, of course, the result of his suspension midway between sky and earth in terms of vertical spacetime, at the unstable point of transition between physical infancy and maturity. By pouncing on the shadow and recognizing its ephemeral nature, the jaguar destroys the "shadow" of the boy's past and enables him to move forward.

The bow and arrow

The bow and arrow are the standard traditional hunting weapon of the Kayapo and, as such, are the principal attribute of the prototypical adult male role, that of hunter. They are thus an appropriate token of the attainment of adult manhood and function as such in the fire myth. Although during fieldwork I was on the lookout for symbolic sexual associations with the bow and arrow, I did not find any. We will see later in the analysis that a significant turning point comes in the myth when the "father" jaguar gives the boy a bow and arrows for his own and tells him to shoot the "mother" jaguar with them, which will sever the boy's childish dependence on the maternal household. It is no coincidence that among the cultural artifacts the boy brings back to the village are the bow and arrows, symbols of his masculine identity as a hunter, thus transmitting the powers of this role to the other men of the village.

The cotton string

Some of the Kayapo versions of the myth mention cotton string as one of the cultural items in the jaguars' house. Spinning string from cotton is a woman's task in the Kayapo division of labor and is usually performed only by mothers of families. The string thus constitutes a token of the adult female role, much as the bow and arrows serve as tokens of adult manhood. Along with the bow and arrows, the boy brings back the cotton string to the village—and, of course, a piece of fire and some roast meat, the embodiment of generalized, transformative, socializing power. The acquisition by humanity of both sets of gendered items along with the fire signifies that the possession of the power represented by the cooking fire encompasses the power to replicate the complete male and female adult social roles.

CHAPTER FIVE

The structure of the myth

GENERAL FEATURES OF THE MYTH STRUCTURE

The preliminary task of elucidating the socioeconomic and cultural context of the myth, including the cultural significance of its symbolic elements, is now complete. It remains to formulate the structure of the myth itself, following the general conceptual guidelines laid down at the beginning of this work. The basic notion about the structure of narratives advanced there was the need to recognize the distinct units or significant clusters into which the myth is divided and to analyze each of these separately. The structure of the myth as a whole can then be formulated as a set of higher-level relations or rules governing the permutations within the structures of the various lower-level clusters.

The feasibility and usefulness of this notion as the basis for a practical analysis of narrative structure obviously depends on the possibility of developing reliable criteria for what constitutes a significant cluster or minimal segmentary unit of narrative. Let me say at once that I do not think that this can be done in any mechanical, a priori way. Most, if not all, of the segments into which I have divided the myth for the purposes of this analysis are clearly suggested in the narrative itself by breaks in the action, such as journeys separating one scene from the next. I believe that the breakdown at which I arrived would be replicated by most readers even without an acquaintance with Kayapo culture. Intuitive criteria such as this, however, only beg the question: how are we to know that the particular breaks in the action, upon which our intuitive segmentation is based, mark structurally significant divisions between distinct narrative segments?

A model of the type I have suggested cannot give a foolproof answer to this question, certainly not an answer that eliminates the role of creative intuition from the process of analysis (this would be, in any case, an impossible goal). It can, however, afford a more rigorous and objective basis for defining significant structural units and relations than other forms of structural analysis with which I am acquainted. There are three reasons for this. First, the commitment to the notion that the similarities and differences among the structures of the segments or episodes of a story must themselves form a significant pattern (that is, a pattern with certain overall regularities or invariant features) provides an external check of sorts upon the formulation of the structure of any individual segment. Each segment can then be analyzed in terms of whether it conforms to the general pattern previously analyzed or represents a comprehensible variation of it. If not, two alternatives present themselves within the constraints of the model: either the overall pattern itself needs to be reformulated to take the nonconforming features into account, or the segment or its internal structure has been wrongly or inadequately defined. Second, the commitment to take account of all the significant features of the text within the framework of this sort of model is a powerful constraint against arbitrary judgments or Procrustean distortions of patterns within or between segments to fit a preconceived mold. Third, the commitment to matching the formal patterns revealed by the structural analysis of the text and its segments with homologous structures in the social and cultural context of reference provides an additional powerful constraint upon arbitrary formalism.

An analysis of this type should develop further internal constraints as it attains more powerful levels of formal synthesis and structural integration of the symbolic and formal features of the text. On the basis of my own experience with this and similar analyses, I believe that, beyond a certain point, it becomes extremely difficult to retain arbitrary or erroneous interpretations at the level of fundamental features in this sort of analysis. I suggest, in sum, that the sort of analytical model I develop in this study affords a sufficiently powerful methodological tool for the discovery of structures that are really there.

The diagrams

I employ diagrams as a means of clarifying and simplifying the analysis and exposition of the segmentary structure of the myth. For each segment, I have constructed a diagram of its structure. These diagrams have a uniform basic structure and uniform graphic conventions, which it will be convenient to set out here in advance of the analyses themselves. The following model presents all the essential features and conventions employed in the succeeding diagrams:

There are two axes or dimensions of the paradigmatic structure of the episodes:

1. Vertical ('y' axis): Every segment of the story focuses on an action (either blocked or realized), which always implies some form of transformation on the part of the actor. The dynamic aspect of this action (i.e., its aspect as a gain or loss of energy, force, or level of social integration) is represented by the vertical ('y') axis of the diagram.

2. Horizontal ('x' axis): Each episode is also concerned with classifying the modes and results of action according to their relatively "social" or "asocial" ("natural") character. For the most part, the 'x' axis is divided into two domains, with "society" shown on the left and "nature" on the right. The exception occurs in the sixth episode, where the natural domain is subdivided into the semisocial space of the jaguars' house and the natural forest outside it.

General structural principles

Over and beyond the bidimensional feature defined above, the structure of every segment conforms to the following three basic principles:

1. *Dynamic interdependence of transformations on the vertical and horizontal axes.* A transformation upon one axis implies a corresponding transformation upon the other: where the one is impossible the other cannot occur. For example, no transformation can occur on the 'y' axis in the absence of a suitably differentiated pattern of relations on the 'x' axis; the latter, in turn, cannot come into existence without the requisite prior transformations having occurred on the 'y' axis.

2. *Character of the action (in every segment involving realized action) as subject–alter interaction.* The actions that constitute the focus of all but two of the

segments of the myth (the exceptions comprise descriptions of static situations in which action is blocked) invariably take the form of interaction between a "subject" or actor and one or more "alters," usually other actors (and sometimes objects). The subject is always the principal element whose acts and transformations are expressed on the vertical ('y') axis. The action of the subject on the 'y' axis is always made either in response to or in the process of polarizing an "alter" on the horizontal axis into relatively "social" and "natural" aspects. This redefinition is reflected by an analogous polarization of aspects of the "subject" on the horizontal axis.

3. *Paired transformations.* The transformations upon both the 'x' and 'y' axes of the structure of the segments therefore occur in pairs. This is a corollary of (a) the interdependence of the transformations across the two dimensions, and (b) the dynamic interaction between subject and alter, which dictates that they undergo analogous processes of differentiation into "natural" and "social" aspects upon the 'x' axis. The transformation of a subject on the vertical ('y') axis results in a pair of complementary transformations, one of a "social" aspect and one of a "natural" aspect of the subject, respectively.

Affective structure

With the exception of the initial and final episodes, there is a distinct pattern of affective attitudes and reactions in each segment in which the subject is a human individual. This affective pattern is not reducible to, or analogous in any simple sense with, the formal cognitive structure of the episodes. It nevertheless comprises a vital component of the structure of the myth as a whole and has, as I shall show in the concluding section, a systematic structure in its own right.

Graphic conventions: arrows, signs, and numerals

Movements, relations, and transformations on both vertical and horizontal dimensions are indicated by arrows. These arrows are subject to the following conventions of directionality:

1. Vertical ('y') axis: Vertical arrows may be pointed either upward or downward. In the former case they indicate regressive developments (e.g., the boy returns to an earlier, childhood phase of his life cycle); in the latter case they

indicate progressive developments (e.g., the transition from childhood to adolescence).

2. Horizontal ('x') axis: Pairs of horizontal arrows are either pointed toward one another and away from the left and right ends of the horizontal axis, or away from one another and toward the left and right ends. In the former case, they indicate merging or a state of undifferentiated "social" and "natural" entities or attributes; in the latter case, they signify the differentiation of such entities or attributes.

3. A vertical arrow crossed with two parallel lines signifies an unconsummated transformation (e.g., a move declined or a relationship repudiated because the requisite horizontal differentiation has not taken place).

4. A horizontal arrow crossed with two parallel lines represents a lack of movement across "social" and "natural" domains or, alternatively, a failure or blockage of a differentiation or polarization between "social" and "natural" entities or attributes.

EPISODES OF THE MYTH

The initial situation

The myth begins with a brief description of the state of affairs prevailing before the two brothers-in-law set off on their momentous hunt. At that time, the only form of fire known to human society was the sun. Suspended in the sky, remote from human habitation, it was incapable of being used to cook food in any full sense, even though people nevertheless used it to warm their meat slightly. For the most part, they ate wild foods that could be eaten raw, which, with the exception of honey and palm hearts, are not presently eaten by humans and are considered appropriate only for animals. Human beings, in other words, by virtue of their lack of access to cooking fire and their resulting inability to transform natural food substances into a form recognized by present day Kayapo society as acceptable human food, were much closer to animals ("natural" beings) than they have become after acquiring fire.

The remoteness of fire from human society has implications for the internal differentiation and integration of society itself. In contrast to the fully social form of society at the end of the myth, the society of the initial state has access to fire (such as it is) in only one distant form: the fire itself, or more precisely its control and use, can therefore not become the basis of any significant differentiation of relationships of control or work within society. The lack of differentiation of the fire, in short, is reflected in the lack of differentiation of society itself. This is perhaps related to the fact that society enters into the initial and second segments of the myth only in the form of the individual household of the hero's sister. There is no reference to differentiated men's groups and women's households, which do not appear until the end of the story.

The correlation of the structural lack of differentiation and the lack of control over transformational energy as represented by the fire (amounting to a condition of structural entropy, if the term may be allowed) is reflected in the treatment of the meat, the material to be transformed, in the pre-fire state. To be warmed, meat is cut into small pieces rather than transformed directly in its original form of whole carcasses or joints. This suggests that the lack of direct control over transformational power (fire) means the inability to integrate effectively what is transformed. The mutually separate, homogeneous, faintly warmed, and diminutive pieces of meat thus constitute an apt metaphor for the condition of society itself, composed of mutually separate, homogeneous households unintegrated by any central regenerative (i.e., transformational) mechanism, such as the jaguar's burning log in the final episode of the story. The analysis can be summed up in Figure 1.1.

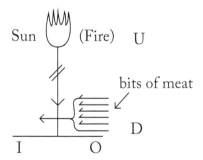

Figure 1.1. Initial situation: lacking fire on earth, humans warm bits of meat in the sun. Key: U = up; D = down; I = inside the house; O = outside the house

Vertical axis: On this axis, transformation remains impossible because of the separation between fire (in the sky) and earth. This means that the earth is still raw.

1. Humans remain untransformed into fully social beings (since they eat virtu-
    ally raw meat and raw animal foods).
2. Animals ("natural" beings) have not been transformed by the fire into their
    contemporary (fully "natural") form, nor has the fire itself taken its fully
    "natural" form (as the red throats of animals).

Horizontal axis: On this axis, the differentiation between "society" and "nature"
is minimal and only incipient at this stage.

1. Fire is itself undifferentiated into "social" and "natural" manifestations;
    it is, in fact, a single, homogeneous entity (the sun) and thus radically
    undifferentiated.
2. "Society" and "nature" are likewise undifferentiated: Human society, with the
    residual exception of warming meat in lieu of cooking, is little differentiated
    from animal nature.
3. Society itself is internally undifferentiated with respect to fire. There is only
    one form of fire, the sun, which can be used only for a single purpose (to
    warm meat, never to light other fires) and which cannot be differentially
    patterned or distributed within human society. A condition of structural
    entropy prevails.
4. "Natural" beings, on the other hand, are not yet fully differentiated from hu-
    man, "social" beings. The jaguar has many social attributes that humans still
    lack.

The macaw episode: ZH, WB, and the developmental crisis of the household

The setting of the initial action of the story is the household of a woman who
has married but whose young brother still lives with her in the same house. The
woman's brother and her husband, who are the protagonists in the first dra-
matic episode, represent successive stages in the development of the household.
The presence of a sister's husband (ZH) and wife's brother (WB) in the same
household implies that the natal family of the woman has entered upon its final
developmental phase of dispersion, one of the main features of which is the
removal of the brother from the sister's household. The confrontation of ZH
and WB thus implies and embodies the contradictory relationships between
the successive families (i.e., the sister's natal and conjugal families) formed in
the same uxorilocal household. This "contradiction" is normally resolved by the

process of family succession, which always takes the form of the displacement of the consanguineal male members of the earlier family (such as WB) from the household.

The dramatis personae of the macaw episode are thus not merely individuals, such as ZH and WB, but the clashing constellations of family relationships each represents. The contrasting relations of the two successive families within the same household is symbolically represented by the contrast between the sister's household, as represented by ZH, and the macaws' nest, with which WB becomes identified through the agency of, and in opposition to, ZH. The macaws' nest is a family household of sorts, specifically like WB's natal family (the bases for the symbolic identification of the young WB with the fledgling macaws have been noted in Chapter Four). Several features of the macaws' nest reflect the main aspects of the socially anomalous situation of WB's natal family relative to that of Z's and ZH's conjugal family within the household. To begin with, the macaws are asocial, "natural" being; similarly, WB's natal family has been rendered socially unviable by the developmental process of the household (in other words, the formation of his sister's conjugal family), so that it, too, has become, in a structural sense, "asocial." It has been transformed into a grouping that no longer has a place within the normative structure of human society. In the second place, the position of the macaws' nest is significant, located in the forest far outside the village. In terms of symbolic space, this places it in the "natural" or asocial zone of concentric space. Third, the position of the nest in vertical space is likewise meaningful; it is suspended above the earth, like the sun in the immediately preceding episode. In terms of the symbolic connotations of vertical space, as we have seen, this position is evocative of the initial stage of a transformational process. The dispersion of WB's natal family is the initial stage of the process of his own transformation into a man. The end of his natal family is thus, in a significant sense, the beginning of his transformation into a social being. The vertical elevation of the nest is thus appropriate in terms of the boy's position relative to his life cycle, while its peripheral location in concentric space is appropriate to its own stage of development in terms of the family cycle. These relationships can be summarized in the Figure 1.2.

The action at the macaws' nest

Let us take it as established, then, that the macaws' nest represents the natal family of the boy in its double capacity as the previous phase of the developmental

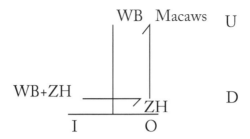

Figure 1.2. WB and ZH leave their household for the forest, where WB climbs up to the macaws' nest on a cliff.

Key: U = up; D = down; I = inside the house; O = outside the house; WB = wife's brother; ZH = sister's husband

cycle of WB's household and as the first stage of WB's own life cycle, at the point when both phases are drawing to a close. ZH, for the reasons that have been given above, is the appropriate agent to precipitate the definitive termination of both phases. Now let us consider the action that transpires at the macaws' nest.

ZH's purpose in the hunt is to capture the macaw fledglings alive and bring them back to the household in order to raise them as sources of feathers (and thus as "permanent fledglings"). This plan implies, as we have seen, an impossible solution to the sociological problem of readjusting the structure of the sister's household in the face of the need for her (and her brother's) natal family to disperse to make way for the conjugal family she has formed with her husband. ZH's proposal to bring the fledgling macaws and WB back with him to the sister's household amounts to an attempt to resolve the problem by arresting the development of WB's natal family (the preservation of the macaws as permanent fledglings in the sister's household implies preserving the social identity of the household as a "nest," that is, an undispersed natal family). By the same token, ZH's plan means arresting the development of WB himself toward adulthood (by returning with WB to the household on the same terms as he had left it to come on the hunt).

Because ZH's proposal is impossible in terms of the developmental process of the household, WB cannot comply with his demand to throw down the fledglings. Although all Gê variants of the myth feature WB's refusal to do so, they vary in the way in which he refused. In the Kayapo version, WB throws down a stone that breaks ZH's hand, which in turn leads the enraged ZH to pull down the ladder connecting the nest to the ground, thus marooning WB in the nest. This action confirms the separation of WB from his natal household in its new developmental phase, which is now dominated by the conjugal family of Z and ZH. The stone-throwing episode, the breaking of ZH's hand, and the absence of parent macaws express the precise nature of the social adjustments that this process of succession implies in the Kayapo household.

I should like to emphasize two further aspects of the scene at the macaws' nest before going on. The first is the way in which ZH's plan and the ensuing action at the nest creates a situational identification between WB and the macaw fledglings on the basis of their common relationship to ZH. WB can come down and go home only if the fledglings are made to do likewise: their destinies are thus not only linked but made explicitly analogous. This identification between the boy and the fledglings is consistent with the symbolic identification between them pointed out above, but, in another sense, it is analytically distinct from it. It provides the more generalized metaphorical identification with a specific situational focus. This point is vital because it in turn implies the possibility of changing the terms of the identification by changing its situational focus. This is precisely what happens when the jaguar comes on the scene, as we will see shortly.

A related point is the nature of the boy's problem of "coming down" from the nest. The manner in which the boy is left stranded in the nest emphasizes, in the most concrete terms, the social nature of his problem. He cannot get down unless someone on the ground puts back the ladder that ZH has pulled down. He must, in short, come down to someone if he is to come down at all. The interpretation that has just been given of his inability to come down to ZH, as well as the general interpretation given earlier of vertical spatial movement as emblematic of a developmental transformation, allow a prediction to be made about the nature of this "someone." To be consistent with our interpretation of the myth up to this point, the boy's rescuer must be someone whose social status is one with which the boy can identify as a viable focus of his own further social development, that is, of his transformation into an adult man.

Affective aspects

Significantly, it is at the point of the rupture of the relationship between WB and ZH that the first expression of subjective feeling on the part of any of the actors occurs in the myth. I never heard WB's trick of throwing down the stone to ZH described as an act of malice or explained in any way in terms of WB's motives as an actor. It is simply related as an objective event, to which the motives of WB are irrelevant. The breaking of ZH's hand by the stone is, by contrast, invariably accompanied by a cry of pain, more or less vividly mimicked by the teller of the myth. More poignantly, as ZH walks angrily away after pulling out the ladder, suffering from the pain of his broken hand, making his intentions of stranding WB in the nest clear, WB screams in terror to him to come back, claiming that there are, after all, fledglings in the nest and that he will throw them down to ZH as originally requested. WB offers, in short, to give up all his prospects for growth and manhood and to accept the lot of a permanent fledgling out of terror of his forthcoming ordeal, but it is all to no avail.

The foregoing analysis can be summarily presented in Figure 1.3.

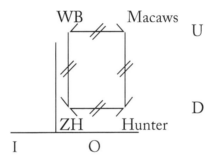

Figure 1.3. WB is stranded in the macaws' nest after ZH angrily pulls out the ladder.
Key: U = up; D = down; I = inside the house; O = outside the house; WB = wife's brother;
ZH = sister's husband

Vertical axis: In this episode, the action on the vertical axis demonstrates the impossibility of transformation from one developmental stage of the life cycle (and family cycle) to the next within the context of the boy's natal household.

1. When they leave the village and find the macaws' nest, where the WB climbs up the cliff and begins his movement away from his Z's house, WB and ZH cooperatively define their relationship between their respective sets of family relations within WB's natal household. This relationship is represented in terms of upper and lower positions in vertical spacetime (i.e., earlier and later developmental phases of the life cycle and family cycle), which corresponds to their relationship in terms of the normative social structure.

2. However, after ZH tells WB to throw down the macaw fledglings, WB's further development toward adulthood (which would be represented by his descent from the nest) is impossible in the terms proposed by ZH, who intends to bring the fledglings and WB back home. This would hypothetically identify WB's natal household as the arena of development, a logical contradiction and therefore social impossibility.

3. ZH, by the same token, provides no possibility of eliminating the macaws, which represent the childhood or "nestling" aspect of WB's identity; on the contrary, he proposes to preserve them as permanent fledglings in his own household. WB therefore cannot throw down the macaws in spite of ZH's demands that he do so.

Horizontal axis: This axis illustrates the impossibility of differentiating between the relatively unsocialized and socialized aspects of the role identities of either WB or ZH within the natal family context.

1. It is impossible to differentiate WB (as a "social" being) from the macaw fledglings (as "natural" beings that represent the unsocialized aspect of WB as a child) because of their analogous position in relation to ZH, who offers them an analogous fate as "permanent children" in his household.

2. ZH affirms this equation both by putting WB up in the nest and then insisting that the macaw fledglings are with WB in the nest. WB repudiates the equation by denying the existence of the fledglings and substituting the stone "egg" for them, which he throws down and thus symbolically asserts his own separation from the natal household (nest).

3. It is likewise impossible to differentiate the social and asocial (or "natural") aspects of ZH in either of his roles, as an affinal kinsman or as a hunter, because of the analogous ambiguity of his relations to WB and to the macaws.

4. Although ZH is a "social" kinsman, he actually plays an antisocial role of displacing WB from the household into the "natural" zone of the peripheral forest and placing him in a situation that identifies him with "natural" creatures, the macaws. "Natural" and "social" elements are thus inextricably mixed in his ostensibly "social" capacity as an affine and coresident household member to WB. By climbing up to the nest, WB collaborates willingly in ZH's "asocial" acts toward him in this capacity.

5. In his role as hunter (i.e., destroyer and transformer of "natural" creatures into "social" food), ZH proposes to play the anomalous role of "socializer"

toward the macaw fledglings; rather than destroy, cook, and eat them, he proposes to bring them back alive (untransformed) and treat them directly as members of his own ("social") household. Again, "natural" and "social" elements are ambiguously combined in this role, which therefore offers no firm basis for WB that would allow him to negate the unviable "natural" aspect of himself represented by the fledglings. WB defies and repudiates ZH's efforts to treat his "natural" aspect in a "social" way. He is therefore left with no means of detaching himself from his "natural" attributes and thus of returning to society. These relationships are represented in Figure 1.4.

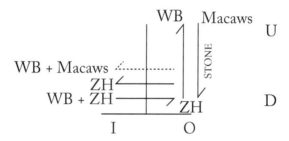

Figure 1.4. WB refuses to throw down macaws, having thrown down a stone instead, and refuses to return home with ZH.

Key: U = up; D = down; I = inside the house; O = outside the house; WB = wife's brother; ZH = sister's husband

Affective structure

1. At the start of the hunt, WB and ZH demonstrate cooperation and mutual trust, that is, social solidarity.
2. Upon the rupture of their relationship, ZH expresses rage and pain, and WB expresses terror. WB's terror drives him to make a regressive offer to throw down the macaw fledglings so that he can return home with ZH.

Affective transformation

Once ZH exits the scene, the boy's situation in the macaws' nest becomes not only unviable but actively contradictory. The absence of ZH removes the basis for the boy's situational identification with the macaws as well as the link to his natal household, which was symbolically represented by the macaws' nest and his identity as a WB. His role in relation to ZH, which was the basis of the "social" aspect of his identity, has been destroyed; he is now simply "the boy." Moreover, by his own action in throwing down the stone "egg" to his ZH, the boy has actively asserted his separation from the natal household, which is analogous to the macaws' nest. With the positive bases of his identification with the macaws destroyed, the boy is nevertheless still situationally identified with them in the negative sense of being trapped in the nest along with them. The boy's relationship with the macaws, in short, has become transformed from one of metaphorical equivalence and situational identification to one of symbolic antithesis and situational contradiction. The problem is the boy's inability to differentiate himself effectively from the fledglings; he thus maintains continued but now negative identification with them.

The nature of the boy's situation is sensitively reflected by two details that form integral parts of the Kayapo variant of the myth. The boy is said to be starving as well as reduced to consuming his own feces and urine (see Figure 1.5, below). Food is supposed to be transformed natural substance. It represents, at the lowest and most concrete level, the dependence of "social" existence upon the transformation of natural entities. Dying, by contrast, is conceived in Kayapo terms as being transformed into an animal, that is, into a natural entity, hence the opposite of keeping oneself in existence as a social being by eating normal food. The boy's starvation (his transformation into a "natural" being) thus represents the consequence of his failure to transform himself into a "social" being (symbolized by his lack of suitably transformed natural substance, i.e., food). Excrement, on the other hand, is naturally transformed food, first ingested as a social substance; it is therefore the inverse of proper food. It is, moreover, self-produced; it emanates not from a social relationship, as does all normally processed and distributed food, but from the "natural" core of the individual, the body. The boy has cut himself off from society, even from the macaws, through his autonomous act of throwing down the stone from the nest. This leaves him in the impossible position of trying to keep himself alive and maintain his identity as a social being, by himself, apart from any social relationship. This is an evidently contradictory situation, aptly symbolized by his desperate but futile attempt to nourish himself with naturally transformed, asocially (autonomously) produced antifood. The act of consuming his own excrement and urine is, to complete the irony, an antihuman, animal-like behavior; thus the boy, by his own efforts to save himself as a "social" being, furthers his transformation into a

THE STRUCTURE OF THE MYTH

"natural" being on the level of an animal. Finally, the regressive associations of a person eating excrement, i.e., returning to presocial infancy, are significant here. In this sense, the boy's action represents an attempt to escape his situation by retreating to an infantile situation of nurturance in the bosom of his lost family at the cost of surrendering his socialization.

Starving and eating excrement have affective connotations for a Kayapo audience so obvious that there is no need to point them out in the text of the story. Starvation has associations of both suffering and fear, while the eating of excrement provokes revulsion, disgust, and the horror of animal-like behavior. Both of these sets of connotations underline the affective corollaries of separation from the natal family: fear and anguish at the separation itself; the sense of weakness and frustration attendant upon the inability to create a viable adult identity by his own efforts outside the family; and finally the regressive tendencies that arise in the face of the frustration, wretchedness, and terror of the situation.

The transformation of the boy's family status (and therefore of his relationship with the macaws) from identity to antithesis also transforms the nature of his problem in escaping from the nest. The change in the boy's relationship to his own past social identity changes his relationship to one of open contradiction. He remains, however, situationally identified with the macaws. This situation means that his identity itself has entered into a phase of excruciating internal contradiction, which can be resolved only by destroying the unviable aspects of that identity. In the concrete terms of the myth, this means destroying the macaws. As the embodiments of his childhood (infrasocial) attachments to his natal family, they cannot be allowed to continue to exist, since they represent actively unviable aspects of the boy's present and future social persona. This means he cannot simply climb down and leave them behind in the nest.

The boy, then, must find a way to destroy the macaws. To destroy an aspect of his social identity, however, is not a thing he can do alone: social identities are defined only in relation to social "others." The boy can neither create nor destroy aspects of his social identity by himself any more than he can feed himself with his own excrement. He therefore cannot get rid of the fledglings by killing them himself or merely by throwing them out of the nest onto the ground. Just as the boy can only define a viable status identity for himself as an adult male by relating to an exemplar of that status, so he can only negate his now unviable childhood status by having its symbolic representatives destroyed by an exemplar of a complementary status.

It thus becomes evident that the boy's problem of escaping from the macaws'
nest (by successfully relating to the proper adult male status) and his problem of
destroying the macaws (and thus definitively surrendering his unviable childish
identity) are complementary and inseparable aspects of the same problem. For
it is clear that there is only one relationship in which the status of the boy's now
unviable childhood family identity was defined and toward which the boy must
orient his development into mature manhood. This is the pivotal male status
identity of father, which was described in our earlier discussion of Kayapo family structure. The stage is set, then, for the entrance of the bearer of the pivotal
status of father.

The set of symbolic elements and relations associated with WB and his situation in the macaws' nest cannot be described as a full-blown episode like the
preceding and following segments of the narrative, but they nevertheless form
a distinct significant cluster with a structure recognizably analogous to those of
the other clusters and episodes of the myth. This becomes obvious by formulating it in a diagram, as shown in Figure 1.5.

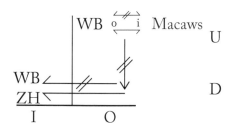

Figure 1.5. After ZH returns to the village, WB languishes in the macaws' nest, dying
of thirst and starvation and resorting to consuming his own urine and excrement.

Key: U = up; D = down; I = inside the house; O = outside the house; WB = wife's brother;
ZH = sister's husband

Vertical axis: This axis here represents the impossibility of passage out of childhood (i.e., of "downward" transformation).

1. The boy cannot get down by himself from the nest for lack of a viable social
    alter to assist him.
2. The lack of a viable social agent to help the boy down from the nest also
    means the lack of a viable social basis for negating his lingering identifica-
    tion with the macaws. They must be eliminated in order to begin the next

phase of his development, or, in terms of the symbolic values of vertical spacetime, thrown down to be destroyed by the appropriate social alter, who has not yet appeared on the scene.

Horizontal axis: This axis here represents the boy's inability to separate the viable ("social") and unviable ("natural") aspects of his identity.

1. The lack of differentiation results in a structural contradiction. When the ZH leaves, the boy's connection to his natal household is severed, removing the basis for the boy's identification with the macaw fledglings. The boy is nevertheless still situationally identified with the macaws in the negative sense of being stranded with them in the nest, unable either to get down himself or to throw them down. His relation to the macaws thus becomes actively contradictory and without any means of becoming differentiated.
2. As the boy starves, he regresses and becomes less social, more natural (animal-like), and more infantile.
3. This contradictory state is utterly unviable, as seen in his eating his own feces and drinking his own urine. His attempt to survive as a "social" being ends by transforming him into a "natural" being. The absence of an alter to precipitate movement out of the contradiction and development forward is the crux of the situation.

Affective structure

1. The boy's starvation is experienced as suffering and fear over being separated from his from family.
2. His consumption of his own urine and excrement represents his revulsion, frustration, and wretchedness over his untransformed, "natural" condition.

The first jaguar episode: The encounter

The jaguar episode begins when the jaguar attacks the boy's shadow (a separated, "natural" aspect of the boy), which he sees projected before him on the ground. The separation of the shadow from the boy, as we have seen above, is an indication of the unviability of the boy's physical ("natural") condition in his asocial situation. In its downward projection in vertical space, it represents a preliminary expression of the separation of the boy from his socially unviable ("natural") childish identity. It is significant, in the light of the role played by the jaguar in this episode, that it is this tentative token of the polarization of the boy's contradictory attributes that serves to bring the boy to the jaguar's attention.

The ensuing exchanges between the boy and the jaguar constitute a process of reciprocal polarization of "social" and "natural" attributes on the part of both boy and jaguar. The jaguar's antisocial natural attributes as a beast of prey become focused upon the boy's shadow and the macaw fledglings, which represent the unviable (natural) aspects of the boy's situation. The jaguar's positive ("social") attributes, on the other hand, as embodied in his civil behavior and especially in the social relationship of "father" he adopts toward the boy, become focused on the boy himself in his capacity as a youth already beginning to develop into a man. This developing aspect of the boy's identity is communicated to the jaguar by the boy when he tells the jaguar how he has, in effect, severed his childhood ties with his maternal household by breaking his ZH's hand and how, in return, he has been stranded in the macaws' nest. This information, provided by the boy in answer to the jaguar's questions as to how he came to be in the nest, thus confirms, in a positive way (in the "social" medium of language), the negative implications of the boy's shadow (a "natural" medium). The jaguar's persuasion of the boy to climb down to him and ride home on his back is, correlatively, the positive counterpart of the jaguar's devouring of the macaw fledglings, which the boy readily throws down at his command.

The key to the jaguar's ability to mediate, in opposite terms, both the viable and unviable aspects of the boy's social identity is his assumption of the pivotal status of father. By this ploy, the jaguar becomes at one stroke a "once and future" father, as it were. As a representative of the boy's own ("once") father—the dominant figure in the boy's natal family (who primarily defined the boy's family status)—the jaguar annihilates the macaw fledglings and thus the boy's now outgrown identity. This, however, implies that, by the same act, he also annihilates the antisocial aspect of his own role in relation to the boy. From this point on, the male jaguar is a purely supportive and "social" figure in relation to the boy. As the embodiment of the father the boy must eventually become—a "future" father, so to speak—the jaguar brings the boy down from the nest. The significance of this act, in terms of the symbolic values of vertical space, is precisely that of establishing the course of the boy's development into a man. The jaguar says he wants to take the boy home and feed him so that he may grow up to become the jaguar's own equivalent, his "hunting companion." In avowing this purpose, the jaguar overtly takes on the function of a future role model for the boy.

The jaguar thus precipitates the polarization of the contradictory qualities that had coexisted within the boy in his structurally undifferentiated situation in the macaws' nest. He accomplishes this by presenting differentiated "social" and "natural" aspects with opposite values (positive, emulative, and viable, on the one hand, and negative, outgrown, and unviable, on the other). These aspects become the foci of coordinated but inverse transformations (one positive, consisting in the development of the boy's adult social identity, and the other negative, consisting in the severance of the boy's connections with the unviable aspects of his past identity).

The essential structural property of the jaguar's role as a "pivotal" figure can thus be stated in two ways: on the one hand, the jaguar acts simultaneously as a mediator of processes of transformation and of differentiation; on the other, he serves as the coordinator of parallel but inverse transformations. These structural properties of the jaguar's role in the myth are analogous to those comprising the two "father" roles in Kayapo social and ritual life, that of the true father and the "substitute father."

The jaguar works as the symbolic vehicle for this complex and crucial pivotal role since, as has been shown, it is a focus in Kayapo culture of a cluster of ambivalent attitudes and qualities that are directly associated with mature manhood. For this reason, the jaguar overtly figures in Kayapo ritual in precisely the same way that it functions as a symbol in the myth, to wit, as a mediator of positive qualities (of socially esteemed mature males) and, simultaneously, as a symbolic sieve for sorting out these qualities from among the relatively undifferentiated characteristics of boys of the same age as the hero of the myth. Recall from an earlier description (see Chapter Four) that it is precisely at this age that boys go through a liminal ritual phase in which they eat jaguar meat as a means of imbuing them with manly attributes and suppressing their childish ones.

The episode of the boy's encounter with the jaguar can be structurally represented in the diagram shown in Figure 1.6.

Vertical axis:

1. A successful transformation occurs along this axis, in opposite senses, of the "social" and "natural" aspects of boy.

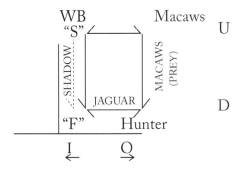

Figure 1.6. The boy casts a shadow on the ground, which the male jaguar mistakes for prey; once he recognizes it is different than the boy, he pounces on the macaws and assumes a friendly attitude toward the boy.

Key: U = up; D = down; S = son; F = father

2. The jaguar, in his "social" aspect as "father," replaces the ladder and induces the boy to climb down to him, thus establishing new link to society on basis of the pivotal male status of "father." The boy cooperates.

3. The jaguar, in his unambiguously "natural" aspect as hunter-predator, destroys and eats the (raw) macaw fledglings that the boy throws down to him, thus negating the "natural" (outmoded, childish) aspect of the boy's identity.

Horizontal axis:

1. Over the course of this episode, a successful differentiation occurs on this axis of the "social" and "natural" aspects of both the boy and the jaguar.

2. At the outset of the episode, the boy finds himself in an undifferentiated state. Casting a shadow is both a symbolic expression of the unviability of his undifferentiated state and a tentative act of differentiation. The jaguar responds by treating boy's shadow as natural prey (unaware that it is differentiated from the boy).

3. When the jaguar realizes the boy and his shadow are different, he relates in two contrasting modes to boy as a "social" being and as the macaws as "natural" beings. The boy responds cooperatively by distancing the macaws from himself, allowing differentiation to occur between his "social" and "natural" aspects.

Differentiation of jaguar

1. The jaguar assumes the pivotal social status of "father" toward boy, behaving toward him in the approved "social" manner by courteously covering his fangs with his paw. He helps the boy to get down from nest and takes him home to the jaguars' house. By associating this aspect of himself with the boy's survival and downward transition to the next phase of his life cycle, the jaguar links this aspect of himself with the boy's future development. The boy cooperates with the jaguar in these respects.

2. The jaguar redirects his "natural," predatory attributes away from the boy (in the form of his shadow) to the macaws. By destroying them in his "natural" capacity as a hunter-predator, thus preventing them from persisting into the next phase of the boy's life cycle, the jaguar also links this hostile aspect of himself with the previous stage, now closed and surpassed, of the boy's cycle. This aspect of the jaguar embodies the negative, superseded aspect of the social role he assumes toward the boy, i.e., the boy's own father, with whom the boy must break connections in order to become, in his own future development, a father in his own right. The jaguar thus represents the boy's "once and future" father. The boy cooperates in these transformations.

Affective structure

1. The jaguar's support and fatherly encouragement enable the boy to overcome his fear and to take the step of separating himself from the natal "nest" on the basis of identifying himself with the appropriate mature male status.

2. The jaguar's menacing, feral attack on boy's shadow (his tentatively differentiated, progressive "social" aspect) is displaced to the macaws (his outmoded, childish aspect). The boy's terror at the jaguar's attack on his shadow is transformed into cooperation with him in the destruction of his childish status identity.

3. The friendly jaguar persuades the boy to come home with him (Figure 1.7).

The second jaguar episode: At the jaguars' house

Cognitive structure and dynamics

The boy's problem at the outset of the myth is to differentiate the two aspects of his social identity that pertain to the successive developmental phases of

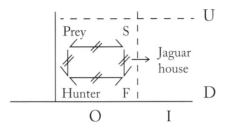

Figure 1.7. The male jaguar persuades the boy to come down and come home with him, where he will feed and care for him. The boy's development is thus incorporated into a new setting.

Key: U = up; D = down; I = inside the house; O = outside the house; S = son; F= father

childhood and mature manhood. These two aspects are associated not only with two successive phases of development but also with two successive levels of the structure of family relations: the intrafamily level, represented by the child's individual natal family; and the interfamily level, represented by the adult affinal status of father-husband. ZH fails to get the boy and the macaws down from the nest because he represents only a single phase and structural level. He is therefore unable to serve as the template of the differentiation of the two temporally and structurally contrasted phases or levels of the boy's identity. The male jaguar succeeds where ZH failed because the pivotal social status of father that he adopts toward the boy functions as an axis connecting the intra- and interfamilial levels of structure and, by the same token, the two successive developmental phases of childhood and maturity. It thus allows the negation of the one to be treated as directly reinforcing the other.

It is not enough, however, for the boy simply to "identify" with the proper mature male status and to shuffle off his childish identity, as it were, in social isolation. These developments also depend upon the readjustment of relations with other aspects of family structure. The brief account of Kayapo social organization presented earlier indicated what the most prominent aspects of this readjustment are: the basic framework of the boy's development toward mature manhood is provided by the opposition between female-centered households and family ties, on the one hand, and the collective men's groupings of the central village plaza, on the other. This opposition takes the dynamic form of the displacement of boys from their natal households, accompanied by the attenuation of their relations to their female relatives, particularly their mothers and sisters.

The polarization of the mythical female and male jaguars in their relationships to the boy faithfully reflects the form of this process, taking into account, of
course, the lack of a collective association of male jaguars. The fire and the meat
it cooks become the active agents of the boy's transformation into a physically
robust young man. This "natural" metamorphosis is given social direction by the
re-polarization of the jaguar symbol into "social" and "natural" aspects. In contrast to the first polarization of the jaguar in the preceding episode, which took
the form of the contrast between the "social" (fatherly) and "natural" (predatory)
aspects of the male jaguar, the polarization now takes the form of the opposition
between the male jaguar and the female jaguar. It is of the essence of the marital
relationship between these two figures that they are both jaguars: their interaction takes the form of a polarization of the ambivalent complex of meanings
associated with the jaguar in Kayapo culture. This new polarization of the jaguar
symbol is more pronounced in this episode, becoming more and more intense
and extreme. The more the boy grows to be like the male jaguar, the more hostile
and feral ("natural") to him becomes the female jaguar; this, in turn, prompts the
male jaguar to become more "socially" supportive of the boy.

This pattern of polarization of the "social" and "natural" aspects of the jaguars
takes concrete form, as we should by now expect, on the horizontal dimension
of symbolic space. Note that all of the boy's interactions with the female jaguar,
from her first hostile greeting, take place at the threshold or inside of the jaguars'
house, whereas all of the boy's interaction with the male jaguar takes place outside it. This is consistent with the emphasis on the boy's identification with the
male jaguar's role as a hunter, given that hunting is an outdoor activity. The bow
and arrow are the distinctive tools of the hunter, and their use thus betokens
the boy's attainment of the status of hunter (i.e., a physically mature, jaguar-
like male). The associations of the male and female jaguars with the outdoors
and household domains, respectively, means that the boy's attainment of mature
male (bow-using) status will require his separation from the intrahousehold
domain of the female jaguar, where he remains while he is still growing.

The female jaguar is thus forced into a relation with the boy analogous to
that of the boy's own mother. She is a mature female, a nurturing, family, household figure with whom the boy must sever his relationship in order to become
a mature man. The male jaguar, on the other hand, takes on a role that is the
opposite of the boy's own father, that is, the figure serving as the focus of the
boy's future development. Both the "once" and "future" and the "natural" and
"social" concomitants become polarized in the form of the opposition of the

female jaguar, associated with the maternal household and oriented toward the past, and the male jaguar, associated with leaving the household and oriented toward the future.

The temporal polarization of the boy's relations to the male and female jaguars is concretely associated with the recurrence of "vertical" spatial imagery. The female jaguar's threats always cause the boy to flee the house and climb up a tree. It is always the male jaguar who coaxes him down again.

The past and future aspects of the female and male jaguars' roles are also associated with distinctive roles and behavior patterns that mark them as "natural" and "social," respectively. The male jaguar's role of father is eminently social, whereas the female jaguar, at the outset, rejects the counterpart "social" role of mother. Her negativity becomes progressively more extreme as she resorts to "natural," predatory jaguar behavior like growling, extending her claws, and baring her fangs in protest against the socially anomalous situation into which her maternal relationship with the boy has forced her.

The foregoing discussion can be summed up in the diagram shown in Figure 1.8.

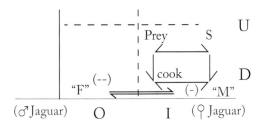

Figure 1.8. The boy's relationships to the male and female jaguars become progressively more polarized: increasingly positive toward the jaguar "father," increasingly negative toward the jaguar "mother."

Key: U = up; D = down; I = inside the house; O = outside the house; S = son; F= father; M = mother

Jaguar's dual personality

Although the boy's transformation in the jaguars' household is accomplished under the social rubric of the pivotal status of father that the male jaguar assumes toward him, he does not actually attain this status as a father in his own right while living with the jaguars. The aspect of the male jaguar's status that he does manage to acquire is that of a hunter's ambiguously "natural" activity conducted with the "cultural" attributes of bow and arrow. It should be noted that the role of hunter is the complementary role played by both of the adult male figures in the myth: first, the ZH at the macaws' nest, and second, the male jaguar, in his feral hunting role as animal predator when he meets the boy at the macaws' nest, and then in the present episode that emphasizes the "socialization" of the hunter's role through the use of the bow and arrow. Both ZH and the jaguar have a "social" status identity through which they relate to the boy in his capacity as "social" being, but it is through their complementary roles as hunters that they relate to the boy's "natural" aspect. This function of the hunter's role has obvious analogies to the role of the human hunter in real life as a mediator between the "social" and "natural" domains. In the present episode, it is thus significant that the jaguar relates to the boy not only as a hunter but as a teacher of hunting techniques, specifically "social" hunting techniques (using the bow and arrow). The boy is clearly being prepared, in symbolic terms, to deal with nature, which here means primarily the regressive aspects of his own character-istics through the mastery of social techniques. He is, in short, being socialized.

The male jaguar's role as father to the boy serves as a provisional formula that provides the indispensable social orientation for the boy's socialization as a hunter, but it is not a status the boy can achieve for himself in "jaguar" society, precisely because there is no jaguar "society." The single jaguar household pro-vides no structural basis for the social transformation of family role identities upon which human society is based. What is specifically lacking is a basis of social differentiation between child and adult roles (i.e., differentiated sets of consanguineal and affinal relations, or, in the simplest terms, a family of orienta-tion and a family of procreation). The jaguars have, in effect, only half a family, since there are no jaguar children. Like the jaguar's fire, the jaguar household lacks the crucial social ability to reproduce itself. Because it is one of a kind, it has neither a more generalized social context to relate to nor the wherewithal to regenerate itself by detaching its own members (i.e., children) to start new families.

These considerations explain why the boy's separation from the jaguars and return to human society is the structurally appropriate outcome of his "sociali-zation" among the jaguars, which culminates in the redefinition of his childish relations to them along adult lines. This is recognized by the male jaguar himself when he tells the boy that, if he kills the female jaguar with the bow and arrow (an act that, as we shall see, marks the culmination of his socialization), then the two of them must separate, the boy returning to his village while he, the male jaguar, goes off in the opposite direction.

This analysis also explain why the boy's act of separating from the jaguars' household (and simultaneously of detaching from it pieces of fire, roast meat, cotton string, and the bow and arrows) comprises the essential basis for his re-integration into society as the product of a completed family cycle, represented by his development within and exiting from the jaguars' household. The boy's achievement thus becomes the basis of the transformation of society as a whole into its present generalized, self-replicating form.

Affective structure

The affective structure of this episode is a triumph of composition. It amounts to a comprehensive template for the transformation and reorganization of a boy's childish emotional relations toward the mother and father into the affective "set" of the mature male personality.

The female jaguar's hostility to the boy stems directly from the contradictory position in which she is placed by the boy's (her "son's") development toward physical and social maturity in her household. The contradiction here arises in terms of the Kayapo norm of uxorilocal residence. The female jaguar is asked to feed and nurture the boy, while his growth, the direct result of her nurturance, is precisely what renders his position in her house—indeed, his entire relationship to her—increasingly anomalous in terms of the normative residential pattern, which calls for adolescent youths to be removed from their mother's households. She tries in vain to impede the pace of the boy's growth by offering him only weak varieties of meat such as venison, but he defies her by demanding the meat of the tapir, the biggest and strongest animal of all (since the Kayapo have a notion that the nutritional value of a species of meat is directly proportional to the size and strength of the animal). The boy's defiant demand for tapir meat is thus, in one sense, an assertion of his relationship of dependency and nurturance toward his jaguar mother. In another sense, however, the demand for tapir meat is in direct contradiction to this relationship, since it is what will most strongly promote his growth beyond the point at which a nurturant relationship with the mother, or even coresidence with her in the same household, is socially appropriate. The boy's behavior in demanding the meat in itself implies that this point has already been passed, for he asserts his demand in an autonomous, independent, and, in the end, defiantly aggressive way—in short, in a way that embodies precisely those qualities that make the continuation of his dependent childlike relationship to his "mother" anomalous. She, for her part, responds in a correspondingly ambiguous and ambivalent way, first threatening him by baring her claws and fangs and then, as she moves murderously toward him, hissing softly but menacingly, "Don't be afraid!"

Both the boy and the female jaguar thus relate to each other in contradictory ways. The behavior of each toward the other is, in fact, a good example of a "double bind" (Bateson 1972). The myth shows each double bind as arising ineluctably from the basic contradiction represented by the continuing coresidence of the growing youth with his mother. She remains his only source of food, so he must continue to demand food from her that he needs to grow; she must resist his demands in spite of her nurturing, motherly tendencies ("Don't be afraid"). His double-bind behavior generates hers. Hers, in turn, has the ironic result of reinforcing the very regressive behavior on his part that originally gave rise to it, for when she succeeds in driving the boy out of her house, it is only to have him climb a tree. In terms of the symbolic spacetime of the myth, this amounts to his regressing to the position of a dependent child in a natal household, which he has only just painfully and tentatively left behind in the macaws' nest. It is precisely this regressive role, of course, which the "mother" jaguar had originally set out to deny and destroy.

The actions of the male jaguar serve, on the one hand, to complete and reinforce the vicious circle set up by the double bind between his wife and "son" but, on the other hand, to point the way toward the eventual transcendence of the problem. The effect of the male jaguar's role in getting the boy to come down out of the tree jaguar is to rechannel the regressive tendencies and fears that propelled his climb up the tree into the motivating force for the identification with the male jaguar associated with climbing back down it. In this sense, the male jaguar continues to play the same constructive role as a socializing figure that he first undertook in the episode with the boy at the macaws' nest. Having rescued the boy from the tree, on the other hand, he takes him back into the house, remonstrates with his wife for threatening the boy, orders her to comply with whatever requests he makes for food, and encourages the boy to ask for anything he likes. In short, he serves as the final link in the vicious circle through which the double-bind interaction between the boy and the female jaguar is perpetuated and intensified.

It is precisely the intensification of the contradiction in the relationship between the boy and the female jaguar, however, that becomes the force that drives the boy to identify definitively with the male jaguar and, by the same token, to break the regressive cycle of the interaction with the "mother" jaguar. This identification of the two males in opposition to the female is initiated by the male jaguar when he takes the boy out of the house and down to the river, where he makes a bow and arrow for the boy and shows him how to use it. He instructs the boy to use the weapons to defend himself against the female and then sends him back to the house to repeat his intolerable demands for tapir meat, which once again lead to the female's hostile behavior. The inevitable result, the triggering of the female jaguar's menacing double-bind response, then becomes the trigger driving the boy to take the final, decisive step in his transformation from child to man. In terror and imminent peril of his life, he uses the bow and arrow to kill the female jaguar. He thus achieves symbolic identification with the male jaguar in his adult male role of hunter and simultaneously breaks his regressive ties to his jaguar "mother" and her household (which is, in symbolic terms, his natal household). His acts of shooting her through the paw (or in other versions, the nipples) and leaving the house for the last time reinforce the symbolism of the murder. Shooting the outstretched paw (or the nipples) of the "mother" plays on the aspect of the break that represents the destruction of the nurturant role of the mother. It is analogous to breaking the outstretched hand of the ZH with the stone in the macaw episode (recall that this involved a pun on the Kayapo term for "my child," such that the incident connoted the breaking of the child's tie to his household).

This episode, taken together with the preceding episode of the boy's encounter with the male jaguar at the macaws' nest, may be taken as exemplifying the Kayapo pattern for the reorganization of a boy's emotional attitudes to his parents and to himself as a male developing toward future adulthood, modeling the pattern of the mature male personality. The jaguar crisis is, in these terms, the Kayapo counterpart of the Oedipal crisis in Western psychology. Its difference from the latter in respect to the roles of "mother" and "father" figures, and the pattern of the boy's affects toward them, are largely the products of the uxorilocal household structure that provides the setting of Kayapo family organization and sex roles.

The use of the jaguar as the symbolic vehicle of the parental roles in this crisis makes sense in terms of the strong affective ambivalence of Kayapo attitudes to jaguars, documented in the previous chapter. The jaguar symbol, with its associations of terror and antisocial ferocity, on the one hand, and emulative, highly valued adult male qualities, on the other, becomes the "objective correlative" of the ambivalent affective associations attaching to human parents in their roles as socialization figures. The child's emotions of terror and emulation, as well as the tension between his regressive panic over being expelled from his role of a nurtured dependent and his aggressive assertion of his development toward adulthood against the restraints imposed by the parents are the elements that propel the narrative actions at this point.

The jaguar, in short, works as a symbol at the affective level in the same way that it works at the cognitive level. At both levels, it serves first to condense, then to polarize the conflicting and ambivalent aspects of the boy's relationship to his parents, and finally to restructure the field of polarized, contradictory effects and attributes. This restructuring of the jaguar's field of meanings, accomplished through the transformation of its relations with other polyvalent symbols, is directed in such a way that the negation of the unviable components of the field becomes the corollary of the definitive affirmation of (or identification with) the positive aspects. This dynamic capacity of the jaguar symbol to restructure the pattern of meanings it condenses around itself and to actually change its meaning in the course of the story by eliminating or recombining components of this field, is, I would suggest, a key feature of mythical and ritual symbols as a general class.

The structure of the boy's interaction with the jaguars in this episode can be represented in Figure 1.9.

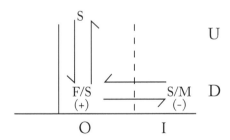

Figure 1.9. The boy repeatedly flees the menacing female jaguar and climbs a tree; the friendly male jaguar repeatedly persuades him to come down again.

Key: U = up; D = down; I = inside the house; O = outside the house; S = son; F= father; M = mother

Vertical axis: "Socialization" occurs on this axis as the coordination of progressive (downward) and redirected regressive (upward) transformations.

1. The boy is coaxed down from the tree by the male jaguar, enabling him to develop in proper direction from a child to mature male status identity.
2. The boy climbs the tree in flight from the female jaguar, thus regressing to his position as a nestling among the macaws and, symbolically, to that of a child in his natal household. The efforts of both the female jaguar and the boy to break off their contradictory relationship within the household thus ironically result in reinforcing the regressive pattern at the root of the contradiction.

Horizontal axis: This axis shows the differentiation of the progressive and regressive aspects of family relations.

1. There is a polarization of the boy's regressive aspect as a dependent child and his progressive aspect as developing adult, which supersedes his regression.
2. Correlatively, there is a polarization of the regressive and progressive aspects of the parental jaguar figures. Through his encouragement, the male jaguar becomes the focus of the boy's development toward a viable adult social identity. The female jaguar becomes the focus of the boy's regressive tendencies through a double-bind situation in which he independently asserts his dependent relation with her, while she menacingly rejects him while telling him not to be afraid.
3. The arrows in the diagram form a continuous cycle moving counterclockwise, which corresponds to the "vicious circle" of the analysis. It is intensified by several repetitions of the set of events that comprise it. The process of intensification reaches its climax and denouement when the youth shoots the female jaguar with the bow and arrows given him by the male jaguar at the river, thus simultaneously breaking off his relation with the former and identifying with the latter.

Affective structure

1. A two-way double bind between boy and female jaguar is set up. The boy over-asserts his dependent, nurturant relationship with the female jaguar in an aggressive, independent manner, to which she replies by threatening him with murderous displays of fangs and claws.
2. The boy seeks to escape from this double bind generated by his contradictory relationship with his jaguar "mother" through "regressively" climbing a

tree, thus symbolically returning to the role of a dependent child in a natal family, which was the original source of the conflict with his "mother." The original double bind is thus transformed into a potential vicious circle.

3. The male jaguar coaxes the boy down again from tree and urges him to be more assertive (more like himself) in relation to female jaguar while continuing to press his demands for nurturance, thus intensifying the double bind and completing the vicious circle.

4. The episode traces the ultimate resolution of the vicious circle and double bind in the affective structure. The female jaguar's hostility and rejection forces the boy, out of terror, to complete his identification as a "hunter" with the male jaguar through the use of the bow and arrow the latter gave him at the river. Furthermore, the boy's use of the bow and arrow to shoot the female jaguar completes the redirection of his fear and anxiety toward her into a defense against his dependent relation to her, and thus a rejection of his regressive tendencies to revert to childhood as an escape from the tensions inherent in the process of becoming an adult male.

The boy's relations with the jaguars are not the only relationships in this episode to become decisively transformed in terms of the spatial contrast of inside and outside the house. The fire appears on earth for the first time at the beginning of the episode, inside the jaguars' house; by the end of the episode, a small piece of it appears again (on very different terms) outside it. These movements of the fire, along with the roast meat, bow and arrows, and cotton string, indicate transformations in the nature and relations among the members of the jaguars' household, thus condensing within themselves the entire significance of the action in the myth up to this point. These can be distilled into the diagram portrayed in Figure 1.10.

The bow and arrows, fire, roast meat, and cotton serve as class emblems that represent the identity of a certain type of being. At this stage, the bow and arrows represent the masculinity and father role of the male jaguar, while the cotton represents the femininity and mother role of the female jaguar. The fire and roast meat, at this point in the myth, represent the jaguar couple as an ambiguously "natural" and "social" household, requiring further differentiation as the myth progresses. As class emblems, these items can be detached and taken from their original bearers and transferred to other beings. They are also capable of serving as prototypes, which will then be generalized and replicated in the village ad infinitum, as we will see in later episodes.

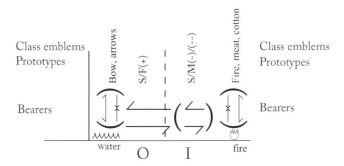

Figure 1.10. The male jaguar gives a bow and arrows to the boy at the river and tells him to shoot the female jaguar next time she threatens him while he takes his meat from the fire. He does so and gathers a piece of fire and emblems of each gender as he leaves.

Key: U = up; D = down; I = inside the house; O = outside the house; S = son; F= father; M = mother

A reconsideration of the broader implications of the developments in the myth so far will shed light on the the metamorphosis of the fire up to this point and provide an explanation of the close association between the jaguar's family household and fire. It is not a coincidence that the fire appears on earth at the same point in the story as does the jaguar's house and wife (a quasi-"social" family) or that these symbolic entities are presented as interrelated aspects (the fire being inside the hut and the female jaguar being occupied with cooking over the fire). Reviewing the preceding episodes of the narrative will also allow us to revisit the transformations in terms of the dialectics of "inside" and "outside," a dimension indicated in the diagrams but which has so far been rather neglected so as not to weigh down the analysis at the outset with too many layers of complexity. Now that we have unraveled the basic dynamics of the vertical and horizontal dimensions, it will perhaps now be clear how the inside–outside dimension operates and, more specifically, how it helps us comprehend the transformations of the fire in relation to the main characters up to now. Since the concentric structure of the myth becomes especially marked in the final two episodes of the myth, we will be in a better position to appreciate it after contextualizing the preceding analysis within this broader set of dynamics.

The boy's dilemma at the outset of the myth, as reflected in the two macaw episodes, can be succinctly restated in terms of the same contrast of "outside" and "inside" the household that emerges as a decisive dimension of the action in the second jaguar episode. The fundamental task facing the boy is to become socialized, that is, to transform himself from a "natural" to a "social" being. His progress in this respect is, however, blocked by a contradiction. He is faced, on the one hand, with the impossibility of staying inside his natal family household, which would imply his remaining a natural being in terms of Kayapo concepts of natal family relationships (as we saw, the implied equation between the boy, in his capacity as "child," and the macaw fledglings expresses this aspect of his situation). He is swiftly confronted, on the other hand, with the impossibility of staying outside the household in the macaws' nest, where he is likewise in the position of a "natural" being without social ties (this aspect of his situation is again expressed by his situational identification with the macaw fledglings, after he is stranded in the nest and begins starving to death).

The terms of this contradictory situation are determined by the existence of the family household, at the outset of the myth, as the sole form of social grouping or, in other words, the singular level of social organization. This means that leaving the natal family household entails passing completely outside of society. With the family household as the only social unit, there is no solution for the boy, since both outside and inside it he has no opportunity to become a "social" being.

Given that the boy must, as a concomitant of his socialization, make his way outside his natal household (in both the physical and the social sense), the only way for him to avoid the unviable and antisocial alternative of passing outside of society altogether is therefore to preserve some form of social link with his natal family household, even as he passes outside of it. This would amount, in a certain sense, to turning his family household inside out, since it would necessarily involve transforming a relationship with its roots inside the family household into an external link between that household and the boy, once he succeeds in moving outside it. The image of turning the household "inside out" also applies in a more general sense, since the boy's task of socialization can be thought of as consisting in transforming himself from a "natural" entity within the "social" group constituted by the household into a "social" entity by virtue of his position outside it. From this socialized vantage point, the household would then appear to him as a relatively "natural" unit (the setting of his "natural" childhood and natal family relations).

The boy cannot accomplish this "inside-out" transformation of his family relations by himself, because to do so would imply access to the social framework within which the family is embedded; the boy's dilemma, however, arises precisely because he has no access to that framework. This inability to escape from the family on his own is represented in the myth by the boy's inability to get down from the macaws' nest by himself. To make possible the boy's progress from inside the family household into society (i.e., the community at large), therefore, the structure of the family itself must have built into it some outward-oriented component to serve as a channel for the boy's outward-oriented development (socialization). The structure of the family, then, must already include a component that has been, so to speak, turned outside-out, in order to enable the boy, in his terms, to turn it inside out.

These are, at any rate, the general principles spelled out by the myth in the concrete language of the macaw fledglings, the macaws nest suspended in its cliff, and the jaguar, with his odd mixture of bestiality and civility. The arrival of ZH has redefined the boy, as WB, as an "outsider" in his own household. The macaws' nest expresses the terms of this situation: on the one hand, it represents, with its fledglings, a "natal family" inside its household; on the other, it is decidedly outside the boy's own natal family household. The young WB is taken outside his house and made to climb up into the macaws' nest by his ZH and is then left there with no way to get back inside his own natal (i.e., his sister's) household. This means, in one sense, that the boy has been displaced outside his natal family household, but, as we have already seen, the terms of his "displacement" are in fact specious and contradictory. In another sense he is still prevented from extricating himself from within his natal family (represented by the macaws).

The ambiguity of the relationship between the macaws' nest and the boy's sister's household is reflected, in parallel terms, in the relationship between the ZH's two roles as ZH and as macaw hunter. Both of these roles mediate the opposition between outside and inside the household. A ZH is, in one sense, a member of the same extended-family household, but he is, in origin, an "outsider" from another household. A hunter normally kills wild animals outside the household in order to bring them back inside to be transformed (cooked) into social matter (food). The ZH, however, transforms the terms of this relationship into an attempt to introduce "natural" beings (the fledglings, and by implication, the boy) into the household as permanently unsocialized members of it.

Both aspects of ZH's role identity are therefore defined, in relation to the boy, in terms of an outside-inward orientation. This means, on the one hand, that these aspects do not in themselves afford the boy a viable channel for his own socialization, that is, his development from inside the family outward. On the other hand, their very "outside-in" orientation precipitates the formation of a corresponding pattern of "inside-out" orientations on the part of the boy. The definition of both of ZH's roles with reference to the inside–outside contrast, moreover, makes them potentially viable structural channels for the boy's development, once their "directionality" is reversed from "outside in" to "inside out."

This reorientation is accomplished in the second macaw episode and the following encounter with the male jaguar. The boy reorients himself to the macaws' nest (and thus, symbolically, to his natal family household) in terms of an "inside-out" perspective. The corollary reorientation of both the "hunter" (i.e., natural) role and the "member of the same family household" (i. e., social) role from "outside in" to "inside out" is achieved thereafter by the male jaguar. The social role the jaguar adopts toward the boy is, as we have noted, the critical attribute of the latter's future adult status identity, thereby pointing the way out of the natal family and household. As a "hunter," on the other hand, the jaguar devours the macaws' nestlings (representing the aspect of the boy associated with his childhood attachments inside the family and household), thus preventing them from being brought back inside the house as sister's husband wished to do. This act simultaneously cancels out the inside-oriented aspect of the "father" role the jaguar assumes toward the boy (that is, the aspect of the "father" role associated with the boy's own father and natal family).

By combining the definitive destruction of the macaw fledglings (i.e., the aspect of the boy associated with his position inside the household) with the overt affirmation of an adult male family role directed outside the family, the jaguar re-polarizes the ambiguous and contradictory role pattern created by the ZH and the equally ambiguous and contradictory relation between the boy's natal household and the macaws' nest.

This clarified and consistently polarized role pattern is a result and a permutation of the initial structure of role relations created by ZH. It represents, in other words, a manifestation of the same pattern (albeit in a disambiguated form) at the same structural level of contrast (i.e., the contrast between outside and inside the individual family household). This disambiguated pattern of differentiation between positively affirmed outward role orientations and negated inward role orientations reappears as the structure of the jaguars' household itself where, as we have just seen, its implications are worked out to their logical conclusions.

The structure of the jaguars' house thus represents a detachment of the pattern of contrast between "outside" and "inside" orientations from its original setting (the relations between the boy, his ZH, the macaws, and the boy's sister's household) and its transposition to another setting (the jaguars' household), where it is then replicated. Although the permutation that the pattern undergoes in the course of this transition does not represent an actual transition between social groups or levels of social organization, it nevertheless provides a viable framework within which the development of both the boy and the family itself can go forward from inside outward (i.e., toward dispersion and reintegration at the higher level of community structure).

Thus, the establishment of the pattern of differentiation between "inside" and "outside" orientations between the male jaguar and the boy at the macaws' nest leads directly to the appearance of a jaguars' domestic family household and, simultaneously, to the appearance of the fire as the central feature of that household. The jaguars' family household appears when a pattern of differentiated outside and inside orientations is created that allows an outside-oriented transformation to take place inside the household; this therefore makes it possible for both the boy and the fire (as the principal and agent of transformation) to be brought into the household.

The changes that the fire goes through from its original form as the undifferentiated sun in the sky to its reappearance inside the jaguars' house parallel the transformations in the structure of role relations and inside–outside orientations that have just been described for both the boy and the family. Like the pattern of differentiation in the jaguars' family, it has been detached, transposed to a new setting, and replicated there in a form that will permit full transformation to take place (that is, a genuine cooking of meat rather than the mere warming generated by the undifferentiated sun). Like the boy, it has been detached from its vertically elevated setting in the sky and has come down to earth. Downward movement in vertical space, as we have seen, connotes transformation or growth in "natural" respects within a given social unit or level (i.e., a transformation that does not involve crossing any social boundaries, such as divisions between groups or levels of social structure). In the fire's case, this transformation consists of the intensification of its own powers of transformation to the point at which it is now capable of fully "socializing" both food and the boy, as well as the structure of the family itself. As a final point of correspondence, the fire, in its form as a single log of symbolically "raw" wood, bears a formal analogy to the untransformed (undetached, unreplicated, and ungeneralized) character of the jaguars' household in which it is located and to the as-yet unsocialized boy (as explicated in Chapter Four).

The fire, the boy, and the pattern of progressive polarization between constantly reinforced outside orientations and constantly undermined attachments to the inside of the household are transposed to the jaguars' household. This ensures the eventual dispersion of the household or, in the terms of the present discussion, turning it "inside out." The boy, as we have seen, goes through a progressively intensifying series of oscillations between the contradictory, outside-male and inside-female aspects of the pattern until, by the time he breaks away and returns to the village, he has fully and consistently defined himself in relation to both aspects of the pattern (see Figures 1.9, 1.10, above). In other words, he comes to represent within himself a detached and replicated instance of the pattern of relations within his family. He thus comes to embody the generalization of that pattern. This dual process, the myth implies, is the essence of socialization.

The replication of the family pattern, however, implies a replication of the fire. This is so because the fire, in its capacity as the principle of transformation, forms part of the family pattern, the essential feature of which is that it is not merely a static pattern of roles but a pattern of progressive transformations, which constitute the developmental process. The detachment of the boy from the jaguars' household (upon his definitive passage outside it) therefore parallels the detachment of a bit of the jaguar's fire and its passage outside the household in the company of the boy.

The movements of both the boy and the fire from outside into the household and from inside out of it again are thus not only formally analogous but causally interconnected. They represent the product and the dynamic principle, respectively, of a generative process that turns out products that are replicas of itself.

The outside–inside contrast plays a relatively latent and secondary role in the structure of the early episodes preceding the boy's stay in the jaguars' household. It is, as it were, an overdetermined but unmarked component in the vertical separation of the fire (as the sun) from society in the initial significant cluster of the myth and, subsequently, in the vertical separation of the boy from his sister's household to the macaws' nest. In the boy's flight up the tree from the female jaguar in the second jaguar episode, however, the inside–outside component of the vertical spatial dimension becomes salient, just as it does on the horizontal spatial dimension (see Figure 1.9, above).

The metamorphosis of the fire on both the vertical and horizontal dimensions reinforces the shift in emphasis from the contrast between the vertical and horizontal frames that have served as the structural axes of the earlier episodes to a structure in which the vertical and horizontal axes become increasingly joined. This tendency is fully realized in the final pair of episodes, in which both vertical and horizontal axes assume the shape of a "concentric" spatial contrast. The significance of this development will be dealt with in the following chapter. What I want to stress at this point is the way in which the outside–inside contrast serves as a transition between the heterogeneous spatial structure of the earlier episodes and the homogenous structure of the final episodes.

The inside–outside contrast serves as a sort of common denominator capable of subsuming the values of both vertical and horizontal axes under a common form of polarity that is focused on the natal family household. As such, it becomes the formal basis upon which the homogeneous spatial structure of the later episodes is extrapolated. The inside–outside contrast serves as the transitional link between the heterogeneous vertical and horizontal coordinates of the earlier episodes and the homogeneous yet internally differentiated concentric space of the final episodes. The two levels of the vertical and horizontal axes of the final pair of episodes are collapsed when the youth walks out of the jaguars' house and returns to his village, then when he walks out of his mother's and sister's house to the men's house in the central plaza, and finally when the men go out of the village to fetch the cooking fire and bring it triumphantly back.

CHAPTER SIX

The macaw and jaguar episodes

Up to this point in the story, all the significant clusters of relations into which we have divided it have proved to be identical in their general structural features. All share the bidimensional form, with a horizontal dimension representing the polarity between "nature" and "society," and a vertical dimension signifying dynamic, developmental transformation, represented by movement upwards or downwards in vertical space. In all of the episodes involving action between the boy as subject and an "alter," upward, regressive change on the vertical dimension has instigated differentiation on the horizontal dimension, which then provokes downward, successful changes on the vertical, thus leading to a continuous cycle of coordinated pairs of transformations.

The final pair of episodes of the myth preserves these general formal principles and constraints while systematically inverting most of the particular features of the form and content of the earlier episodes. Since the final episodes are identical with one another in these respects, it will be convenient to begin their analysis with a listing and interpretation of all of the significant points of structural contrast between them as a pair and the preceding episodes.

The first and perhaps most salient difference is that the final two episodes lack vertical spatial movement and therefore also the bidimensional form of the vertical or 'y' axis of the structure in relation to the horizontal axis of the earlier episodes. This contrast, with its basic value of dynamic, developmental transformation, persists as a dimension of the structure of the final episodes, but it is represented in them by movement in "concentric" space.

The second difference is that the symbolic form of the horizontal ('x') axis of the structure, representing the dimension of classificatory contrast between "nature" and "society," also changes from the various forms it had assumed in the preceding episodes to a graded series of contrasts arranged in a concentric form (see "Cosmology, objectification, and animism in indigenous Amazonia," this volume). The series moves out from the central plaza (and the communal groups associated with it) to the village periphery (which consists of extended-family households, primarily associated with women and children) and, beyond that, to the *a-tuk* zone, where rituals of transition occur (such as initiation and mortuary rituals) and then, further yet, to the concentric contrast between village and forest. These gradations mean that there is a significant interplay between micro- and macrospatial dimensions and contrasts as actors move through their world.

The third point that should be mentioned is the contrast between the linear structure of the earlier group of episodes and the cyclical pattern of the later pair. The macaw and jaguar episodes all develop in the same way: they proceed in a linear, irreversible manner from an initial point or situation to a final situation that is different, both substantively and structurally, from their starting points. The two final episodes, however, are alike in returning to their starting points, thereby achieving reversibility. Moreover, the modifications caused by the intervening departure and return of the subjects are constructive rather than destructive in character, in contrast to the destructive aspects of the linear development of the earlier episodes.

A fourth difference is that the order of causal priority between the classificatory differentiation and successful developmental transitions is inverted in the latter pair of episodes from what it was in the earlier set. In the macaw and jaguar episodes, classificatory differentiation, represented on the horizontal 'x' axis, is the prerequisite of successful (downward) transition, represented by the vertical 'y' axis. As mentioned above, the distinction between the horizontal and vertical axes are recombined into the concentric dimensions in the final two episodes, but the coordination of transformations between classificatory distinctions and developmental changes persists nonetheless. Their causal relationship, however, is reversed: in the episodes of the boy's return from the jaguars' house and of the men's collective theft of the fire, successful developmental transitions become the prerequisites of classificatory differentiations between "natural" and "social" entities and spaces.

This change is related to a shift in the identity of the initiator of the action in the earlier and later sets of episodes. In the earlier episodes, the role of "subject" (the boy) is essentially reactive: it is always the "alters" (ZH or the jaguars) who initiate the action or precipitate the situations to which the "subject" responds. In these episodes, the subject is always represented as the entity undergoing vertical transformation, while the alters remain at ground level, directly involved only in classificatory differentiation on the horizontal axis. In the final pair of episodes, by contrast, the subjects (the boy and the collective men's group, respectively) initiate the action and precipitate the reactive polarization of the alters.

The last salient point is that the final pair of episodes differs from the earlier parts of the story with respect to the relatively greater prominence of unambiguously "social" actors rather than the symbolic, equivocally "natural" jaguars and macaws of the earlier episodes.

A satisfactory structural analysis should be able to account for all of the differences between the earlier and later episodes just enumerated, as well as the similarities between them. I shall take up the differences first and defer an analysis of the basic common features of both sets until the conclusions.

CONTRASTIVE STRUCTURAL FEATURES IN PRIOR EPISODES

To get a clear idea of what is involved in the pivotal transformation in the story that underlies the contrastive features of structure and content just enumerated, it is necessary to briefly consider the significance of the forms assumed by these features in the earlier (macaw and jaguar) episodes.

In general terms, the earlier group of episodes deals with processes of differentiation within single, low-level social units (the individual household or family) as they are precipitated by the onset of natural developmental processes (for instance, the physical growth of the boy and the arrival of the boy's sister at marriageable age and her acquisition of a husband). In the macaw episode, the boy's natal household is polarized into its component family units (specifically, the boy's natal family and the conjugal family of his sister) on the basis of their relative structural position as consecutive stages of the developmental cycle of the household. Then, in the two jaguar episodes, the boy's natal family itself is polarized in two ways with reference to the boy's relations to his parents: his identification with the male parent is encouraged at the expense of his relation with the female; and his relation to both parents is polarized between their roles as future role models and as past childhood natal family bonds that must be broken if the future adult role identity is to be attained.

The polarization of the temporally differentiated role attributes of the alter in these episodes always occurs on the horizontal dimension ("x") axis, while the vertical ("y") axis always represents the subject's dynamic transition between temporally contrasted role relations or identities. The initial vertical polarization (the boy's climb to the macaws' nest) denotes that the essentially "natural" processes of the boy's psychophysical growth and the development of his natal family toward dispersion have reached a point at which they cannot continue merely as natural processes but require a more complex framework of social differentiation for their successful completion. Successfully completing these processes is, in other words, incompatible with the persistence of the insufficiently differentiated social-structural framework afforded by the single family household. Consummation of the processes therefore requires the destruction of the latter and the reincorporation of its transformed components into a more complexly differentiated system of relations.

This brief résumé of the content and structure of the macaw and jaguar episodes provides the necessary basis for the explanation of the form assumed in the contrastive features, listed above, between the earlier episodes and the final pair.

To begin with the vertical dimension, the appropriateness of vertical spatial movement for the expression of the "natural" processes of growth or development in terms of Kayapo notions has been explained in the foregoing discussion of Kayapo symbolic values (see Chapter Four). The 'y' axis of the earlier episodes is represented by vertical spatial movement because the dynamic, transformational process represented by this axis (the growth of the boy from one stage of development or role identity to the next) is as yet unsocialized and therefore "natural."

Second, the horizontal ('x') axis of the structure of the earlier episodes does not yet take on "concentric" form, as it does in the final episodes, because concentric space, in Kayapo terms, is articulated in terms of contrasts between distinct social groupings of different degrees of sociality (e.g., the communal men's societies in contrast to the women's extended-family households, or the village as a whole in contrast to the forest). The action of the macaw and jaguar episodes, however, takes place within the boundaries of a single household or family group; in other words, it is not yet structurally significant at the level of contrast represented by "concentric" space. The concrete form of the horizontal dimension of these episodes therefore progresses from a merely virtual or logical space (for instance, the contrast between the two role aspects of the ZH, or between the two attitudes of male jaguar in the macaw episode) to the "proto-concentric" contrast between inside and outside the jaguars' house. In the latter case, the natural domain of the forest is further divided as social space inside the jaguars' house (the female jaguar's domain) and the unsocialized space outside of their house, which is the forest with animals to hunt and solely inhabited by the male jaguar.

Third, the vertical and horizontal axes of these episodes are heterogeneous both with regard to their content and their symbolic form. The vertical axis represents "natural" processes as yet unsocialized by incorporation into an adequate social framework; the horizontal axis represents the inadequate social framework within which these processes are taking place, as well as the development within it of polarities that it cannot possibly accommodate on the basis of its existing structural resources.

The substantive continuity of the horizontal axis throughout the first group of episodes is provided by the repeated contrast between the male role of hunter (which is ambiguous on the natural–social dimension of contrast) and a series of social roles, which provide variously unviable or partially viable solutions for the hero's predicament. The boy's problem throughout the first set of episodes is to attain the hunter's role in his own right (thus consummating the "natural" aspect of his growth, represented by the vertical structural axis) on terms that simultaneously align him with the viable male social status represented by the male jaguar (thus successfully reorienting himself toward the "social" pole of the horizontal axis). His attainment of this double alignment duly precipitates the destruction and transformation of the structural framework of the action itself, which is concretely represented by the jaguars' household.

With reference to the fourth point in the list of features, a specific hierarchical relationship exists between the two forms of spatial contrast on the 'y' axis in the earlier episodes that, to some extent, parallels that noted as obtaining on the concentric dimension of the action of the final episodes. This is the contrast between the fire's position as the sun in the initial cluster of relations presented in the myth, thus placing it at the upper pole of vertical macrospace, and the position of the macaws (and thus of the boy while he is in the nest as the upper pole of vertical microspace). The effect of the juxtaposition of macro- and microspatial dimensions is to emphasize the parallelism between the essentially social, microspatial poles of the boy's structural predicament (between his relatively unsocialized and socialized role identities) and the cosmic, macrospatial polarity between utterly asocial, natural powers (epitomized by the sun) and the increasingly socialized and replicable human society. The point of this parallelism lies not in the static, metaphorical equation between the polar values of the two forms of the opposition but, rather, in the implied analogy between the dynamic, metonymic processes of mediation between them.

It will be convenient to defer discussion of the fifth point, the contrast between the linear and irreversible form of the action in the macaw and jaguar episodes and the cyclical organization of the final episodes, until the characteristics and implications of the latter can be clarified. This will be done immediately following the present review of the features of the earlier episodes.

Sixth is the relative priority of differentiation on the horizontal axis over successful transformation (through downward movement) on the vertical axis in the earlier set of episodes. Note that this problem has two consecutive aspects. Upward vertical movement (representing the incipient "natural" transformation of the household in terms of the strain between consecutive developmental phases) precedes and is presented as the precondition for the manifestation of polarities on the horizontal dimension. Downward vertical movement is then made to depend on successful polarization of relations on the horizontal dimension. In terms of the foregoing summary of the content of these episodes, this sequential action between the vertical and horizontal dimensions can be accounted for as follows. Upward vertical movement (the boy's ascent to the macaws' nest) precedes differentiation on the horizontal dimension (the two aspects of ZH) because the latter impetus toward differentiation in the structure of the household and family is initially generated by the natural forces of growth and development manifested by the vertical pole. Successful mediation of the vertical opposition (i.e., downward movement), on the other hand, cannot occur without an adequate differentiation on the horizontal axis, which frames the evolving social structure.

The seventh point concerns the relatively passive or reactive role played by the boy as "subject" in the earlier episodes (a role that contrasts strongly with the forcible character of the adult "alters," the ZH and the jaguars, who initiate the action in them). This contrast is the result of the fact that the boy has not yet acquired the structural basis for shaping his own situation without the decisive inputs (helpful or otherwise) of the adult "alters." He is in a manifestly contradictory situation: on the one hand, he is not able to extricate himself from his series of predicaments (being stranded in the macaws' nest, being kept in the jaguars' house) because he is not a mature male hunter, that is, a naturally grown man; on the other hand, the terms of his predicaments, which are all some variant of the structure of his natal family and household, are precisely what prevents him from attaining his manhood. He cannot break out of this circular dilemma by himself. As the myth shows, it requires the male and female jaguars working together (or, more precisely, in tandem against each other) to do the job.

The eighth and last point is the relative predominance of natural creatures (the macaws and jaguars) in the earlier episodes in contrast to the relative preponderance of normal human beings, playing recognizable social roles, in the concluding segments of the myth. The key to the understanding of this contrast is the realization that both types of "natural" creatures in the earlier episodes represent (from the boy's point of view) changed "social" beings, that is, role aspects of the boy himself (as in the case of the macaws) or of his parents (the jaguars). The social and subjective character of these roles has been transformed by the changes in the structure of the boy's family and household that accompanied his own growth. These changes have a threatening aspect, since they represent a cracking of the social veneer by the natural processes of psychobiological development at a point where the latter are not yet reintegrated into society through being channeled into social forms of a higher level. This is a point between levels of social structure, as well as between consecutive phases in the developmental processes of the family and household units that make up the lower level of social structure. This transition mediates between the role attributes of the childhood of the boy and those of his transition away from childhood toward independence. This movement asserts itself most acutely as a contradiction from the standpoint of a boy at the particular stage of life in which he finds himself; however, it is not a contradiction from the standpoint of the higher level of social structure at which it is resolved, but this point has not yet been reached. It is therefore not yet relevant to a boy going through the crisis of the end of childhood. To him, the changes in his own social position and his relations with his parents manifest themselves as monstrous, "natural" forces, alien to and disruptive of the only social order he knows and trusts—the order of the family and domestic group.

To view the change in a boy's childhood family status and role relations as the result of "natural" forces is not only subjectively appropriate from the standpoint of the boy undergoing the changes; it is also objectively accurate in terms of Kayapo notions of "nature," in two senses. In the first place, the changes in question are the results of the impact of infrasocial, natural processes of psychobiological development. In the second place, the disruption, polarization, and transformation of the low-level order of social relations comprising the family and household are reconfigured by transformational processes emanating from the highest level of communal structure, which are regarded in Kayapo cosmology as themselves of natural origin.

This doubly ambiguous (infrasocial and suprasocial) character of the transformations of the boy's family status and role relations is reflected in the doubly asocial character of the jaguars. They are alien to the prevailing low level of human social organization both in their infrasocial bestiality and in their possession of the attributes of a higher level of sociality (the fire, the bow and arrow, the cotton string, and the roast meat) than that yet obtaining within human society itself. The jaguars (but not the macaws) possess this ambiguous character because they represent not only the parental figures of the natal family from which the boy has begun to turn away (the bestial, infrasocial aspect) but also the future adult roles which he must now turn toward (the suprasocial aspect). The macaws, who represent only the boy's past role as a child, remain unambiguously bestial (infrasocial). The general point, which holds for both the jaguars and the macaws, is that they, as natural beings, are appropriate vehicles for transformations in the boy's social identity and relations because the level of social structure to which the boy remains attached (namely, the individual natal family and household) is unable to accommodate them within its own structure and thus to transform them into "social" tendencies. The boy's escape from the space of the macaws and jaguars represents a leap to a higher level of social organization, the village community as a whole. As the myth indicates, it is at the community level that the very changes that could only be expressed at the family household level by monstrous, natural figures like the jaguars are now invested expeditiously by the boy's family relations and fellow villagers, acting in their normal human capacities and social roles.

The departure of the boy from the jaguars' household and his return to the village can be summarized in Figure 1.11. Note that the contrast between "inside" (I) and "outside" (O) becomes more complex at this point: whereas in previous episodes, it essentially represented the contrast between the inside and outside of the house, it now is duplicated to represent contrasts between the inside and outside of the house, and the inside and outside of the village.

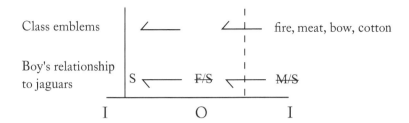

Figure 1.11. After killing the female jaguar, the boy takes a piece of the fire, along with the bow and arrow, roast meat, and cotton string, and heads back alone to the village.

Key: U = up; D = down; I = inside the house/inside the village; O = outside the house/outside the village; S = son; F/S= broken father/son relationship; M/S = broken mother/son relationship

CONTRASTIVE STRUCTURAL FEATURES OF CONCLUDING EPISODES

The boy's attainment of the role attributes of male physical maturity (the use of the bow and arrow and the role identity of hunter that this betokens) in a way that aligns him with the appropriate adult male social role (the "pivotal" role identity of "father," also borne by the male jaguar) completes his socialization, characterized as an intrasubjective or psychological process of redefining his individual identity and social orientations. The climax of the second jaguar episode presents this subjective transformation as the corollary of the transformation of the boy's natal family, which attains its final dispersion with the destruction of the female jaguar "mother" and the separation of the boy, now a physically and subjectively mature youth, from his male jaguar "father" and role model.

The transformation of the boy as subject into a socialized youth and the dissolution of the overly static and constricted order of social relations represented by his natal family and its macaw and jaguar counterparts transform the nature of the basic problem with which the myth is concerned, to wit, the creation of a fully human social order. Nevertheless, they do not, in and by themselves, resolve it. Neither the boy nor his transformed natal family has yet been integrated into society at large. Clearly, such integration will require changes and accommodations on the higher levels of communal structure, which are analogous to those that have already taken place at the intrasubjective and intrafamily levels. Until this happens, the problems of individual socialization and the developmental cycle of the family cannot be considered to be definitively solved from a social point of view. The problem posed by the myth therefore shifts focus from the problems of developmental transformation and restructuring within the individual subject and family to more complex problems: first, the issue of reintegrating the results of these processes; and second, the overarching problem of reintegrating the basic principle of the transformational process *itself* into a more complex order of social relations that are capable of embracing them all on a noncontradictory basis.

The myth portrays the accomplishment of this task in the concluding pair of episodes by means of a systematic series of inversions of the form and content of the earlier episodes. In the earlier group of episodes, "society," as exemplified by the individual family household, is presented as a static, relatively undifferentiated structure unable to accommodate within itself transformation or the structural differentiation it entails. This means, on the one hand, that, at this stage, society still has a relatively "natural," animal-like character; on the other hand, it means that it is alien to the very processes of transformation and differentiation that form the core of contemporary human society. These processes of differentiation, when they occur within society (as the juxtaposition of the sister's husband and wife's brother in the same household at the beginning of the myth implies that they have begun to do) therefore have the effect of transforming the framework of the social group itself into progressively more asocial, natural forms (the macaws' nest and the jaguars' household) and finally of destroying their framework altogether, leaving the socialized youth as a free-floating particle thrown off by the fission of the parent group.

The later episodes, by contrast, present society as transforming itself from its original, relatively "natural" state into a fully human or "social" form by integrating into itself (through its own dynamic action) the concrete embodiment of natural transformational power—the fire. This transformation is brought about as a direct result of society's successful reintegration of the youth upon his return from the jaguars' household. The youth (now no longer a boy) takes the objects from the jaguar family, the fire and roast meat, and the cotton and bow and arrows, back to the village. In the process of removing them, he transforms them from singular entities into prospectively generalized entities, which we have called class emblems.

The youth, upon his return to the village, replicates (in overtly social terms) the pattern of the transformation of the structure of his relations in the jaguars' protosocial household. He terminates his childish relations to the women of his natal household and, as a corollary of this, removes himself physically from the household to join the mature males of the community, who assemble for the purpose of receiving him in a collective group in the central plaza of the village. The youth's movements on returning to the village thus generate two contrasting social groups: his maternal family household, in its form after dispersal (i.e., the form it assumes after he has left it to join the men in the plaza); and the collective men's association. These two groups, moreover, represent distinct levels of social organization, a lower, relatively "natural" level, and a higher, fully "social" level, respectively. This pattern of differentiation represents two complementary forms of social grouping and different levels of social organization, the higher associated with males and the lower with females. These levels can be recognized as a replication of the pattern of differentiation within the jaguars' household. In this case, however, they reflect a pattern of transformation and polarization of the intrafamily level of organization within a higher level of social structure that is sufficiently complex to accommodate its fulfillment within the bounds of society per se.

The pattern of communal structure generated by the youth's return from the jaguars' house not only replicates the pattern of the process of structural transformation and differentiation occurring at the intrafamily (jaguar) level but, in addition, the pattern of the youth's journey between the jaguars' household and the village. In terms of the interpretation developed here, this return journey has the form of a mediation between the relatively natural, intrafamily level of social structure (the jaguars), on the one hand, and, on the other, the fully social level of social organization represented by the community as a whole, because the process that produces one of them also results in the production of the other. The structural homology between this process and the resultant differentiation of the community as a whole implies that the highest level of social structure embodies the process by which it is itself generated. This generative process, in turn, is structurally homologous with the developmental processes occurring in the lower-level, segmentary units of the social order. The effect of this triple homology is thus to create a hierarchically stratified system in which the dynamic process of mediating between levels simultaneously regenerates both levels, since it represents the culmination of the developmental process of the lower-level units and the regenerative recruitment process of the higher-level units.

The key element in this elegant resolution of the problem of accommodating the contradiction posed by the developmental process occurring at the lower level of family structure, then, is clearly the transformation of the basic generative process itself from its lower-level expression as a "natural" force, alien to and disruptive of social order, to the status of a "social" process, specifically, the central generative principle of the social order as a whole. The model for this replicative process follows from the communal men's act of retrieving the fire from the jaguar's house and then dividing and generalizing the fire for each household. The collective activity and the replication of the fire instantiate the generative processes that perpetuate the social order as a whole. This meta-transformation (for it is a transformation of a transformation) consists of two formal features: the detachment of the process from its original association with the lower-level groupings of the social order (families and households); and its generalization as the foundation of the pattern of the organization of the community as a whole.

The central transformation that creates the social order in the final episode of the myth consists of homologizing the structure and process at the lower level. In response to the boy's return from the jaguars, the creation of a differentiated social order consisting of dispersed maternal households, communal men's association, and a coordinated pattern of relations between them (embedded in the recruitment procedures of the communal men's association) represents the highest level of social structure. It also ensures that the processes of transformation and polarization of lower-level (family) units will continually regenerate the system at both levels, while the highest level, in return, sets the pattern for the process of transformation, polarization, and dispersion among the lower-level units. Society thus transforms itself into a self-regulating, self-generating system by transforming its collective structure in the image of the processes that, at a lower level of organization, perpetually threaten to overwhelm and destroy it. The system is perpetuated by the individual acts of Kayapo boys becoming men who act communally and also become fathers who reproduce the form of the individual households that produce the next generation of actors.

This summary exposition of the thematic content of the final pair of episodes provides the necessary basis for understanding the inversions in the form and content of the structure of these episodes in relation to the earlier episodes of the myth. I shall go over these points in the same order as I dealt with them in relation to the earlier set of episodes and then proceed to a separate consideration of the structure of each of the two final episodes.

To begin, then, the change in the concrete form of the dimension of dynamic, developmental transformation, represented by the 'y' axis, shifts from vertical to concentric spatial movement. The final episodes deal not with the continuation of a natural transformational process regarded as alien to, and at cross-purposes with, the order of social relations but, rather, with the integration of this process and its product(s) into society. "Vertical" spatial symbolism, for reasons that have been given, is appropriate to the former process but not the latter, since the latter does not involve "natural" growth or development of a linear or nonrepetitive kind. Instead, it concerns the transposition of such a linear process from its original natural setting to a social setting. The appropriate symbolic vehicle for the mediation of the relations between "nature" and "society," or between relatively natural and social levels of social structure, according to Kayapo notions of space and time, is movement in "concentric" space.

The horizontal ('x') axis of the structure of the final episodes takes on a concentric form for related reasons. The horizontal axis, as we have seen, represents the classification of relations with reference to the nature–society contrast. The horizontal structural contrast in the macaw and jaguar episodes always remains within the bounds of a single household unit: it could not, therefore, attain concentric form, which is appropriate only to the contrast between units or categories of different degrees of sociality. The interaction in the final two episodes, between the jaguars' household and the village as a whole, as well as the relations within the village between women's family households and communal men's societies, straightforwardly exemplifies this concentric contrast in Kayapo terms.

The assumption of the same concentric spatial form, involving both the 'y' (dynamic) and 'x' (classificatory) dimensions of the final pair of episodes, means that, for the first time in the myth, the dynamic process represented on the 'y' axis and the structural order represented on the 'x' axis become formally homologous. The significance of this formal development is the coordination of structure and process by the grand culmination of these episodes.

The concentric contrast of the final episodes can be divided into two levels: concentric macrospace, defined in terms of the opposition between the village as a whole and the forest; and concentric microspace, consisting of the contrast within the village between the men's societies of the central plaza and the women's extended-family households of the village periphery. This is in accord with the foregoing discussion of the subdivision of the village into concentric zones. The subdivision of the village into peripheral women's extended-family households and central men's communal societies replicates, as we have seen, the form of the process by which the nature–society polarity is transposed from the intrafamily (natural) level to the village (social) level. We can now see that these processes in the myth can be considered as: (1) an instance of that process; (2) a product of it; and (3) a template for it.

Both of the final episodes have a circular or cyclical form, in contrast to the linear, unidirectional form of the action in the macaw and jaguar episodes. The subjects of both of the final episodes return, that is, to their starting points and in each case modify them in some decisive way as the result of the events that have transpired since their departure.

This cyclical character is directly obvious in the final episode of the men's collective theft of the fire, in which the men start out from the village and return to it after taking the fire and other cultural artifacts from the jaguars' house in the forest. The preceding episode of the boy's return implicitly has the same structure, since it complements and completes the action of the boy when, as WB, he left the village at the beginning of the macaw episode. The macaw and jaguar episodes occur within a spatiotemporal setting of the periphery ("nature" and forest) set apart and removed from ordinary "social" spacetime. The boy's return serves to close this separate space and to integrate the action back to ordinary social spacetime. I would argue, therefore, that the departure of ZH and WB from the village for the macaws' nest at the beginning of the story forms part of the same significant cluster as the events of the boy's return to the village from the jaguars' house. Those episodes bracket the events in the forest as distinct from the episodes in which actors can move between these different domains.

The cyclical form of these two final episodes affords a particularly crisp example of the correspondence between form and content typical of the myth as a whole. The cyclical process of separation and return that forms the action of the episodes also constitutes a feedback process of interaction between levels of lesser and greater differentiation within the whole. The essence of what happens in both episodes is the modification of the social group from start to finish (the natal household for the youth in the penultimate episode, and the village as a whole for the men of the final episode). In both cases, the group is transformed from a relatively undifferentiated entity into a more hierarchically stratified set of related units connected in dynamic, cyclical interaction. The final form of social structure arrived at in both episodes thus replicates the form of the episodes themselves. In essence, both the myth and the social structure become situated in reversible spacetime.

The pattern of events that served as the point of departure is, by the end, itself transformed from a linear, nonrepetitive process (i.e., the process of development and dispersion occurring within the family) into a repetitive, cyclical process that continually integrates the lower and higher levels of the system. Since these lower and higher levels correspond to the starting and ending points of the action of the episodes, this transformation also directly reflects the structure of the action in the episodes.

The actions that make up the pattern of the episodes are, as has been repeatedly stressed, patterns of interaction between a "subject" and an "alter." In the final two episodes, the subject initiates and dominates the action. The correspondence between the form of the episodes themselves and the structure of the social transformations and organizational patterns created in them is thus more than mere metaphorical patterning; it represents the final instantiation of society as the product of purposive, consciously directed, and appropriately motivated subjective action. This is, in my opinion, the central message of the myth. It is significant that the pattern of action by which socialized subjects are shown as creating society in the final episodes is the inverse of the form of the process by which those subjects are "socialized." The socialization of immature persons and the creation (or cyclical, repetitive, reversible recreation) of society by mature, socialized persons are thus presented as complementary aspects of the same structure or, more precisely, complementary phases of the same process.

This is perhaps the most appropriate point to mention a further aspect of the structure of the final two episodes, which I did not mention in my general list of contrastive features of the earlier and later episodes, since it applies only to the contrast between the two final episodes themselves. It nevertheless bears directly upon the interpretation of these two episodes, taken together, as an elegant and sufficient image of a hierarchically organized, self-regulating system. The point in question deals with the reversal, from the penultimate to the last episode, of the direction of the interaction between the upper and lower levels of the system, from bottom up to top down, and the displacement of the locus of the causal or dynamic force motivating the action from the lower to the higher levels of the social system. The episode of the boy's return shows the transposition of the pattern of the developmental process occurring within the lowest-level unit of the system to the highest level; it is formulated, so to speak, "from the bottom up." The final episode of the men's collective theft of the fire replicates the same pattern of action but is formulated "from the top down"; it shows the community collectively appropriating the generative principle of this pattern (the fire) from the lower-level unit represented by the jaguars' family household to serve as the basis of its own institutional structure. The symbolic particulars of the handling of the fire by men and animals in this episode nicely bear out this interpretation, as we shall see below.

As I noted earlier, the pattern of temporal and causal priority in the interaction between differentiation on the horizontal axis and dynamic transformation on the vertical axis undergoes a permutation from the earlier to the later groups of episodes. In the earlier episodes, upward vertical separation is the precondition for the appearance of differentiation on the horizontal axis, but the appropriate pattern of differentiation on the horizontal axis is then made to appear as the precondition of downward vertical transition. In the concluding episodes, on the other hand, this pattern is reversed: progressive, developmental movement (which now involves inward movement toward the center, since the vertical axis has assumed a concentric form) now appears as the prerequisite of the definitive differentiation of natural and cultural categories on the horizontal axis.

The emergence of dynamic movement in the later pair of episodes is directly correlated with the transformation of the role of the subject in the same episodes from being the object of the actions of a dominant alter, as in the macaw and jaguar episodes, to that of initiator of the action. The direct correlation of these two developments is a function of the fact that, in both sets of episodes, the subject continues to be associated with dynamic transformation, while the "alter" or "alters" are primarily associated with structural differentiation on the horizontal axis. The earlier episodes show the process of formation of the subject (the boy) as a social being, that is, his socialization, through the dissolution and dispersion the family and domestic group. The latter pair of episodes reverses this pattern. They show the subjects (the youth and the collective men's society, respectively) as already formed and, in turn, as forming, through their decisive actions, the definitive structure of society as a whole.

CHAPTER SEVEN

The theft of fire in the final pair of episodes

SOCIAL FEATURES AND SYMBOLIC STRUCTURE

Much of the analysis of the final episodes has been accomplished in the preceding chapter, but it remains to tie together the points that have been made concerning certain specific features of these last two episodes and to construct formal models of their structures, as was done for the preceding episodes. Chief among the features that have so far been ignored are the numerous homologies between details of the structure and content of these episodes and actual Kayapo social organization.

The boy's return to the village

A good example of the homologies between these episodes and Kayapo social organization is the manner of the youth's return to his village. His first contact with human society is not with the village as a whole but with his sister and then his mother. It is only from their house (i.e., his natal family household) that he makes his way to the communal men's grouping in the plaza. His interaction with his mother and sister, moreover, is fraught with actions indicating the attenuation and transformation of their earlier relationship. In most of the versions of the story, the sister plays a more prominent role in making the first contact with the youth than the mother. These details accurately reflect the dominant patterns of actual Kayapo family and community structure (described in Chapter Three). The mythical role of the sister and, secondarily, of the mother, as the contacts between the youth's past social identity as a child in his natal household and his future identity as a mature male and member of a communal men's society is analogous to the prominent role played by the sister and mother, in that order, in Kayapo social life as the links a youth has with his natal family and consanguineal kindred in general. During both the initial period while the youth resides as a bachelor in the men's house and later, after his marriage, when he resides in his wife's household, the sister and mother serve to mediate the structural cleavage between the family level of structure and higher levels of social organization (the communal men's groups and other families and households). It is precisely this boundary between structural levels that the boy crosses on his symbolic return to the village from the jaguars' house; the roles of his sister and mother in the myth thus correspond to their roles in everyday social life. Even the relative prominence of the sister over the mother in this connection is deftly indicated in the most common version of the story, in which the youth's sister is the first to meet him outside the house and then becomes the bearer of the news of his return to the mother within.

The responses expressed by the youth's sister and mother to him (by their weeping salutation) and his reaction to them (by his restrained demeanor) also reflect socially appropriate attitudes. The weeping salutation is a formal pattern among all Gê groups for expressing the grief the weeper feels about his or her separation from the person who is the object of the salutation. Occasions for such weeping are the return of a kinsman from a long journey, his or her death, or any rite de passage. The convention is that the stronger the relationship and the more severe or prolonged the separation, the louder and more prolonged the wailing. Women are supposed to wail loudly, men to be more subdued, but otherwise the pattern is reciprocal. The weeping salutations of the hero's mother and sister may be taken in these terms as expressing his absence and their recognition of the change that has occurred in their relationship. The youth's subdued response, on the other hand, is appropriate to the now sharply attenuated character of his maternal and sororal relationships, from his point of view. His failure to respond with the same force indicates both that he has distanced himself from them and that he has acquired the relative sangfroid of a mature man.

The alternate version of the story, in which the hero returns at night and is able to locate his natal household only by identifying his mother and sister by touch, makes the same basic point about the attenuation of his relationship to them. The mother, sister, and the natal household remain, in this version as in the more common one, the point of re-entry of the youth into the community.

Once they are together inside the house, the youth's interaction with his mother and sister continues to emphasize the latter's recognition of his transformation and its social significance. He shows them the fire, roast meat, bow and arrows, and cotton string he has brought, prompting his mother to exclaim over them in surprise and admiration.

The men of the community respond to the news of the boy's return with the bit of fire and other token objects by assembling as a group in the men's house in the plaza. They summon the boy to come there from his mother's house to tell them of his experiences and show them what he has brought. This reflects the ordinary social procedure of separating youths of the hero's age from their maternal households and recruiting them into the communal men's societies. The manner in which this is done in the myth emphasizes the circular interdependence between the two levels of social organization represented by the men's house as distinct from the mother's and sister's house. By making the boy himself the occasion for the men's assembly, the myth stresses how the completion of the process of socialization and family dispersion by individual youths is simultaneously the source of the new recruits necessary to regenerate and maintain the collective men's societies (in the "bottom-up" view). At the same time, it stresses the role of the latter in providing the necessary structural framework for channeling socialized youths away from their natal households and thus allowing the latter to complete their developmental cycles with an orderly pattern of dispersion (in the "top-down" view).

The analysis of the boy's return to the village is depicted in Figure 1.12.

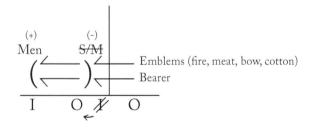

Figure 1.12. The boy arrives in the village and goes to his sister's and mother's house, showing them what he has brought back. The men then summon him to the men's house to show them the items.

Key: U = up; D = down; I = inside the house/inside the village; O = outside the house/outside the village; S = son; F/S= broken father/son relationship; M/S = broken mother/son relationship

Concentric microspace

Vertical axis: In this episode, the distinct levels of social structure and developmental stages on this axis are resolved into continuous concentric zones.

1. The initial transition occurs at the beginning of the myth from a relatively undifferentiated social context (in the mother's and sister's house) to a context of incipient differentiation (in the jaguars' household).
2. A reverse transition occurs in the final episodes from a lower-level context (the jaguars' household) back to the starting point (the mother's and sister's house), with the effect of integrating these two levels. The relations in jaguars' house are imported back to village, but they are not yet embedded in the higher level of communal group relations.
3. The boy's identity is differentiated into a positive, future-oriented role aspect as a mature man versus a negative, past-oriented role aspect as an ex-child (now separated from his natal household).

Horizontal axis: A differentiation of "social" and "natural" attributes in concentric microspace occurs along this axis.

1. The jaguars' household represents the lowest (intrafamily) level of social structure as the starting point for higher level communal organization. A further polarization of "social" and "natural" attributes, respectively, takes place within the context of the jaguars' family household.
2. Correlatively, human society is transformed through differentiation over the course of the myth. The initial state of society before differentiation is represented by the mother's and sister's household before dispersion (i.e., while the boy is still a resident member). The incidents in the jaguars' house impel the dispersion of the lower-level, "natural" natal family household, which, in turn, propels the formation of a higher-level "social" organization (the collective men's groups), which encompasses the natal family households. The final state of human society is thus based on the differentiation between these levels.

Affective structure

1. The youth leaves the jaguars' household on terms that align him positively with the status of the male jaguar, with the latter's support.

2. At the same time, his departure aligns him negatively against his dependent, nurturant relationship to the female jaguar "mother," who opposes his assertion of independence and separation from her even while driving him away.

3. Back in the village, the youth is summoned by the assembled men to join them in the men's house, and he complies willingly.

4. The mother and sister weep over the youth, thus affirming the attenuation of their previous relationship to him, but he does not reciprocate their wailing greeting, thus affirming the attenuation of his previous close relationship to them.

Episode of the collective theft of the jaguars' fire

If the foci of the penultimate episode are the returning youth and, with him, the process of transformation and differentiation of family and communal relations that his symbolic trip brings about, the foci of the final, climactic episode are the fire and, with it, the definitive reordering of "society" and "nature" that its theft from the jaguar precipitates. To grasp the significance of the events in this concluding episode, it is therefore essential to understand the symbolic connotations of the fire and the transformations it undergoes in the course of the episode, both in form and in use.

It has been shown earlier in this article (Chapter Four) that the form of the fire in the jaguars' house (in one piece, thus both undetachable and ungeneralized in relation to its source, the jatoba log) and the nature of its source (the blood-red, symbolically "raw" jatoba wood) serve alike to convey that the jaguars' fire, like the jaguars and their infrasocial "family," is not fully "socialized," even though it possesses an essential feature of the socialization process, the power to transform "natural" into "social" entities (i.e., cooked food).

The fire is itself a "natural" phenomenon, as the myth makes clear by introducing it in the initial form of the sun. It has the power to transform other things from "natural" to "social" or vice versa, depending upon the circumstances and how it is used. At the jaguars' house, it catalyzes both directions of transformation at once. It stimulates the boy's growth and thus promotes his "socializing" identification with the male jaguar; at the same time, it promotes the increasing "naturalization" of the boy's putatively social relationship with the female jaguar. The fire thus reveals itself as the generative power of transformation that establishes the basic structure of human sociality at all levels of organization (intrasubjective, intrafamily, and communal).

While the jaguars' fire serves the generative, transformational functions of cooking, transforming the hero from child to grown youth, and precipitating the transformation of the initially undifferentiated jaguar household into "social" and "natural" elements, it does not, in that setting, exercise its most distinctive and powerful property, to wit, the capacity to reproduce or replicate itself. Insofar as the fire is identified as the generative agent of polarization of the jaguars' household, however, the replication of that pattern (initiated by the dispersion of the household and the breaking away of the youth) is further propelled by the replication of the fire. The import of this action is embodied by the boy's act of breaking off a piece of the fire to take along with him—for the first time using fire to replicate itself.

The youth's feat represents a provisional "socialization" of the fire that parallels his own incipient socialization. His return to society with the fire marks his first separation from the setting in which he mastered his development into a socialized youth. Society's acceptance of the youth, along with his social accoutrements of the fire and of the roast meat, bow and arrow, and cotton string, confirms these preeminent social products. It does not, however, imply the definitive socialization of the socialization process itself, as it were, or of the fire as the generative principle of that process; society does not yet possess the power to create these things for, within, and by itself.

It is significant that the collective men's group is formed for the purpose of acquiring the fire by stealing it from the jaguar. This is the first time we see collective human action, which starts with the symbolic induction of the youth. Only after the men bring back the fire do they fully transform both themselves and the fire as renewable social products. Before this, society lacked the power to regenerate its own structure, in other words, to replicate and maintain itself. It had fire, but it still could not make fire. The men are thus correct in making the acquisition of the jaguar's fire, which can serve (unlike the boy's diminutive coal) as the source of fire for the whole village. That is why it is the first item on their agenda after the induction of the boy.

The men's self-transformation into animals for the actual fire theft signifies the manner of collective transformation upon which they are embarking. Their association of themselves with animals reflects, in the first place, their relatively "natural," animal-like condition as members of a society that is still without fire. It should be noted, however, that the species of animals they assume are all game animals—animals of the sort normally cooked, transformed, and thus socialized by fire. The men change back into human form only after they return to the village with the fire and commence to light other fires with it. In the forest, they are "raw," animal-like, unsocialized, natural beings who are as yet untransformed by fire. Arriving back in the village, they are transformed not into cooked beings (directly transformed by fire) but into cooking fire-making beings. They are not themselves "cooked" but embody the power to cook; that is, they embody "social" reproductive power.

This transformation of the men and, by implication, of the women who share in the process of lighting the new fires, is the direct product of the transformation they bring about in the nature of the fire itself. Before the men take it from the jaguars' house, the fire is as yet undetached from its original "natural" source and unchanged from its original (one-piece, hence particular and ungeneralized) "natural" form.

When the men bring the burning log to the village, they and the women together transform it into a detachable, hence generalized, self-replicating mechanism. The source of the new fires is itself now socially controlled; the nature of fire has thus become inversely transformed, from "natural" to "social." This inverse transformation in the substantive nature of the fire from the earlier to the final set of episodes is the corollary, at the level of symbolic content, of the formal inversion of the structure of the earlier and final episodes described above.

The transformation of the fire and of society is accompanied, with scrupulous logical consistency, by a transformation of nature, which is the inverse of the former two. This set of three transformations effectively generates the structure of the cosmos as it exists today. Recall that the men are accompanied and aided in their theft of the jaguar's fire by genuine animals, specifically, certain game birds and the toad, which have in common that they are red-throated species. They hop along after the men gobbling up the sparks and embers that fall from the burning log, thus achieving the triple result of directly transforming themselves (gaining their red throats), directly transforming the fire (it becomes the redness of their throats), and leaving no fire in the domain of "nature" for either the jaguar or themselves.

The eating of the fire by the animals is not only complementary to the men's theft of the fire; it is symbolically treated as the inverse transformation to that comprised by humanity's acquisition of the fire. As we have emphasized, the first use that human beings make of the jaguar's fire, once they have brought it to their village, is to light other fires with it. These "secondary" household fires are, in turn, used to cook meat and other food. It is this revolutionary use of fire to replicate itself as a generalized transformational mechanism, rather than simply to cook, that makes the men, women, and fire truly social. The jaguars, after all, could cook over their single-log fire; what they could not do was make other fires. The animals, at the other extreme, treat the fire directly as food and, by eating it, transform it into a literally "raw" form as it becomes embodied in their own bodies. The reddening of their throats, by the same token, repre- sents a direct transformation of themselves, which is analogous, in one sense, to cooking (it is a transformation induced by fire), but it results, unlike cooking, merely in an altered raw, "natural" condition. The reason for this is that it lacks even the partial indirectness of cooking (which, after all, consists in the use of fire as a tool to transform one's food rather than oneself). The animals prove themselves incapable even of this minimal degree of deferment or indirectness in their relation to the means of their own transformation. They therefore fail to attain even the quasi-socialized status implied by the ability to cook. Their self-transformation remains trivial; they remain animals, the fully "natural" be- ings they always were.

This formulation of the relationship between nature and human society ac- cords with the notions of "nature" and "society" outlined earlier in the general ac- count of Kayapo social and cosmological notions (see Chapters Four and Five). It should also be clear that the spatial form of the social distribution after the fire has been brought into the village conforms neatly with the essential char- acter of Kayapo social structure as a hierarchically oriented feedback system, in which the upper level (composed of the communal organizations located in the central plaza) functions both as a "model of" and a "model for" the lower levels (Geertz 1973). The men collectively bring the burning log to the central plaza of the village. The women then come out of the extended-family households around the periphery of the plaza, light their individual family fires from the central log, and return to their houses. The result is that the fire of each separate family unit of the village is a microcosmic replication of and, by the same token, generated from the centralized men's fire of the plaza. The analogy between the two differentiated forms of the fire and the two differentiated levels of social structure (the communal men's societies of the central plaza and the women's family households of the village periphery) is obvious. The analogy, moreover, holds for function as well as form: the communal societies of the central plaza, as was explained earlier, serve as "models of" and "models for" the lower-level family households; and they function in practical terms in such a way as to bring about the replication of the family and household structures in their own image. The central fire functions in exactly the same way in relation to the individual household fires: it is not only replicated by them, but because of its relative size, causal priority, and central position, it becomes their generalized model. This generalization completes the socialization of the fire that began with its detachment from the jaguars' house, just as it completes the modeling of the dynamic structure of Kayapo society through the symbolic medium of the fire.

It is worth emphasizing that the differentiation of the communal and family-household levels of social structure at the end of the final episode is prefigured by the men's acquisition of the emblems of the sexually differentiated adult roles—the bow and arrow for men and the cotton string for women—along with the fire and roast meat. Earlier, we saw that these items express the implications of the socialization process represented by the fire and roast meat for both sexes. We can now appreciate that they thus represent the objective correlatives of the pattern of differentiation between the adult male and female members of the family that accompanies the transformation of Kayapo boys into "socialized" youths. In many respects, the jaguar's relationship to the boy is analogous to the relationship of the Kayapo "substitute father" to boys who are leaving their natal household and entering the men's house as junior members of the men's communal groups (see Chapter Three). This pattern becomes the model for the differentiation of the two levels of social organization (the women's family households and the men's communal groupings). It is therefore consistent with their structural connotations that, in the myth, the bow and arrows and the cotton string should be taken by the men, along with the jaguars' fire and roast meat, as tokens, this time not merely of individual adult sex roles but of the hierarchical differentiation of society with which those sex roles are associated.

The collective fire theft condenses two further aspects of Kayapo social structure directly involved with its relationship to "nature." The more obvious of these is the character of Kayapo society, as analyzed earlier, as a mechanism for integrating the two forms of social organization associated with the two primary modes of production, to wit, the permanent agricultural village and the hunting-and-gathering trekking group. The men, in stealing the fire, constitute themselves as a trekking group for their sortie into the forest. The creation of fully socialized human society, symbolized by the incorporation of the fire into the community, is thus situationally associated with the reincorporation of the men's trekking group into the permanent village. This act epitomizes society's capacity to transform itself from one form of structure to another. This capacity, as we have already shown, is based upon the hierarchical integration of infrastructural productive units (individual families) into the community as a whole, through the intermediacy of a flexible system of collective (men's) associations (e.g., moieties and their subdivisions), which can serve either as trekking groups or segments of the communal village. The production of the means of subsistence, occurring predominantly within the family, is, in Kayapo terms, at best a "quasi-social," "quasi-natural" process: hunting epitomizes the ambiguity of food production in this respect. Communal social control over economic processes, the highest expression of which is the ability to transform the structure of the community from the social form associated with one mode of production to the other and back again, thus consists essentially in the social control of relatively natural, family-level transformational (productive) processes. In sum, this communal control is exactly the type and level of reversible control symbolically achieved at the end of the myth by the men and women of the village when they collectively appropriate the means of the most fundamental of all processes of production of the means of material subsistence, the cooking of food.

At a different level, the collective transformation of the men into animals and their return with the burning log has the form of a typical Kayapo communal ceremony. Not only are such ceremonies conceived as "natural" in origin, as we have noted, but they typically include ritual hunting expeditions and other symbolic excursions into the natural space surrounding the village. Several actually involve carrying huge logs (cut as far from the village as possible) into the village by members of the collective men's groups. These ceremonies may be said to have essentially the same function as the men's theft of the fire in the myth: the transformation of relatively natural phenomena (typically, intrafamily relationships) into fully social form.

The final episode, taken together with the immediately preceding episode of the boy's return to the village from the jaguars' house, thus condenses all four modes in which the Kayapo ordinarily experience their society as interacting with, transforming, and controlling "nature": their economic rhythm, their ceremonial celebrations, their family household cycle, and their individual socialization.

The structure of the final episode can be summarized in the diagram depicted in Figure 1.13.

Vertical axis: This axis, now integrated into concentric spacetime, is the dimension where the dynamic aspects of the socialization of humanity and the fire

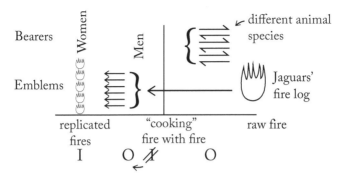

Figure 1.13. The men go to the jaguars' house to fetch the jatoba log and bring it back to the men's house, where the women come to light their own fires and bring them to their individual houses.

Key: I = inside the house/inside the village; O = outside the house/outside the village

occur. Both are separated from a lower, relatively "natural" level and transposed to higher, fully "social" level; correlatively, it is where the "naturalization" of animals occurs.

1. The men, as a group, separate themselves from the as-yet relatively unsocialized village, enter the forest, and are transformed into animals (thus expressing their relatively unsocialized state) as they trek to jaguars' house to take the fire.
2. The men seize the burning jatoba trunk and carry it back to village. They thus detach the fire from the jaguars' household and transpose the socializing power embodied in the fire from the forest to the village, and from a single household to the communal level, simultaneously "socializing" both the fire and the social community as a whole, including themselves.
3. Some of the animals gobble up random bits of fire that fall from the log as the men carry it back to the village. They thereby achieve the inverse of the men's transformation: instead of "socializing" the fire by transposing it to a higher level of organization than that represented by the jaguars' family, they "naturalize" it by transposing it to a lower level (incorporating it directly into their bodies).

Horizontal axis: This is the dimension representing the classificatory aspects of the socialization of humanity and the fire (generalization of fire and transformational capacity it represents on the basis of differentiating levels of social structure) and the naturalization of animal nature.

1. As we have seen, the jaguar's fire is "raw," "natural" transformational power. It has been provisionally differentiated by the boy's feat of detaching the bit of fire to take back to the village (thus using the fire to replicate itself), but it is as yet ungeneralized through the collective replication of the boy's individual act.

2. "Society" and "nature" are relatively undifferentiated before the collective acquisition of fire; after it is acquired by the men and animals, they are strongly differentiated.

3. Furthermore, society becomes fully differentiated into hierarchically distinct levels (the family households and the collective associations), which contrast with one another in terms of their relative power of generalization and replicative functions.

4. The fully "socialized" fire is brought by the collective men's group to the central plaza, where the women come to light pieces of wood and bring them back home. The fire in the men's house thus serves as the generalized form and source of the relatively "natural" women's household fires, which, conversely, replicate the form of the fire in the central men's house as their common source.

5. Animals are transformed into their final and thus fully natural forms through the transformation of the fire they eat into "raw," inert, directly attached, particular features of their own bodies.

CHAPTER EIGHT

Conclusions

NATURE AND SOCIETY, FIRE AND COOKING

The Kayapo myth of how human beings came to possess fire uses fire and cooking as indices of the contrast between "nature" and "society," as Lévi-Strauss has pointed out for this and many similar South American myths (Lévi-Strauss 1969b). It does not, however, formulate either the relationship of nature to society or the significance of fire and cooking in the terms he suggests in his by now familiar formulation:

$$\text{nature:culture :: raw:cooked}$$
$$\text{(Lévi-Strauss 1969b)}$$

The basic shortcoming of Lévi-Strauss' formulation is that it ignores the sophistication and power of indigenous conceptions both of "nature" and "society" (a term I have preferred to "culture" because the myth so obviously treats social organization as the structural basis of "culture" in the more general sense). Lévi-Strauss' formula rests upon the notion of nature and culture or society as essentially static, metaphorically related orders of classification. "Transformations" enter only in the form of mediations between semantically contrasted categories of the same paradigmatic order or level (e.g., raw to cooked, fresh to rotten, etc.).

In contrast, the Kayapo myth, interpreted in the light of its full power and range of cultural meanings, formulates "nature" and "society" in essentially dynamic terms as modes of action, specifically, as modes of interaction between "subject" and "object," in which different aspects of the acting subject, as well as different categories of social actors or of humans and animals, may assume the subjective and objective roles.

This set of notions is based upon an ordered system of categories, such as different modes and zones of space; predators and game animals as different orders of nature; men, boys, and women as different categories of social beings, etc. Some of these categories stand in metaphorical relationships to others; for instance, the contrast between the central men's space of the village plaza and the peripheral ring of women's family households is metaphorically analogous to the concentric spatial contrast between "society," as central space, and "nature," as peripheral space. Although such metaphorical correspondences are significant, they are not the predominant basis of the ordering of the system of categories involved in the myth. This role, as we have seen, is played by coordinated sets of transformations, when changes in one reflect, instigate, or create changes in the other.

Lévi-Strauss' dictum that mythical thought always proceeds from an awareness of polarities to mediation is, in these terms, incomplete and one-sided. The other half of the story is that mythical thought is equally concerned with the polarization of ambiguous, insufficiently differentiated situations in order to enable contrastive "mediation" or transformation to occur at all. Transformations, in short, play a far more important and dynamic role in mythical thought than structuralist formulations have so far recognized, both as mediators between hierarchically differentiated levels and as catalysts of further differentiation of categories within the same levels.

It is precisely in formulating the contrast between "nature" and "society" not as two states but as contrastive modes of action that the role of transformations in the structure of mythical thought emerges most clearly. As the Kayapo myth makes clear, the social state is not merely transformed nature, "the cooked" as contrasted to "the raw." It is not even the interposition of a detached transformational mechanism or process (fire and cooking) between socialized humanity, as the eaters of cooked food, and the natural beings (animals) who become transformed into food by cooking, although this marks a halfway point in the transition between "nature" and "society." The stage of full sociality is attained, in the myth's terms, only when humanity becomes able to generate and thus to manipulate in a generalized way the detached transformational tool (the cooking fire) it has interposed between itself and nature. In other words, when humanity becomes able to make fire, and thus to use fire both to replicate itself and to cook, it reaches the supreme level of sociality.

These notions are succinctly stated in the concrete form of the actions of the animals and the men and women of the village in the final episode of the myth. On the basis of this episode alone, Lévi-Strauss' formula might be amended to read: nature:society :: fire-eating:fire-making. As our discussion has by now made clear, however, any such binary formulation distorts and oversimplifies what in essence is a more complex and sophisticated conception. Let us attempt to formulate this conception in general terms.

Society is defined in the myth as the domain of mediated (indirect), self-replicating operations. These may in turn be differentiated into first-order and second-order operations. First-order operations consist of the differentiation of the fire, as an external, objectified medium of manipulation and transformation, from both the subject (eater and cook) and the object (the cooked food), and its use by the subject (as cook) to transform the object (the cooked food). The first-order capacity for manipulating the fire as a detached transformational medium, however, gives rise to the power to replicate this capacity, e.g., by teaching it to other members of society. The replication of the pattern of first-order operations, however, implies an operation of the second order: the differentiation or detachment of the fire from itself, its generalization, and its use to replicate itself. This generative ability inaugurates the era of full human control over fire, thus marking the advent of fully socialized human existence. The transition from first- to second-order operations is embodied in the myth by the transition from dependence upon the "raw" jatoba log as the unique source of the fire to the direct use of fire as its own source. In concrete terms, fully human society is born when humanity learns to cook the fire.

Nature, by contrast, can be defined as the domain of direct (nonmediated, unreplicable) operations. The treatment of the fire by the animals in the final episode exemplifies such direct operations. They directly consume it, thus simultaneously identifying it, as a transformational principle, with both subject (eater) and object (food). The state of nature can thus be simply stated as the implicit lack of differentiation between subject and object. Nature is thus contrasted with the social state in three ways: 1) the differentiation of subject and object; 2) the differentiation of a medium of manipulation of an object by a subject; and 3) the distinction between the manipulation by the subject of objects through the use of the medium of fire, on the one hand, from a level of second-order operations dealing with the use of the medium to generate itself and to adapt itself to differentiated uses, on the other.

This relatively complex pattern of differentiation between "nature" and "society" is embodied in a series of contrasts that assume a triadic rather than a dyadic form. The basic structure of all of these contrastive triads can be stated in terms of the generalized model put forward in the preceding paragraphs as this proportion:

society:medial (quasi-social, quasi-natural) state:nature :: second-order operations:first-order operations:direct (unmediated) operations

Cooking, in terms of this schema, plays the role of a middle term, halfway between "society" and "nature," not, as Lévi-Strauss would have it, of the criterion of society in its fully socialized form. The latter function is in fact reserved for fire-making. A representative set of contrastive relations between "society" and "nature" developed in the myth within the terms of this triadic formula is set down in the following table:

SOCIETY	TRANSITIONAL	NATURE
fire-making	cooking	eating raw (including eating fire raw)
fire made from fire ("cooked" fire)	fire from "raw" jatoba log ("raw" fire)	fire in totally "raw" form of animals' red throats
socialized humans	jaguars, adolescent boys	macaws, unsocialized children
communal groups	adult (conjugal) family*	childhood (natal) family**

Table 1. Contrastive relations and transitional forms between "society" and "nature."

*represented by future-oriented aspects of jaguar family and male jaguar's "pivotal" role as father-husband.
**represented by past-oriented aspects of jaguar family and parental roles of both jaguars, as well as by sister's and mother's household.

This schematic pattern of the differentiation of "nature" and "society" leaves unresolved the question of the character of both human society and the fire (in the form of the sun) at the beginning of the myth. Neither can be fitted conveniently into any of the three categories of the differentiated formula just presented. Society at the outset of the myth is certainly not fully "socialized" (it does not control or make fire). It is not, however, fully "natural," since people already use the sun to warm meat. This operation is really only a quasi-operation, since the sun is not under human control, its "detachment" is not a function of its manipulation by humans, and "warming" is not the same thing as cooking. "Society" therefore does not yet qualify at this stage for the "transitional" category. The sun, as the initial form of the fire, presents a similarly ambiguous set of characteristics. It is not social fire, since it is not made by human beings; it is not "raw" like the red throats of the animals who gobble the sparks from the jaguars' log, and therefore not wholly "natural" in the full, differentiated sense; but it is not a "transitional" fire either, since it not only does not cook, but neither does it depend upon a "raw" source like the jaguars' fire. In short, it is its own source, and it is neither raw nor cooked, but warm.

These considerations point to a solution consistent with the overall analysis of the structure of the myth developed above, to wit, that both the sun and the village at the beginning of the myth represent undifferentiated forms of both the fire and human society along the nature–society continuum. Both their natural and social aspects are, accordingly, still only weakly developed; neither has achieved their final differentiated form. The contrast between the undifferentiated and untransformed state of nature and the fire at the beginning of the myth and the differentiated forms assumed by all three at the end of the myth can thus be formulated in terms of the following proposition:

Undifferentiated:differentiated :: untransformed:transformed :: low energy:high energy

FIRE AND BOY: THE MYTH AS A MODEL OF SOCIALIZATION

At the beginning of the analysis, I observed that, upon first reading, the myth seems to consist of two distinct but intertwined stories, that of the boy and that of the fire. This first impression has received some confirmation in the course of the analysis, since it has shown that the movements and transformations of the fire are both causally and formally related to those of the boy. A provisional interpretation of the fire has been given based on its overt relations with the jaguars, the boy, and society as a whole, which seems to account for both their causal interdependence and their formal parallelism. The fire represents the dynamic energy necessary to carry through the transformations of family structure and the boy's subjective and social role identity involved in socialization. The fire, as such, necessarily forms part of the pattern of transformations of the boy and the family, both in the formal and causal-functional senses.

This interpretation, it seems to me, is all right as far as it goes, but it leaves some basic questions unanswered. To begin with, why should the transformational capacity or dynamic energy essential to the boy's growth and the development of the family be treated as external to the boy and, originally, to the family and household as well? Put more concretely, why is the fire, as the embodiment of transformational power, originally presented in the form of the sun, totally outside of human society? Second, why must the boy—and human society in general—get the fire from the jaguar? Third, if we grant the interpretation of the fire as the boy's power of growth and self-transformation, what accounts for the oddly indirect relation between the boy and the fire? By this, I mean the fact that his initial contact with the fire, the contact that actually precipitates his transformation into a physically and socially mature youth, is in the indirect form of roast meat, over which he repeatedly argues with the female jaguar. Furthermore, the direct control of the fire, which comes as the culmination of this process (when he breaks off the piece of the jaguar's fire to take with him on his return to his village), is still only exercised for indirect purposes and in an indirect way. After all, the boy does not use the fire directly to eat, as the animals do, or even to cook for himself, as the female jaguar does, but to show the villagers and thus secure his final and definitive integration into the community.

These three questions suggest that the provisional interpretation of the relationship between the fire and the boy offered above does not go far enough. It does not, in short, deal adequately either with the question, what is the fire? or, to raise the question directly for the first time, what is the boy?

To begin with the last question, it is clear that the boy is a representation of the Kayapo notion of a real boy undergoing socialization in Kayapo society. The question we are really asking, then, is this: what is the Kayapo notion of a boy undergoing socialization? More precisely, what do the Kayapo conceive to be the outcome of "socialization"? What, in other words, is their notion of the person?

The myth, as we have seen, represents socialization as a process of the boy's detaching himself from a series of relatively unsocialized family contexts (the sister's household at the beginning of the myth, the macaws' nest, the jaguars' house, and finally the mother's and sister's house). These acts of detachment always take the concrete form of the boy's going outside the contexts in question, which has the effect of "externalizing" the contexts. Each instance of detachment and externalization is made in relation to, and with the support of, an adult tutelary figure represented as also being in some sense "outside" that context (the ZH, the male jaguar, and finally the collective men's association of the village). Each step in the socialization process, in short, consists of shedding a role (and its context) in which he has been defined as a child in order to relate to and become more like some adult male figure represented as "outside" his current role. Kayapo boys and youths, having listened to this myth throughout their lives, may use this model to ease their own transitions from childhood to adulthood.

Socialization, as far as the formation of the boy's mature social identity is concerned, thus comes down to the boy's building a set of identities through which he can transform his past externalized role—the role identities which he aspires to fulfill in the future but has not yet "internalized." Thus, for the boy, socialization means defining and redefining himself as a nexus of relations among an externalized system of roles.

As the process of "externalization" proceeds in each successive episode, the boy is called upon to relate to new external figures and to simultaneously shed aspects of his own past role identity. In the encounter with the male jaguar at the macaws' nest, for example, the boy is able to throw down the fledglings to be eaten by the male jaguar because he has already "externalized" them (that is, effectively detached himself, through his interaction with ZH, from the childhood natal family household that the fledglings represented). In the episode of the jaguars' household, he is able to detach himself from the household as a whole, this time specifically including both the "paternal" and "maternal" jaguars, and to complete his development toward functional equality with the male jaguar (while remaining detached from him). What the boy accomplishes in these successive episodes, then, is to apply the same basic pattern of "externalized" relations to increasingly complex and demanding social situations. Each transformation increases the generality and power of the pattern itself. Each new set of transformations is presented as a variation of the transformations made in the preceding episodes. The basic relational pattern thus increasingly assumes a more generalized form as a set of coordinated transformations, since all the transformations are presented as transformations of itself. It is in this sense that it becomes a more powerful structure. Its power manifests itself in its ability to handle more permutations of the basic situations to which it applies (i.e., family, household, and, ultimately, community structure). This power enables the boy (as the subjective locus of the structure) to detach himself from each increasingly complex variant of the set of situations (e.g., developmental phases of the family) to which the structure applies. The culmination of these transformations is the power of the boy to detach himself completely from the family as a whole, thus transforming himself into an autonomous, mature, and socialized actor.

While the boy learns to externalize relations, the complementary aspect of this process is the "internalization" of these features of the boy as "subject." As a subjective actor (in his role in the myth), the boy develops his character as a nexus of relations which he himself helps to generate. The myth indicates that "internalization" in this sense has occurred by making the boy, as "subject," initiate patterns of action in which he had played only a passive or reactive role in earlier episodes. Examples of such initiated acts are throwing down the stone from the macaws' nest, casting the shadow before the jaguar, shooting the female jaguar, and, finally, returning to the village and interacting there with his mother and sister.

The notion of socialization implicit in the myth, then, is of a coordinated process of externalization and internalization, in which the "person" or "subject" is formed not as an additive sum of his past roles and introjected parental figures or other "alters" but, rather, as a nexus or pattern of relations among role identities conceived as external to, or detached from, the acting subject itself. On the basis of this coordinated pattern of transformations, the subject becomes able to adapt his actions in appropriate ways to variations in his social situation and, ultimately, to act with an adult degree of autonomous detachment.

The entire process of socialization described in this myth requires energy. The more abstract and powerful the nexus of subjective structure becomes, the greater the inputs of energy required. This energy is embodied in the fire, which, as we have seen, functions in the myth as the source of generalized transformational power: first, to transform meat into food, on the concrete level, and then to transform "natural" to "social," boy to man, and family structure to communal structure, and vice versa.

The fire thus embodies, at the level of the boy's transformation into a man, what we might call libidinal energy, defined in a general rather than a specifically sexual sense. As a representation of libidinal energy, the most striking characteristic of the fire's relation to the boy is how it is external to him. The boy as subject, that is, as a developing nexus of relational principles, never comes to "contain" the fire in the sense that Western notions of personality or the selfhood conceive of libidinal energy or the "id" as being contained within the body. Over the course of the myth, the boy becomes able to control the fire, to use it indirectly (in the form of roast meat) to transform himself, and to use it directly to make other fires. He is thus able to transform it in the sense of detaching and replicating it and, in this way, provisionally generalizing it. The boy's relation to the fire, in short, develops along the same lines as his relations to the family role identities that form the "externalized" pattern of his "internalized" subjective structure. He does not "internalize" the fire itself but, rather, the pattern of relations (detachment, replication, generalization, and indirect use) involved in its control and use as a catalyst of his own transformation.

The development of each new level of complexity in the boy's pattern of family relations is accompanied by a transformation in his relationship to the fire. His initial displacement from his sister's household to the macaws' nest brings him closer to the sun in the sky. His subsequent descent to the jaguars' household brings him together with the fire under the same roof, where he eats the food that has been cooked with it. Finally, his return to the village is marked by his actually taking possession of a piece of the fire for himself. Each of these transformations clearly involves a closer relationship with the fire; at the same time, the relationship is always defined in terms of the developing pattern of family relations itself. There is thus a direct relationship between the development of more complex internalized role structures, greater access to libidinal energy, and the development of the ability to control ("externalize") libidinal energy in terms of internalized role structures. The higher the level of complexity of the internalized structure, the more control over (and access to) libidinal energy it requires, and, by the same token, the greater its capacity to channel libidinal energy into forms that it can exploit (such as cooking food and using fire to make fire).

"Socialization" is thus presented in the myth as consisting of two parallel processes: one of these is the "externalization" and "internalization" of the family role system, similar to the Kayapo institutions of the "substitute father" and subsequent initiation ceremonies; the other is the externalization and internalization of the fire, as the libido or dynamic energy of the subjective system. In both processes, what is "externalized" are the specific, concrete forms taken by role patterns or the libido at particular stages of development of the family and the person; what is "internalized" are the formal, increasingly abstract, and dynamic patterns that structure instances of libidinal control. Such instances are transcended and brought under control by being subsumed into the developing nexus of relational rules and transformations that constitutes the structure of the "subject" or person. This is why the stories of the fire and the boy parallel one another. On the one hand, they both pass through analogous transformations in their respective relational patterns; on the other, they converge, drawing progressively closer together in concrete spatial terms and, more abstractly, in terms of the directness and intensity of their functional interaction. The stories of the fire and the boy, although they appear as distinct though interwoven stories, must be understood at the deepest level as complementary aspects of a single complex tale: the story of the transformation from child to adult. This trajectory moves from concrete patterns of relations and behavior based on direct, unmediated (though feeble) libidinal gratification to abstract relational patterns based upon the principle of mediated (detached, indirect, generalized, and thus far more flexible and powerful) libidinal energy, and ultimately from the "natural" to the "social" condition.

This interpretation of the fire also clarifies the final formal characteristic of its treatment in the myth so far left unexplained, to wit, the fire's structural role as a "subject" in its own right, that is, as an entity that undergoes dynamic transformation on the vertical axis of the structure of the myth. The fire is treated structurally as a "subject" on a par with the boy because it is, at the deepest level, an aspect of the boy's own subjectivity, albeit an aspect of his subjectivity that he must objectify ("externalize") as the precondition of his development as a social being. In this connection, it should be noted that the fire shifts from the role of an active "subject" (i.e., initiator of its own actions) to a passive "subject" (reacting to the actions of others), in direct relation to the boy's inverse shift from passive to active "subject." As the boy gains more control over his own actions and his relations to his family, the fire loses its autonomy and becomes increasingly controlled, first by the boy and finally by the community as a whole that has integrated the boy into itself.

It is both consistent and appropriate, in the light of these considerations, that the boy becomes able to detach and to carry with him (i.e., to control) his own fire at the point in the story at which he becomes able to overcome his childish attachment to his parents, and that this is also the point at which he becomes ready for integration into communal society as a mature ("socialized") youth. The bow and arrow and the cotton string he takes with him on his return to the village from the jaguars' house carry out and complete the parallelism between the externalization of the libido (represented by the detached bit of fire) and the externalization of the family role pattern itself. The bow and the string represent externalized expressions of this pattern in the same way that the boy's piece of fire represents the externalized form of the libido.

It is worth emphasizing that the myth explicitly stresses the correlation between the attainment of control over libidinal energy (the fire), the generalized level at which that energy then becomes available to both the individual subject and society in general, and the external, indirect nature of the relationship this implies between human beings and their libidinal energy. In this respect, the animals that eat the fire in the final episode represent the opposite of human beings. Their animality (i.e., their "natural" character) is exemplified by the way they directly relate to their own libidinal impulses: they eat the fire rather than use it to cook their food, much less light other fires for themselves. They thus fail to exercise any degree of control over their own libidinal energy (i.e., any degree of detachment, indirectness, or "externalization" in relation to the fire). By the same token, they fail to preserve and develop their libidinal "fire" in a generalized form in which it could become an energy source capable of supporting a system of transformations of a basic pattern of relations. They are left instead with their single, concrete, and invariant pattern of species characteristics, symbolically embodied in their red throats. Humans, to the contrary, keep the fire outside themselves ("externalizing" it) on the basis of their ability to generate and thus to control it ("internalizing" it). They thereby succeed in transforming it into a generalized energy source that can be channeled into different shapes and uses (e.g., to kindle other fires or to cook food) and thus, symbolically, to support varying patterns and levels of social relations. The essence of "socialization," and of human sociality in general, might be succinctly formulated in Kayapo terms as the trick of being able to have one's fire and eat it too.

The generalized level of control over libidinal energy represented by the youth's culminating seizure of the fire is not achieved without agonizing struggle and emotional trauma at every point along the developmental route when more concrete forms of affective attachment must be surrendered. The myth presents the emotions of each step in the process of the internalizing new principles of role relations while simultaneously externalizing existing role relations. From his panic and subsequent suffering at being abandoned by ZH in the macaws' nest to his fear of the male jaguar after the latter devours the fledglings, and, most of all, his terror of the "mother" jaguar, the myth shows how the boy's terror and suffering are transformed into a positive force in his development by serving as a motive leading him to form or further his relation to the supportive male jaguar. We could say that this aspect of the myth deals with the repression of relatively direct, concrete social and emotional attachments, as well as the traumas attendant upon this repression. The point to emphasize is that the myth provides a model whereby repressive energy can be rechanneled and turned to good effect in furthering the socialization process by helping to motivate the proper pattern of realigning family relations with the support of the appropriate parental figure.

The youth demonstrates that he has surmounted the traumas of socialization by his display of sangfroid toward his human mother and sister as they wail over him when he returns to the village. In a situation that invites regressive emotionalism, the youth stands firm and retains control over his feelings, thus attesting to the strength of the internalized controls he has developed.

In addition to modeling the socialization process, the myth may be said to contain a model of the basic cognitive and affective features of normative Kayapo mature male subjectivity or "personality." Various aspects of the myth contribute to this model. To begin with, it has been shown that the myth accurately presents the key features of the concrete pattern of family role relations, which serves as the social framework of the adult personality structure: the pivotal male role of father-husband; the ambivalent affinal relation between ZH and WB; and the attenuated but nevertheless continuing bond with mother and sister. In the second place, the myth takes the form of an interaction between a subject and one or more "alters." We have seen that the total set of the patterns of "subjective" interactions between subject and alters forms an overall structure focused around the decisive transformation from intra- to extra-family relations. It may now be suggested that this structure not only reflects the social form of the socialization process and, at a higher level, the structure of society itself but, in addition, the framework of subjective orientations or personality structure of the normative Kayapo male. Third, the form of the individual relational components in each episode as intersubjective interactions becomes the primary vehicle for relating the interpersonal, social macrolevel of relational patterns to the intrapersonal, subjective microlevel.

The modeling of adult male cognitive relational patterns to male subjectivity or personality is complemented and completed by the emotional dynamics of the mature male personality embodied in the overt affective patterning of the action in the episodes. The explicit affective values of the action in each of the episodes in which the boy participates as "subject" can be interpreted, when taken together as a set, as a systematic model of the repression of childish family attachments and needs for direct libidinal gratification, and the positive redirection of the affective energy involved in repressive traumas into adult motivational patterns.

The fire imagery of the myth constitutes a dynamic model of what would be called in psychoanalytic jargon the sublimation of the libido. I have made a case for this interpretation purely on the basis of the structural analysis of the myth itself, supported by such symbolic interpretations as could be directly justified on the basis of ethnographic documentation. I have most explicitly made no appeal to symbolic interpretations of the usual Freudian type, since I could neither elicit such interpretations from informants nor document them from independent ethnographic sources. This being said, however, it would be remiss to ignore the possibility of sexual symbolism of the fire and the burning log, the more so since the most straightforward interpretation of the fire in these terms directly supports the interpretation at which we have already arrived on other grounds. The burning log with its fiery tip, which showers sparks of fire and reproduces itself in all of the women's family fires of the village, would be hard to improve upon as a phallic symbol and thus as a symbolic vehicle of male libidinal energy. The Kayapo ritual in which the men collectively carry an enormous, weighty log and charge into the empty central plaza of the round village, while the women watch from their family houses ranged around its periphery, could be interpreted, in a similar vein, as a collective version of the primal scene. This would, of course, be fully consistent with our more anthropological interpretation of the same scene as the primal act of social reproduction.

It should be clear that, in speaking of the myth as constructing a model of adult male "subjectivity," I do not mean to refer to the subjectivity of individual persons per se or to subjectivity in the sense of the immediate content of consciousness or perception. I have employed the term to denote the culturally prescribed modes of orienting the person as actor, and therefore also as re-actor, in the society and physical environment in which he or she lives. Every society depends upon, and its "culture" in great part consists of, collectively stereotyped subjective orientations in this sense. These are sometimes articulated overtly as rules of behavior, but more often (especially in the case of the more basic patterns) they are only indirectly communicated, never brought to consciousness or articulated in so many words. I now want to suggest that collective symbolic forms such as myths encode models of socially standardized subjectivity in this sense and that they function as vehicles for conveying these collective subjective forms to, and impressing them upon, individual members of the society. They thus constitute an important means through which societies are able to channel motivation and shape behavior into collectively prescribed organizational patterns.

The myth in question, since it concerns the socialization process, is a particularly clear-cut instance of this function, but I do not mean to suggest either that all myths are about socialization or that the function of shaping individual

subjectivity into collectively established patterns is confined only to the socialization of children and the myths that describe it. I would maintain, on the
contrary, that the need for such social conditioning of the "subject" arises across
all points of conflict, transition, or ambiguity in the collective social and cultural
order. Moreover, this need tends to arise even outside of structural foci of conflict due to the constant and cumulative tendency for individual experience and
sensibility to diverge from collectively established norms. This process, if not
countered in some way, would lead to the erosion of the meaning and effective-
ness of the collective forms of social life. Myths and other collective symbolic
genres deal with virtually all aspects of this process. By providing patterns of
action, feeling, and response that underscore the normative patterns of social
organization and behavior, as well as being viable and appealing in concrete, affective terms to individuals in their continual struggle to reconcile their personal
lives and experience with their social environment, myths may serve as powerful
devices for supporting a given form of social organization.

Quite apart from this functional relationship to the collective order, however, the conflicts and ambiguities of subjective experience in relation to the
forms and premises of collective order, which I am suggesting is the focal theme
of all myths, is a universally absorbing topic for the members of all societies.
Myths are therefore often told simply for the fun of telling and listening to
them. Certainly this is true of Gê myths and specifically of the myth that is the
subject of this study.

I have attempted to show that the myth does, in fact, model both the structure of society and the structure of a particular collective category of subject
(a young male undergoing socialization), as well as indicating the ways in which
these models are connected to each other at the lower levels of myth structure
(i.e., within the individual episode). The highest level of both the social structural and subjective aspects of the myth has been shown to consist of an ordered
sequence of transformations extending from the first to the last episode of the
myth. It remains to identify the principle by which these two aspects of the
structure of the myth are related to each other at this highest level.

MYTH STRUCTURE AND SOCIAL STRUCTURE

The functional relationship between myth and society that we have just suggested operates on the principle that life imitates art. Nevertheless, the power

of myths to engage their hearers and thus move them to action depends largely upon their correspondence, at the level of underlying structure, if not of overt content, to the actual experience of the hearers, on the principle that art imitates life. There is, then, a circular, mutually reinforcing relationship between the structure of myth and the structure of social and cultural reality.

The question becomes this: what is the focus of this relationship? What specific aspects of social organization are myths most essentially concerned to reflect and thus, in turn, to project as patterns of feeling, motivation, and behavior for their listeners? The foregoing analysis has demonstrated a series of comprehensive correspondences between the form and content of the myth and social organization at both the family and communal levels. At the level of family structure, the myth accurately reflects the role composition and developmental cycles of the uxorilocal family and domestic household. At the level of the structure of the community as a whole, it reflects the main features of village structure: the opposition between the uxorilocal extended-family households on the periphery of the village and the collective men's organizations in the central plaza; and the oscillating pattern of economic adaptation between dispersed hunting-and-gathering bands and the centralized village community with its pattern of ceremonial organization.

The analysis has also suggested, however, that the myth, at least at the level of structure, does not refer to these specific features of social organization and experience as ends in themselves, as if its main concern were to serve as a "charter" for them or, alternatively, as a sort of collective information source or memory bank from which data on the proper forms of social relations could be retrieved as needed. Most of the specific points of correspondence of the kind we have noted (particular role patterns or status identities, concrete details of village structure, etc.) represent relatively low-level components of the structure of the myth. They serve, for the most part, only as concrete points of reference for the pattern of transformations that constitute the higher level of myth structure. This pattern of transformations corresponds to a key component of social organization: namely, the generative process through which the structure of society at all levels is reproduced. This process, as we have noted, can be structurally described as a series of transformations of a basic pattern of family relations, which, in turn, is identical to the basic paradigm that serves as the constant structural component of the successive episodes of the myth.

At the basic level as well as at the higher (transformational) levels, then, the structure of the myth is homologous with the model of Kayapo social structure as a dynamic, hierarchically structured, self-regenerating system, as developed in Chapter Three. The order of transformations of the basic structure encoded in the succession of episodes of the myth (which, in general terms, follows the pattern of detachment, replication at a higher level, and generalization) becomes the framework of the system at the social level. The dynamics of Kayapo social structure essentially consist, it has been suggested, in the transposition and replication of the same pattern of relations "upwards" and "downwards" between the family household and communal levels of social organization. In sum, myths, in their overall structure as well as in their specific content, "reflect" social structure, but the aspect of social structure they are primarily concerned with, and which they encode at the highest level of their own structures, is not the static formal framework or the specific content of social relations per se but, rather, the relations of production of both the form and content of social structure. In other words, the structure of society emerges from and structures the processes by which it is produced and maintained in being.

The structure of myths is, for all practical purposes, inseparable from the functional processes and dynamics of producing or reproducing the order of society. This is the fundamental reason why myth structure cannot be dissociated from the real (empirical, concrete) order of socioeconomic relations. The functional process of generating and maintaining the social order provides the focus for the metaphorical correspondence between the structure of myth and the structure of society, and thus for the formal properties of myth structure itself. Myth structure, as this implies and as our analysis has revealed, is essentially and above all dynamic; as structure, it embodies the form of a generative process.

This dynamic, functional aspect of myth structure, both in itself and in its relation to social reality, accounts for the dual character of myth as constrained by social reality and, at the same time, as standing in a creative, dynamic relationship to that reality. Myth, in other words, is not merely a passive reflection or positive copy of socioeconomic organization or, for that matter, of the natural environment; rather, it is the perspective of a "subject" or actor (who may be an individual or a group as the embodiment of a collective category) who is engaged in creating, through their own actions, the order of relations that the structure of the myth reflects.

The demonstration of this determinate (but not determined) relationship between myth and its socioeconomic context has been the major aim of this study. The point has both theoretical and methodological implications that run squarely counter to much of what has come to be identified as the "structuralist approach" to myth and its analysis. For one thing, the perspective on myth presented here implies that the primary reference of the structure of myths is directly to their socioeconomic and cultural contexts, not to a corpus of myths that relate to one another like so many turns of a cosmic kaleidoscope, endlessly recombining the same structural elements in different ways without any true focus or formal unity, either as a set or as individual myths (cf. Lévi-Strauss 1969:5–6). On the contrary, the present analysis has demonstrated that individual myths have both unity and structural focus, and that they serve as both a model of and a model for the generative structure of the social pattern or situation as defined from the vantage point of a particular, culturally defined category of actor or "subject." The subject may correspond to a normative category of social actors, as in the specific myth we have analyzed, or to a hypothetical combination of "subjective" features and attributes, as, for example, in "trickster" figures and other socially marginal beings. In either case, the subjective vantage point and the unity of the myth can be given precise structural definitions.

This general discussion has so far stressed the sequential aspect of myth structure, that is, its aspect as a series of transformations of a constant formulaic pattern. The analysis has, however, revealed a complementary aspect of myth structure that is equally related to its character as a representation of a dynamic, generative process. I am referring to the hierarchical aspect of the structure of the myth and, specifically, to the dialectical character of this hierarchy. The plot of the myth proceeds in the form of a series of apparent contradictions (e.g., the incompatible juxtaposition of a growing boy and his maternal household), which it proceeds to surmount by transposing them to a higher level of structural differentiation of the same basic pattern of relations. The latter is invariably constructed by polarizing or juxtaposing aspects of the basic pattern in relation to one another, thus giving rise to further differentiation within the pattern itself. By this means, the pattern is recreated in a form capable of including a higher degree of structural variation, more powerful transformations, or greater differentiation between aspects of roles and social groups—in short, at a higher level in a hierarchy of differentiation of the same basic system.

This aspect of myth structure bears directly upon the distinctive relationship of myth as a genre to social or historical contradictions. Lévi-Strauss (1963:229) has suggested that "since the purpose of myth is to provide a logical model capable of overcoming a contradiction (an impossible achievement if, as it happens, the contradiction is real)," it will keep on generating variants until the desire to resolve the contradiction that produced it is exhausted. I would suggest, on the contrary, that the definitive characteristic of myth as a genre, exemplified by the Kayapo myth of the origin of cooking fire, is that it treats contradictions in the structure of society and the cosmos as surmountable or resolvable within the terms of that structure itself, by virtue of the transformation of the structure into a more differentiated, more inclusive, and hierarchically encompassing variant of itself.

Myth thus deals with contradictions only to deny them, as Levi- Strauss has suggested, but not in the way he proposes. The implication of the present study is that myths remain alive, that is, meaningful to the members of the societies in which they arise, only so long as they appear to represent viable ways of surmounting and resolving the contradictions with which they deal.

TIME AND STRUCTURE

This manner of dealing with contradiction is related to a further basic characteristic of myth as a genre that has remained implicit in the analysis up to this point, to wit, the mythical treatment of time. The structure of the Kayapo myth of the origin of fire, and perhaps most, if not all, myths and other genres of symbolic narrative, is based upon the juxtaposition, interaction, and final reconciliation of three distinct modes of time. These three modes can be thought of as forming a hierarchy of levels of temporal experience.

At the lowest level, the events of the story present themselves as mere sequences, following one another on the basis of pure chance or, at least, not according to any overall principle of order. It may be said that this level corresponds to the subjective time of the hero of the myth until the episode of his final return to the village. This is the first time he undertakes a concerted program of action oriented toward future time; in the preceding episodes, he merely responded to events as they occurred.

The second level or modality of temporal organization in the myth is the linear, directionally polarized time of the story or stories contained in the myth: the story of the boy's growing up; and the story of how society came to control the cooking fire. At this level, the individual events and episodes of the myth can be perceived as organized in a linear sequence, in which each event has its place; there is a beginning and an end, that is, a direction and closure, to the sequence. This temporal perspective, in which the sequence of events in the story appears as an orderly process, could be said to correspond to the viewpoint of the hero as a socialized youth at the close of the myth, when the pattern of events leading up to the climax becomes clear in retrospect and, accordingly, takes on meaning. This dimension or mode of time has a structural basis in the linear order of events in the story as well as a real basis in the linear, nonrepetitive form of the experience which the story relates, that is, socialization and growth from childhood to adulthood.

A third mode of time, however, lies implicit in the highest level of the structure of the myth. This is the modality of nonlinear, cyclical, repetitive time, which is implied in the use of the same fundamental pattern, depicted in varying transformations, as the basis of the structure of each successive episode. The repetitive use of the same basic pattern means that, in the midst of the linear change and chaotic flux of the lower temporal modes of organization of the myth, there is an element—the most essential component—that persists unchanged. Not only does this basic structural component continually reassert itself in each new episode, but it serves as the final frame of reference for relating all the episodes from the vantage point of the end of the story. In terms of this foundational structure, then, the linear, nonrepetitive time of coherently ordered individual life experience, along with the chaotic, unordered time of spontaneous, unintegrated life experience, are perceived or felt, in the last analysis, to be merely modalities of the repetitive, enduring, unchanging, and, in effect, "timeless" time embedded in the enduring and recurring patterns of society and social life associated with the highest levels of the social system.

The association of cyclical time with society as a whole is achieved in the final episode, in which society collectively appropriates the repetitive, reversible pattern as the basis of its own structure. The basic structure thus takes on the character of the organizing principle of experience and reality itself. It becomes, in other words, both an epistemological and an ontological first principle. As such, it is felt as a unifying force, governing and ordering the superficially chaotic, nonrepetitive events of the story, and thus as both the regulating principle of the socialization and subjective structure of the boy, and, at the collective level, the basic structure of society itself.

This organizing function of this foundational pattern of the story may be unconsciously sensed, I suggest, by the native hearers of the story, who are intuitively familiar not only with the symbolic connotations of the elements of the story but also with the foundational pattern itself in other contexts of their lives, even though they do not overtly perceive it as the underlying structure of the myth. There is nothing mysterious or out of the ordinary in the perception of such unconscious patterns: innumerable examples of the same basic phenomenon could be given from the literature of experimental and Gestalt psychology and from everyday experience in Western culture. A good example of the latter would be a person who is able to feel the power and intensity of a Bach fugue without ever consciously perceiving the structure of the music, based on the constant reintroduction and variation of the same melodic figure. For Kayapo listeners, unconsciously sensing a pattern in a myth as ordering vital forms of everyday experiences (such as growing up, witnessing the dispersal and formation of families, dividing the village to go on treks and coming together again) enables them to apply the same pattern to create order out of their own experience and thus their behavior. Behaving according to the patterns unconsciously inferred from myths and other genres of symbolic forms, the listeners recreate their patterns in objective social reality. In this way, by shaping the motivations and orientations to the experience and, ultimately, to the behavior of social actors, myths may play a role in the creation and recreation of social reality in their own image.

To return to the problem of the mythical treatment of contradiction raised in the preceding section, the temporal dimension of myth structure is based upon the principle of the reconciliation and harmonization of three modes (random sequence, linear, and cyclical) of time, by showing that all are simply complementary manifestations of the same basic reversible structure. They do not, in short, contradict one another or even, in the final analysis, run at cross-purposes to one another. There can therefore be no history for the mythical consciousness in the essential Western sense of the term, i.e., an irreversible, linear process of change in the basic structure of society itself. There can likewise be no basic contradiction or incompatibility between the individual subject and the collective sociocosmic order. This is because the sequential and linear (nonrepetitive) modes of time in which subjects perceives their experience (or at least that aspect of their experience that does not readily fit into the cyclical, repetitive temporal frame of reference represented by the collective order of society and the cosmos) are shown to be subsumed at a deeper level within the basic structure of the collective order. Myth, in sum, presupposes, in its most basic structural principles, the absence of truly insurmountable contradictions, the absence of history, and at least the possibility of the perfect integration of the collectively stereotyped "subject" within the social order.

THE STRUCTURE OF MYTH AS STRUCTURE OF MIND AND AS STRUCTURE OF SOCIAL ACTION

One of the goals of this study announced in Chapter One was to develop a model of myth structure based upon the principle of a "hierarchically organized system of transformations of a single set of symbolic oppositions that recurs as a basis for each successive episode." A model of this description, I suggested, would be able to "give an account of the narrative or temporal dimension of myth structure, and the type of message it conveys, as well as giving proper weight to the nontemporal, paradigmatic aspects of the myth structure." The analysis presented in the course of this study has fulfilled both of these formal goals.

Having done so, however, it has raised an even more general issue: that of the origin and nature of the structure that has been revealed. The general nature of this question derives not from the structure of the myth alone but from its resemblance to certain models of the basic structure of language and the human intellect.

Let us briefly review the general formal characteristics of the model of the structure of the myth that has been developed in this study. The structure of the myth, in terms of our model, consists at the lowest level of a bidimensional matrix or paradigm that is repeated, with relatively slight variations, in each of the successive episodes or segments of the myth. At the next higher level, the pattern of interrelations between the actors and symbolic elements within each episode is transformed by a pair of coordinated transformations. At the third level, the pairs of transformation in consecutive episodes are connected with one another by a set of higher-order transformations in such a way that they form a cumulative sequence or linear pattern. At the fourth level, the substantive content of the two dimensions themselves, as well as the pattern of coordination of the pair of transformations carried out with reference to them in each episode, are transformed at the midpoint of the myth, thus defining two main clusters or sets of episodes (the earlier episodes and the final pair).

This hierarchy of structural levels is cross-cut by two essentially parallel series of transformations (each involving the same pair of dimensions and series of levels), comprising the stories of the fire and of the boy, respectively. Finally, at the end of the final episode, the general form of the structure of both society and the socionatural cosmos emerges, subsuming both the sequence of episodic transformations and the two hitherto separate but parallel story lines of the boy and the fire within a single dynamic whole.

The formal structure of this dynamic totality is intriguing. It is a grid structure of two dimensions, of which the vertical is a dimension of dynamic, continuous development or transformation with kinetic, causal properties, while the horizontal is a dimension of essentially static, classificatory differentiation. In linguistic parlance, the vertical dimension would be defined as the modality of metonymic or syntactic relations, while the horizontal would be defined as the modality of metaphoric or paradigmatic relations. The basic triangle of myth structure, in these terms, obviously represents a specimen of the same genus as Jakobson's "primary phonemic triangle" or the basic triangular structures Lévi-Strauss has sought to identify as the root form of such diverse cultural structures as kinship relations and culinary symbolism (Jakobson and Halle 1971:51–53; Lévi-Strauss 1963:31–54; 1966a).

The basic structure of the Kayapo fire myth can be reduced, in the simplest terms, to a dimension of dynamic action involving a transition between varying levels of energy or intensity, and a dimension of differentiation among classes of acts or the products of action of the same level of structure or of intensity or energy. A glance over the graphs of the structures of the episodes of the myth should suffice to reveal that they all conform to this general schema. Seen as analogous to the diagrams of both Jakobson and Lévi-Strauss, the overall structure of the myth can be seen to conform to the general schema depicted in Figure 1.14.

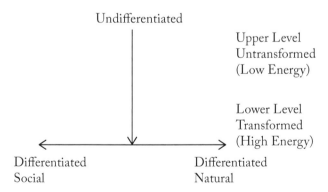

Figure 1.14. The general triadic schema underlying all the episodes of the myth of the origin of cooking fire.

This schematic pattern serves, on the one hand, to classify and identify all of the symbolic elements of the various episodes in relation to one another. On the other hand, it serves as a model of the action that transpires in each episode. Reduced to its simplest form, it represents a minimal model of any significant (social) act, since any such act must necessarily comprise a vertical (energetic, metonymic, or kinetic) component and a horizontal (interpretative, classificatory) component, in terms of which it can be related to other acts or objects of action.

Broadly speaking, the paired sets of transformations on either side of the vertical axis represent mirror images of each other; in other words, they are related in logical terms as reciprocals of one another. The individual transformations within each paired set, on the other hand, take the form of inversions, that is, of reversals of the status of an actor or element as defined with reference to polar oppositions such as up:down, inside:outside, social:natural, differentiated:undifferentiated, and so on. Now it so happens that exactly such simple systems of transformations, involving the coordination of reciprocal and inverse transformations of simple matrices of relations, such as the basic bidimensional structure of the myth, have been identified by Piaget as the basic structure of human intelligence (Piaget 1970a, 1970b).

Jakobson, particularly in his studies of aphasia, and Lévi-Strauss, in several of the works already been cited, have suggested a much broader role for the basic triangular structure that Jakobson first isolated in his studies of sound patterning in language. They have asserted that it represents the fundamental structure of human intelligence or of the human mind (Jakobson and Halle 1971; Lévi-Strauss 1966a). Similarly, when interpreted as a paradigm of meaningful action, the Jakobsonian triangle can be seen as homologous with Piaget's (1970a, 1970b) model of the basic structure of the mind.

At first glance, the congruence of these two models of the fundamental structure of the mind with the basic structure of the myth might also appear to reinforce the "intellectualist" bias of Lévi-Straussian structuralism, especially with regard to myth:

> Mythology has no obvious practical function... it is not directly linked with a different kind of reality [i.e., social or environmental factors: T.T.], which is endowed with a higher degree of objectivity than its own and whose injunctions it might therefore transmit to minds that seem perfectly free to indulge their own creative spontaneity. And so, if were possible to prove in this instance, too, that the apparent arbitrariness of the mind. . . and its seemingly uncontrolled inventiveness imply the existence of laws operating at a deeper level, we would

inevitably be forced to conclude that when the mind is left to commune with itself and no longer has to come to terms with objects, it is in a sense reduced to imitating itself as object; and that since the laws governing its operations are not fundamentally different from those it exhibits in its other functions, it shows itself to be of the nature of a thing among things. (Lévi-Strauss 1969b:10)

The whole thrust of the present analysis is, however, diametrically opposed to this interpretation. To begin with, the insight that the Piagetian and Jakobsonian models of the fundamental structure of the intellect are homologous was based upon the interpretation of the latter as a paradigm of action, that is, of meaningful interaction between an actor (or subject) and an "object" (which may, in the simplest terms, be simply the act itself, regarded as an object of classification). Piaget's model of the structure of the mind is based on precisely the same notion: for him, behavior (i.e., concrete, motivated interaction with objects) always precedes intellect, and intelligence always develops through the introjection of the principles governing concrete action.

This pragmatic notion of the nature of the intelligence and, hence, of the fundamental structures of thought and the mind runs squarely counter to the assumption implicit in Lévi-Strauss' formulation that the structure of the mind is itself unconditioned by having "to come to terms with objects," being, rather, inherent in the mind in an a priori capacity. The mind, in Lévi-Strauss' terms, is itself conceived as an inert "thing," defined, for essential structural purposes, in isolation from other "things," and therefore as having the same "nature" as other inert, isolated objects.

This static, passive, and objectified notion of mind (and of human culture as a whole) is perhaps the most central and pervasive tenet of "structuralism" as it has taken shape as a crypto-philosophical position, which is at the root of the pessimistic and quietist tone of a number of the canonical structuralist works. It is, however, precisely on this basic issue that both the notion of intellectual structure and of the structure of myth advanced here conflicts most dramatically with the structuralist view.

As far as the structure of myth is concerned, the present analysis has indicated that myths have a "practical function" that "directly links" them with social reality. This function is that of shaping the patterns of feeling and behavior of "subjects," defined as stereotypic categories of social actors, toward the socioeconomic system that forms their collective arena of action. This function, as I have argued, is directly related to the structure of the myth, which is both a metaphor of social action and a model of the structure of the acting subject. I have sought to demonstrate this interpretation by showing that at every point and at every level at which the basic "triangular" structural pattern asserts itself, it can be shown to correspond directly to some dynamic process of social action.

Insofar as an argument from the structure of myth to the structure of mind may be admitted (which is, of course, the sort of argument upon which the structuralists have based their position), the analysis of the structure of the Kayapo fire myth carried out in this study constitutes an argument for the Piagetian and Marxist notion that the structure of the mind is formed through dynamic interaction between itself, in its capacity as acting "subject," and "things" or objects of action. It consists precisely of the pattern of this interaction, introjected as a guide to the action of the "subject," which in turn tends to replicate the pattern in the objective world of relations among "things."

The structure of the mind and the structure of myth are therefore homologous—but for the opposite reasons as those asserted by Lévi-Strauss. It is not that myth and the mind are alike as symbolic structures removed from the necessity "to come to terms with objects" but, on the contrary, that both myth and the mind or intellect are symbolic structures for coming to terms with objects.

Perhaps it would be well to reiterate at this point that the structure of society (at least that aspect of social structure "reflected" by the myth) is not merely a static table of the organization of collective groups or a network of non-native role relations; it is itself a dynamic pattern of action of the same type represented by the structure of the myth. At the level of the individual actor, this takes the form of patterns of interaction between role actors; at the collective level, it takes the form of the cyclical processes through which families and collective groups form, dissolve, interact, and exchange members. To "reflect" such a structure of social relations, as the myth does, from the standpoint of one of the categories of actors within it is simultaneously to lay down a pattern of action, as well as of knowing and experiencing and deeply feeling that structure of social relations.

There is, in sum, no contradiction between the notion that myth reflects aspects of social organization and the idea that it stands in a dynamic, creative, functional relationship with that social organization. By the same token, there is no contradiction between the notion that myth structure reflects social structure, on the one hand, and, on the other, the notion that it reflects the structure of the intellect or "mind." Given the basic notion of the function of myth put forward in this study, namely, that of directly connecting the "subjectivity" of the social actor with the objective structure of the socioeconomic system to which he or she belongs, this is precisely what one would expect to find.

I have presented in this study an analysis of only a single myth. The question arises of how far general propositions of the order put forward above can be justified on the basis of such a study. The answer is, of course, that they must be considered only as hypotheses, to be confirmed or discarded on the basis of further studies. An analysis of the Greek Oedipus legend I made (Turner 1969) before fully working out the concepts and techniques employed in the present study revealed a repetitive paradigmatic structure similar to the one turned up in this analysis. Even these two studies are perhaps enough to suggest the potential usefulness of the model of narrative structure developed in them as a device for investigating systems of structures of subjective meaning and systems of objective relational categories, either within the same society or in different societies. There is, for that matter, no reason why it could not be adopted to the study of individual fantasy material or, at the other extreme, to non-narrative forms based upon the repetition and variation of motifs or themes. The major point of the present analysis is that such a model—or, indeed, any model of the structure of symbolic forms—must be undertaken with close attention to the relations between such forms and the social, economic, and cultural contexts in which they arise. I hope to have convinced the reader, through this fine-grained analysis of the Kayapo myth of the origin of cooking fire, of the possibility, validity, and value of doing so—and of thereby coming to appreciate the profoundly creative and intellectually sophisticated capacities of so-called "savage thinking."

PART TWO

Later articles

Beauty and the beast
The fearful symmetry of the jaguar and other natural beings in Kayapo ritual and myth[1]
The 2011 R. R. Marett Lecture

As an aging anthropologist, I have found that one of the more congenial ideas of the Mebengokre Kayapo, the indigenous people with whom I have been doing research since the 1960s, is that, as people grow older, they tend to become more beautiful. The Kayapo terms I translate here as "beauty," *mêtch*, or in its more enthusiastically approbatory forms, *mêkumren* and *mêtire*, connote aesthetic beauty, perfection of performance, or finesse of execution in such valued modes of public performance as oratory, singing, and dancing, admirable qualities of character, and the satisfactoriness of social relations and transactions. These valued cultural qualities constitute the most desirable aspects of social identity, a cultural ideal of humanity that is attainable, to varying degrees, by all social persons and things but is generally expected to be exemplified in the highest degree by senior men and women who have attained communal prominence as leaders and "teachers." Such leadership is manifested through public oratory in communal political and ceremonial activities, especially those

---

1.   First presented as the Marett Memorial Lecture, "Beauty and the beast: Humanity, animality, and animism in the thought of an Amazonian people," at Exeter College, University of Oxford, on May 6, 2011. Published in 2017 in *HAU: Journal of Ethnographic Theory* 7 (2): 51–70.

associated with the possession and circulation of ritually prestigious "beautiful" names and "valuables" (items of personal adornment and rights to perform specific acts in communal ceremonies). They may be distinguished as such from "common" (*kakrit*) persons, who lack such prestigious social attributes or qualities. There is a parallel but less formally constituted classification of food animals: "beautiful" people should on the whole only eat "beautiful" animals, birds, or fish, while "common" or undistinguished folk may be pejoratively referred to as *mē ngwòy tam bôrô*, "those who eat birds thrown directly on the fire without removing the feathers" (i.e., without skinning or cleaning them, resembling the way animals would eat prey).

The ideal of beauty, as reflected in socially refined and distinctive behavior, is thus bound up with ideas about the relation of humans and animals, or humanity and animality as existential conditions. Humans and animals are not conceived as either entirely different or originally identical kinds of beings, but, rather, as comprising differential points on a continuous scale of relative distinction and refinement (i.e., "beauty") of qualities of identity and conduct. The Kayapo consider humans, animals, and, to varying degrees, other nonhuman beings as sharing fundamental aspects of existence, such as processes of growth, health, energy, strength, proneness to rage and violence or to tameness and affability, and as experiencing the processes of sickness, aging, and death. In the cases of some animal, fish, and bird species, they also practice such cultural and social traits as having names, ceremonies, language-like communication, and elementary family life. However, in no cases are these features and activities fully identical with their Kayapo human analogues. For example, it is believed that fish or animals may hold ceremonies, but they have only a single form that is fixed for the whole species, like the physical forms of the creatures in question; furthermore, the performers move or dance about in circles, repeating the names of their own species rather than bestowing their individual names on younger-generation kin of specific relationship categories, which humans do.

This implies that the distinction between humanity and animality is not conceived simply as an external difference between humans and animal species, but as levels or qualities of being, which are shared to varying degrees by different species; humans share aspects of animality, but humans alone share certain unique features that set humanity apart from animals. These distinctive features themselves, however, comprise developments or elaborations of prototypes originally shared by the ancestors of contemporary animal and human beings. The distinction between humanity and animality, in sum, is internal to humans as a relation between levels of being human as well as external in the relations between human and animal species. Moreover, the distinction is not a fixed and stable boundary as an internal component of specifically human existence; rather, it is a fluctuating and variable process of transformation of basic animal powers into human cultural forms—a process that can run in either direction. In this process, animality functions as the boundary condition of humanity; in the Kayapo perspective, we begin and end as animals.

The development and ultimate dissolution of human personhood is grounded in, and interdependent with, transformations of human bodiliness, which involve the containment, control, channeling, and appropriation of animal energies and forms that are fundamental parts of human existence through the processes of socialization and enculturation. The social development of the person is treated in Kayapo ritual and social practice as a process consisting of repetitive transformations of internal bodily energies and affective dispositions as well as external social relations. These transformations take the form of framing and regulating spontaneous affects and energies within consciously objectified forms of socially valued behavior. The Kayapo consider these spontaneous affects and energies to be shared, to varying degrees, by all living beings and some entities that we would consider inanimate. The transformation of these essentially animal features into social forms of human bodiliness, personality, and behavior is achieved through participation in social relations in the family and through public activities, notably rites of passage. They are accompanied by changes in bodily adornment and recruitment to membership in communal groups such as age sets. The animal aspects of human existence, however, are not limited to bodily needs and drives, but are also imbued in elementary social relations, such as close family relations between parents and children, and between adults of different genders in their roles as mates and subsistence providers. These relations are the locus of physical reproduction and primary socialization, and as such are the context for transforming the affective dispositions involved in intimate, precultural relations in socially coordinated, culturally valued forms of relationship and behavior. Myths such as the Kayapo myth of the jaguar's fire record the affective and social terrors and adjustments of such attachments, as well as the social and cultural stakes involved in such crises of reframing and transforming personal identity and social relations. While the Kayapo regard themselves and their fundamental social relationships such as the elementary family as sharing some traits with animals and certain other nonhuman entities, however, they do not represent humans and animals as essentially identical in either subjective or objective terms. On the contrary, human personhood, bodiliness, and social relations are conceived as different in critical respects from their animal counterparts and prototypes, despite the extent to which humans may share, or may once have shared, some of their forms.

The essential distinction between contemporary humans and animals, as represented in myths, ritual practices, and various culturally framed attributes of social identity, amount to a distinctive Kayapo conception of the essence of humanity. The fundamental aspect of this distinction is the human development of objectified formulas (frames) of feeling and activity, and the ability to communicate and inculcate these frames through symbolic communication. The struggle to internalize and put into practice these objectified patterns of personal behavior and social activity is the focus of the traumas and triumphs of individual socialization and the social regulation of activity. In Kayapo terms, this is the essence of the struggle to achieve "beauty," the proper integration of personal identity and social relations.

As I developed my ethnographic understanding of the Kayapo ideal of "beauty," however, I became aware of a troubling ambivalence pervading Kayapo attitudes toward the notion of beauty as a social ideal. This ambivalence is expressed in a sense of the inherent instability and susceptibility to a dizzying collapse of even relatively well-integrated, highly valued, and beautifully framed specimens of social identity into its antisocial opposite: raging, chaotic, and even murderous rampages. I found that this culturally recognized form of berserk, antisocial madness, called in Kayapo *aybanh*, is associated with jaguars. It is thought to be caused by the penetration of the skin by the hairs or blood of jaguars, as when a hunter has contact with the body of a jaguar he has killed or brings its body into a village to be roasted and eaten by boys of the junior age set. The hairs or blood of other wild animals or even human enemies may also give rise to the antisocial madness of *aybanh*, but the jaguar is thought to be the most potent etiological agent in this regard. A person who becomes *aybanh* loses partial control of his or her bodily movements and becomes functionally blind, or at least incapable of visually coordinating bodily movements in a normal way; the eyes tend to roll up so that only the whites show (the Kayapo expression for a person who has become *aybanh* is *no kaykep*, "eyes roll around"). The *aybanh* person becomes violently, even murderously aggressive toward everyone without regard to identity, gender, or social relationship. His or her body becomes extremely hot to the touch, sweat pours off the skin, and the muscles become powerfully tensed. As I was to discover from personal experience, persons in this trance-like state become extremely strong. The qualities of the *aybanh* condition, ranging from extreme body heat (internalized fire?) to fierce aggressiveness to the loss of cultural faculties like language and motor coordination, can be understood as the assumption of a jaguar-like identity and the accompanying loss of social characteristics. As I learned about the condition from informants, I was intrigued by its affinities to jaguars and above all by the insistence that the most "beautiful" or culturally refined people seemed particularly vulnerable to sudden onsets of the jaguar-like state. In their accounts, it seemed that the very elaboration of perfected forms of social discipline and cultural behavior, which are intended to guard against relapses into unsocialized, animalistic behavior, might actually be responsible for generating counterpressures for brushing aside social restraints and giving expression to the notionally repressed modes of behavior. In other words, the social production of beauty gives rise to an intimation of a fearful symmetry of beauty and bestiality.

This sense, I realized, is bound up with a Kayapo notion that their constructions of social identity, viewed as transformations of bodiliness and affect in the service of idealized patterns of socially valued feeling and relationship conduct, might give way and fail to hold in check the powerful propensity to identify with the violently antisocial modes of feeling and action exemplified by the jaguar. This social collapse renders them vulnerable to relapses into the bestiality that continues to lurk beneath the veneer of their sociality. The most insidious form of this Kayapo idea is the feeling that that this danger may be aggravated, rather than repressed, by the adoption of ideal ("beautiful") forms of social feeling— even though such forms are intended to control and protect against tendencies emanating from contacts with external exemplars of the animal substratum of bodiliness and affect, above all, the jaguar, or with internal tensions arising from its transformations into cultural forms. The most "beautiful" people may be the most vulnerable to a tendency for human social refinement to collapse into its opposite: violent fits of antisocial aggression and a loss of cultural consciousness, even language, more appropriate to beasts of prey than to social humans.

INSIGHTS FROM EXTREME ANTHROPOLOGY

My first ethnographic intimation of this problem came to me early in my fieldwork in an unexpected sudden and frightening form.

In late 1965, I presented my doctoral thesis based on a year and a half of fieldwork among the Kayapo and immediately returned to Brazil to begin a second bout of fieldwork with a different Kayapo group than the two I had previously studied. This was the Mentuktire Kayapo community of Porori, located on the bank of the Xingu River. After I had been in Porori for a couple of months, an epidemic of flu broke out, and six people out of the village population of 168 died. My wife had returned to Rio, and I was the only person capable of dispensing a semblance of Western medical care, which, in that context, meant essentially aspirin pills and heavy doses of bedside manner. I soon found myself spending most of my waking hours trying to help the many sick and terrified Indians, doing rudimentary nursing, and even helping to bury a few of those who died, if their kin were too sick to do the job.

One afternoon, I spent several hours with a very sick widow who lived by herself in a house built some distance from the village. I returned to the circle of houses when the sun was low in the sky, casting long shadows on the cleared ground of the central plaza. It was oddly quiet—none of the usual noises of household conversations, children playing, or women chopping wood for cooking fires. I caught sight of one person, a senior man I knew and with whom I had friendly relations. Although he was a leader in political activities, he was known for eccentric public behavior. At this moment, he was standing in the center of the plaza with his back to me. He seemed to be holding a shotgun, which had its breech broken open in the loading position, the barrel and wooden stock protruding from different sides of his body. A little odd, but I thought nothing of it. My hut lay ahead on the opposite side of the plaza, so my way led directly past him. As I passed him, I clapped him on the shoulder and hailed him cheerfully by name, "Ho, Krantàytch! What are you up to?"

Several things then happened in rapid succession. Krantàytch, who had not seen me coming, jerked his body around and turned his face to me. With a shock, I saw that his eyes were turned up into his head so that only the whites were showing. He was trembling with intense muscle tension and was extremely hot to the touch. As I registered these disconcerting facts, Krantàytch succeeded in pushing a cartridge into the firing chamber of the shotgun and closed the barrel with a loud click. He spoke not a word and seemed to be in a trance. With a start of fear, I registered the significance of the odd silence that enveloped the usually noisy village: the place was abandoned except for Krantàytch and me. I guessed at once that he had entered the crazed, antisocial trance state the Kayapo call *aybanh* and that the reason the village was so quiet was that all the inhabitants had fled for their lives to the forest. I was alone with a crazed berserk, with my arm around his shoulder as he loaded a shotgun with trembling hands.

I said, "Krantàytch, give me the gun," and seized the barrel. In his trance, however, he seemed unable either to understand or to speak. He was trembling violently and his tautly stretched muscles were as hard and strong as steel. I could not wrench the gun from his hands, but I was able to cover the trigger guard and keep him from taking it away from me so he might have pointed it and pulled the trigger. I dared not let go, thinking that, if I turned to run away, I would likely get a load of buckshot in my back at point-blank range. As we struggled, each of us using all of our strength but neither able to get control of the shotgun from the other, I had a vision of the painting by Henri Rousseau of a tropical forest scene of gigantic trees standing motionless in golden afternoon sunlight (one feels a stillness in it as total as the setting where we were grappling), in one corner of which are the diminutive figures of a man and a panther or jaguar locked in a death struggle, which does not disturb the indifferent calm of the forest.

Fortunately, the silent village proved not to be as serenely empty and unconcerned with human difficulties as Rousseau's jungle. From one of the houses encircling the plaza suddenly burst three men—the old chief Kremoro, another senior man, and a young man of the bachelor's age set. They had been hiding in the hut and watching for a chance to rush Krantàytch and take away his gun. I had unexpectedly given them their chance. They ran out and tackled Krantàytch, and the four of us succeeded in wresting the gun from his grasp. We extracted the cartridge and ran with the gun and cartridge back to the hiding place in the hut where the men had been lurking. Meanwhile, Krantàytch staggered awkwardly away until he reached a house on the periphery of the plaza. He entered it and seized a number of pieces of wood that were smoldering on a hearth. He returned with them to his former place in the middle of the plaza and began throwing them, apparently at random and without aiming, in the general direction of the thatched houses on the periphery of the plaza. He did not hit any houses or succeed in setting any of them on fire, which I supposed was his intention. Our little group stood ready to try to put out any fires he might start, but none of us made any move to restrain him or forcibly prevent more of his crazed behavior.

As we watched from our hiding place in the house, I noticed that the young man standing beside me had begun to tremble violently over his whole body. Startled, fearing that he too might be slipping into a berserk trance like that of Krantàytch, I cried out, "Oh no! Not you, too! Is everybody going *aybanh* around here?" To this he indignantly replied, "What? Am I a beautiful (*mêtch*) person that I should go *aybanh* and run wild (*àkrê*) like an animal? Not me! I'm just a common (*kakrit*) guy!"

My young companion turned out merely to be shivering from fright after his encounter with Krantàytch and the onset of the evening chill. Meanwhile, when Krantàytch ran out of things to throw, he began to show signs of exhaustion. He hung his head, became inactive, and finally fell to the ground. Seeing this, Kremoro, the old chief, shouted from our hiding place for people to come out of the woods, saying it was safe now that Krantàytch's trance seemed to be ending. He sent the first people who emerged to the river with buckets and pans to bring water to pour on the prostrate Krantàytch, who was apparently unconscious but still hot to the touch. Soon he was lying in the middle of a large mud puddle, which effectively cooled him down to normal temperature. He thereupon regained consciousness, although he seemed a bit dazed and had no memory of his lapse into trance. He was not held responsible for his threatening behavior, which was accepted as conduct to be expected from Krantàytch and, in general, from one emerging from an *aybanh* trance, the sort of behavior to be expected from certain "beautiful" or prominent citizens like chiefs or holders of honorific ceremonial names.

From my conversation with my trembling companion, I learned some invaluable lessons about Kayapo ideas of sociality, animality, beauty, and the causes of psychic breakdowns into the antisocial trances. I had thought of the Kayapo value of *mêtch*, which I have translated as "beauty," as the epitome of sociality and, as such, the opposite of *kakrit*, vulgar commonness, and, above all, the berserk craziness exemplified by *aybanh*. I now realized that common sociality was not even on the same scale as *aybanh* trance; rather, the appropriate contrast was that between humanity, in the Kayapo sense of social form, versus animality, in their sense of the animal substratum of human bodiliness.

In *aybanh* trance, I learned, the socialized part of human subjective identity becomes eclipsed, leaving only the unsocialized, unenculturated part. Those undergoing *aybanh* trance lose all or virtually all of their cultural skills, including language and basic locomotion, and ultimately lapse into unconsciousness, from which they may not recover. This state has much in common with shamanic trance, except that, for Kayapo shamans, the coma comes first, then giving way to the trance in which the shaman voluntarily assumes the form of the first creature he sees (usually a flying creature like a moth, bat, or bird). He may go on to assume other nonhuman forms, but he must always remain conscious of his humanity and never lose himself completely in the nonhuman form he has taken on. If he does make the fatal mistake of accepting his adopted form as his real identity, he loses contact with his own body, with the result that both his spirit and his body die. Neither spirit form nor body content can survive without the other: life, in other words, consists of a constant interaction and interdependence between the two.

Aybanh trance, like shamanic trance, involves the separation of the spiritual form of a person—what the Kayapo call the *karon*, his or her socialized and enculturated subjectivity, attached to his or her outward bodily form—from the physical content of his or her body. In most cases, this separation is incomplete, as in sleep or a coma, but in particularly intense or violent cases, the connection between the body and its loosely attached spirit form may be lost, resulting in death. The loosening of the relation of *karon* spirit form to body (¯*in*, flesh, and *'i*, bones) regularly accompanies processes of transformation from one identity to another, as in initiation rituals effecting passages from adolescence to adulthood, or the ultimate transition into death. In such passages, the previously existing physical and social identity of a person is suppressed or separated, following which the initiand is brought into contact with transformative powers and processes that have the power to disrupt or disintegrate ordinary social identities and to form new and different ones. Such transformative powers are the essence of the sacred, as conceived by Robertson Smith, consisting of things needing to be kept apart from ordinary profane or secular social life. Kayapo male initiands, for example, are obliged to live in camps in the forest apart from the rest of society. Their spirits are thought to be so loosely attached to their bodies that loud noises might cause them to fly away, causing the boys to die. On the other hand, the boys take on the character of violent monsters who might rape or kill any woman who stumbles upon their camp. The initiands, in short, have some of the properties of those in an *aybanh* trance. Neither initiands, if they abuse someone who has come too near their seclusion camp, nor people in an *aybanh* trance are held morally accountable for their deeds, since they are not regarded as having been themselves when they did them. Krantàytch, after his cooling off in the puddle, claimed he had no memory of what had happened; he was taken at his word and treated indulgently like a drunk with a bad hangover.

In summary, *aybanh* trance, like the transformative processes and inversions in the medial phases of social rites of passage, is about the power to escape from and transform the identities, relations, and mores of ordinary social life. Persons who become *aybanh* are thought to have accessed such power and thus to have become suspended above ordinary social life and relations, but without the constraints and social safeguards that insulate society from direct contact with them in normal rites of passage. With their normal social identities and morals stripped away, they tend to oscillate between polar extremes of transcendental

exaltation beyond the range of secular social existence and the infrasocial animality that is all that remains of their normal subjective identities. This helps to
understand why some persons who yearn for more power and importance than
is their lot in normal social life—yearnings that cannot be satisfied by conventional tokens of status or "beauty" like beautiful names or "valuables"—tend to
develop a vocation for going *aybanh*. At the very least, it is an infallible way of
commanding attention, concern, and fear from others as a powerful and dangerous person. The performance of outrageous or threatening acts by persons
ostensibly in trance is normally not held against them as it would be if done
by a normal person, because the pattern of asocial or antisocial behavior by
persons in transcendental or liminal states is well established in the culture. It
seems to me, however, that in some cases, at least, such acts may be deliberately
undertaken for the purpose of impressing others in this way. It seemed to me
that Krantàytch was such a person. He was known for past episodes of trance
behavior in which he would stand in the plaza and declaim nonsensical phrases
such as "*ikrê kam ngô!*", which literally means, "water in my body cavity," perhaps
intimating that he was heating up as the result of *aybanh* tendencies and was
in need of cooling. In any case, after emerging from his trance and lapsing into
unconsciousness, his behavior returned to normal. I did not hear of further out-
bursts of violence by him such as I had witnessed, but I saw that people regarded
him as a relatively wild and potentially dangerous character. I took this as an
indication that his trances had perhaps had the desired effect.

Instances of *aybanh* trance behavior help to bring into focus the importance
of the Kayapo notion of spirit as the animating form of the body and their view
that the physical corporality of the body and its spirit form are distinct but interdependent factors in the development of human bodiliness and social personhood. These notions are also fundamental to Kayapo ideas about the character
not only of humans but also of animals and other beings. These ideas need to be
understood, however, in the context of a closer examination of Kayapo social relations—in particular, the relations of the production of "beauty" as a social value.

DISTINCTION, TENSION, AND BEAUTY IN KAYAPO SOCIAL LIFE

The Kayapo, like the other Northern Gê peoples, live in large villages consisting of numerous extended family households built around the periphery of a

large open central plaza. These domestic households conform to a standard pattern of postmarital residence: men are expected to move into the households of the women they marry. Women, by contrast, reside for their whole lives in the households of their mothers and fathers, the same one into which they were born. Their husbands must thus take up residence in the households of their mothers-in-law and fathers-in-law upon the consummation of their marriages.

This pattern of residence is common to all the Gê-speaking peoples, of whom the Kayapo are one, and to a number of other Amazonian societies. The Kayapo version of the common pattern is unusual for its extreme emphasis on the displacement of men from their natal households and corresponding stress on their integration into their wives' households as husbands, fathers, and sons-in-law. This promotes the subordination of in-marrying sons-in-law to their wife's parents, which is expressed in prescribed forms of respect, obedience, and deference of the son-in-law to his parents-in-law. The son-in-law undergoes an extended period of probation and self-suppression as he gradually becomes integrated as a "kinsman by marriage," in the Kayapo expression, into his affinal household. This process is replicated in the relations between the age subset of "young fathers" and the senior male age subset of "fathers of many children" within the men's house. Here, too, the young men are collectively subordinated to, and must show deference toward, the senior men. Senior men, by contrast, are free to express themselves in political discussion and debate. They cultivate the art of oratory and play prominent parts in communal ceremonies as sources of knowledge about details of ritual performance. The office of chief or, in Kayapo terms, "the deliverer of specialized ritual chants" (*ben-iadjuoro*), of which there are usually two or more in a village, is normally recruited from their ranks.

This asymmetrical pattern of transformation in male household relations is both generated and embodied by the Kayapo age-set system and its institutional hub, the men's house, which acts as the focus of the activities of both the men's and women's age-set systems. The men's house is located in the center of the circular village plaza (the word for men's house, *ngà*, means "center"). The plaza and men's house are the setting of the main activities of the age sets, which constitute the ceremonial and political life of the village. The men's house also serves as the dormitory of the youngest age set of boys, who are removed from their maternal houses at about eight years of age and henceforth make the men's house their domicile until they marry. They and their age-mates remain residents of the men's house through their initiation as bachelors and into later adolescence, until they consummate their courtships of girls by getting one pregnant, which the Kayapo regard as the consummation of marriage. The youth's achievement of fatherhood is the essential precondition for his removal from the men's house and his assumption of residence as a father-husband in the house of his wife and wife's parents. This completes the cycle that began with his removal from his natal household to the men's house under the sponsorship of a figure called a "substitute" or "false father," an unrelated man who assumes the role of paternal sponsor of the boy for purposes of men's house activities until he is ready to move into his wife's household as a father in his own right.

The formal severance of the relation of fathers to their sons through the institutions of the "false father" and the boy's induction into the men's house starts the process of maturation and social identity development. The definition of marriage as the consummation of fatherhood reinforces of the role of father-husband and initiates the youth's transfer from the bachelors' dormitory of the men's house to the adult status of resident husband and son-in-law in his wife's household. This transition produces the apparently paradoxical effect of a patrilateral bias of the Kayapo kinship and marriage system, which is juxtaposed with the context of the matriuxorilocal rule of postmarital residence.

This is a relational pattern fraught with structural tension, created and sustained by formal norms of avoidance between youths and their maternal households after their induction into the men's house and then by respect and avoidance behavior enjoined upon young husbands toward their in-laws after they move into their wives' households. Young fathers must show formal deference (which the Kayapo call *pia'àm*) toward their mothers- and fathers-in-law. The new husband, as a son-in-law, spends the first years of his marriage not speaking to his affines unless spoken to, not looking directly at them, and contributing his labor to any household tasks that his affines may call upon him to perform.

Pia'àm, incidentally, the term used to denote the correct attitude of respect by a young son-in-law toward his mother- and father-in-law, is the general Kayapo term for "shame," which is also used to describe the typical attitude of fearful reticence shown by the young of wild animals brought back to the village as pets by hunters who have killed their parents.

Like the animal brought in as a pet, the husband gradually grows familiar with his in-laws, and the more exaggerated forms of respectful inhibition become relaxed on both sides. From his initial status as an incoming affine in the household, he increasingly assumes the identity of a resident kinsman, above all because his children are defined as consanguineal kin by his wife's family. By the time his sons have left for the men's house and his daughters have reached marriageable age, the man is ready to take the place of his father-in-law as the senior male head of the household.

This transition is paralleled by his ascension in the men's house within the senior men's age grade (called "fathers") from the subset of "new fathers" (that is, essentially, sons-in-law) to that of "old fathers" or "fathers of many children." The latter is the age set of senior men who take the lead in political discussion oratory and ceremonial performance. The women of the community, too, are organized in a series of age sets like the men's: the sets of girls and maidens, like the male boys and bachelors, engage in collective social activities, the most frequent and important of which are ceremonial singing and dancing. Women of marriageable age are organized in sets that correspond to those of the men's sets, the "new fathers" and "fathers of many children," with which they are formally associated as "wives of the men's house."

The age sets of both genders thus constitute hierarchies of communal groups, the principal activity of which is to celebrate elaborate ceremonies that involve daily dancing and singing. The most important ceremonies last for two to three months at a time. These are the ceremonies celebrating the bestowal of the honorific names, called "great" (*ruyn*) or "beautiful" (*mêtch*) names, on a small number of children whose parents have volunteered to sponsor the ceremony.

The formal severance of the relations of parents of both genders to their offspring by means of the institution of the "substitute parent" may be understood as a preemptive solution to the contradiction that would otherwise arise from the combination of the emphasis on fatherhood and integration into the father-husband's affinal household, on the one hand, and, on the other, the matriuxo-rilocal rule of postmarital residence. The emphasis on the father-husband's attachment to his wife's household would normally be expected to lead to a strong attachment of father to son, and the son's strong attachment to his paternal (that is, also, his maternal) household, which would conflict with his future integration into his wife's household. Adoption by the unrelated man who becomes his "false father" and his induction by this substitute father into the men's house attenuates these bonds and prevents this problem from arising.

The virtual severance of a boy's relations to his natal family by this arrangement is counterbalanced by the establishment of close relations with other members of his father's and mother's natal families who have been spun off through these same processes. These attenuated kin are the ones who can bestow names and ritual valuables on him. These names and valuables are, in effect, the basic constituents of his social identity; the requirement that these constituents must come in the form of sharing names and valuables with one or more of his grandparents, paternal aunts, and maternal uncles means that his social identity becomes tantamount to his identification with them.

From the perspective of the developmental cycle of the family, the Kayapo pattern of bestowing and receiving names reconnects the end points of the dispersion of a family (its children's children) with its point of origin (the parents of the children's parents). These connections reunite grandparents with grandchildren, and aunts and uncles with nephews and nieces, in a supremely social way. We have seen that the Kayapo system of recruitment to age sets and the development of the men's house, with its conversion of the resident male age sets into corporate associations for collective political and ritual activities, exacerbate the dispersion of elementary families and household attachments. The end result is to reinforce the social and political hegemony of men of the senior age subset of "fathers of many children." These older men are expected to exemplify, in their public personas and activities, the value of beauty (an expectation also extended to women of the corresponding female age subset).

The severity of the dispersion of family and household attachments, and the powerful emphasis on relations of subordination and dominance in men's affinal households and the men's house, give rise to strong social tensions that have frequently erupted in the fission of Kayapo communities. The struggles leading to these secessions and divisions of villages have usually been led by men of the bachelors' and young fathers' age sets.

These chronic tensions are countered by the very elaborate and prolonged ceremonies required for the bestowal of names and valuables. The organization and performance of these rituals are the principal activities of the age sets and societies associated with the men's house. The production of the "beautiful" naming ceremony, in effect, turns the institutional causes of the major fissive tensions of Kayapo society into the instruments of resolving or transcending the tensions. These names and valuables can only be bestowed by certain people— former or current coresident family members of a husband and wife—and given to the latter's children to create social rather than biological bonds.

"Great" or "beautiful" names belong to a small number of classes designated by prefixes: for male names, *Bep-* as in *Bepkororo-ti*, and *Tàkàk* as in *Tàkàk-'i-re*, and for female names, *Payn-* as in *Payn-'ò*, *Bekwoy-* as in *Bekwòy-ka*, *Nhàk-* as in *Nhàk-pôk*, and *Irê* as in *Irê-kaprin*. One class of beautiful names, which begin with the prefix *Kôkô-* as in *Kôkô-ba*, is given to both genders.

There are seven such names in all. All can be conferred only in the elaborate, months-long communal ceremonies performed by the age sets: male age sets and men's house associations for male names, female age sets and associations for women's names. The ceremonies are similar in form although variable in symbolic content. The age sets and associations, however, do not own the names. All names belong to individual persons, and they can only be given by persons of specific relationship categories to young children of the reciprocal categories. Male names, for example, must be given by kinsmen belonging to the termino-logical category that includes maternal and paternal grandfathers and maternal uncles, and the recipients must be their grandsons or sister's sons. Female names are passed between the corresponding categories of female relations (see dia-gram in Chapter Three, p. 183).

The great naming ceremonies are the main social instruments for the pro-duction of the value of "beauty" as embodied in the massive communal effort represented by their performance and encoded by the "great" or "beautiful" names bestowed in the ceremonies as the principal tokens of the value they em-body. They thus constitute a social instrument for the production of beauty as a counter to the major internal social threat posed by the fissive tensions referred to above. The beauty that is produced is two-fold: first, the ritual endows certain members of society with beauty and social prominence; second, it creates a com-munity that works together, embodied in the large, peaceful village that resists fissive pressures—what the Kayapo call, in fact, a "beautiful village," *krin mêtch*.

There is a problem with this elegant solution, however. The massive ceremo-nies required for the bestowal of "beautiful" names are too costly in terms of the resources and collective effort required for their performance to be held for all children. Many families are too small or socially marginal, or else the parents are disinclined to undertake the effort involved in sponsoring such rituals.

As a partial solution to this problem, certain relations of both genders (as de-scribed above), and only they, can also give other names that lack the honorific pre-fixes of the "beautiful" names. These are called "common" (*kakrit*) names. They do not require ceremonies for bestowal, but may be passed directly by their owners to junior relatives of the appropriate categories. "Common" names are always seman-tically transparent, generally referring to common objects, qualities, or activities, whereas the prefixes of beautiful names are, for the most part, semantically opaque.

In addition to "beautiful" names, there is also a large and variegated class of "valuables" or rights, called *nêkrêtch*, which are also considered "beautiful." These valuables are passed down between the same categories of relatives as names (both "beautiful" and common). This class consists of ritual privileges, items of personal adornment, rights to certain portions of the carcasses of designated species of animals, the right to blow whistles made of the bones of certain birds, and so on. Like names, *nêkrêtch* valuables form integral parts of the personal social identities of their owners, and only individual persons (not extended family households, as claimed by Lea 1992) can own and pass on such valuables to others. With a few exceptions, *nêkrêtch* are not linked to names but are passed down separately, although between the same categories of kin. As in the case of "beautiful" names, not everyone receives *nêkrêtch* from his or her senior interfamily relatives.

Not only are people classed as either beautiful or common, but there is a parallel classification of animals as well. The major game animals, such as tapirs, peccaries, and the large tortoises used for ritual feasts, comprise the class of "beautiful" animals. As S. Hugh-Jones (1996) has pointed out, such large game animals are typically hunted collectively and also tend to be consumed in collective social contexts. Their association with social collectivity may be a major factor in their classification as "beautiful." The refinement of "beautiful" people is indexed by their dietary preferences for eating the flesh only of "beautiful" animals (this rule, I have observed, is often broken in practice when only "common" game like monkeys, coatis, or capybaras are available). As mentioned earlier, "common" species are indiscriminately devoured by "common" people, who may be unkindly referred to as *mẽ ngwòy tam bôrô*, or "those who will eat fowl roasted directly on the fire just as they are" (with their feathers still on them).

The Kayapo system of names and ritual valuables results in the division of the whole society into two great status groups. Only about a half of all persons in any village receive "great" or "beautiful" names in ceremonies (the proportion varies, but never approaches one hundred per cent). This is because sponsoring naming ceremonies requires large amounts of labor and the aid of many relatives for the daily supply and preparation of food and other refreshment to the dancers, as well as the support of the father of the name-receiving child, who must lead the hunting of game and tortoises to be slaughtered for the climactic feast. Many families lack the resources and kin connections necessary to undertake the sponsorship of communal naming rituals.

Those who receive only "common" names are called "common" (*kakrit*) people. "Common," in this context, has the pejorative sense that it sometimes does in British English, connoting vulgarity or lack of cultural refinement, resulting from poorly connected or otherwise undistinguished parentage.

Those who receive a "beautiful" name or names collectively make up the status category of "beautiful" people (*mẽ mêtch*). Members of this category share two important attributes: their names that define their honorific status must have been given at the end of a major ritual effort on the part of the entire social community; and they must have come from well-off parents and a relatively large kindred to have sponsored and collaborated in the production of the required ceremony. The "beauty" in question thus derives from the size and communal status of the group involved in making possible the bestowal of the tokens of "beautiful" status.

The Kayapo system thus gives rise to the division of the entire society, including men and women alike, into two status groups roughly equal in size: the category of "common" people, for whom communal naming ceremonies are not held and who receive relatively few "valuables" from their grandparents, uncles, and aunts; and the category of "beautiful" people, who possess names and valuables imbued with the prestigious value of "beauty" (being *mêtch*).

The bisection of Kayapo society by the status distinction between "beautiful" and "common" people does not result in the formation of corporate caste or descent groups. The chiefly office may be filled by a "common" man as well as by a "beautiful" one, and a chief of "common" origin may be counted as, or at least aspire to being considered, one of the "beautiful" elite of the community. As a rule, however, the personal identities of chiefs, like others, are defined by the values attached to their respective social identities. To a certain extent, this value is the product of individual talent and abilities, but much is derived from the investment directed toward the individual, since these values are produced and defined by social activity. The ceremonial action of the whole community is required for the bestowing of "beautiful" names, while "common" names are simply given by the individual uncles, aunts, or grandparents who hold them.

The social connotation of this distinction is that members of the "beautiful" status group must have come from families well established in the community, with relatively extensive kinship networks and social influence to assist them in the labor and resources necessary to perform one of the great naming ceremonies, while "common" people include the majority of those who lack sufficient kin, friends, and political influence in the community.

As we have seen, the Kayapo system of family, kinship, and marriage relations, like the superstructure of collective age sets, men's house associations, and ceremonial performances that embody its cyclical transformations, is constructed of tensely balanced juxtapositions of separation and solidarity. It is fraught with dissonant relations that call for relatively strict discipline and self-control on the part of its members. Even the supreme value of "beauty," as the expression of wholeness and the interconnected coherence of mutually distinct parts, seems precariously balanced against the pressures for centrifugal dispersion of the ordered relations in which it inheres.

There is nevertheless a firm material basis for the social distinction between the value of the "great" names and prerogatives of the "beautiful" people, on the one hand, and those of the "common" people, on the other. It is grounded in the immense amount of time and effort invested by the whole community in the celebration of the ceremonies in which the names were conferred. The resulting distinction and its value is publicly communicated by the names conferred in the rituals and the performance by the "beautiful" ones of their prerogatives mentioned earlier: special ritual roles in ceremonies, the right to blow special bone whistles, the observance of special dietary restrictions, and so forth. Such a division of an entire society into "beautiful" and "common" people does not exist, to my knowledge, in other Gê groups.

The ceremonies that have become the essential instruments for the bestowal of "great" names and valuables on children, thereby investing them with the value of "beauty," are at the same time the main activity of the age sets. The importance of communal organizations in the ceremonial life counters the tendency to fission along age-set lines.

It is significant that in related Northern Gê societies, such as the Ramkokamekran, Kr'ikati, and Krahô, where men have stronger and more continuous relations with members of their natal families and households, names are not divided into "beautiful" and "common" status classes. Instead, names are grouped into fixed clusters that are passed down together between senior and junior relatives without ceremony, like Kayapo common names. Certain names within these groups, however, carry the obligation for the recipient and his or her family to sponsor a ceremony attached to that name. The system is the reverse of the Kayapo pattern: the person who receives the name is required to sponsor the communal ceremony, rather than the ceremony being required to bestow the name, as among the Kayapo.

BODILINESS, HUMANITY, AND ANIMALITY AS TRANSFORMATIONAL PROCESSES: KAYAPO ANIMISM?

Kayapo ideas about bodiliness are founded on the principle that all beings are in active processes of development, transformation, and interaction, which not only produce their own forms but also affect the forms and transformations of other bodies and entities. It follows that no embodied form can be understood solely as the product of its own activity, but always owes its formation in part to its relations with other bodies.

Bodies develop dialectically as internal content meets external relations. These forms develop as the channels of the material energies arising from bodies orient their development and activities, and are in turn shaped by the external relations of the body to other bodies. The forms of things, in other words, are actually embodied processes of formation, which also serve to orient future development and activities. They consist of the directed agency or force that impels the material content of things, including their energetic forces, to assume the specific patterns proper to the species of body or kind of entity in question. This proposition, as we shall see, holds for the cosmos as a whole and all its parts or constituent units.

This set of ideas is exemplified by the cluster of meanings associated with the Kayapo term *karon*, which is used equally to mean "image," "form," "shadow," as well as the "spirit," "soul," or "ghost" of a person or other entity. Although humans are thought of as the *karon*-possessing beings par excellence, mammals, birds, fish, and many trees, vines, and other plants, and even some entities like the sun and moon that might be defined as inanimate, are also thought to possess spirit forms and associated subjective powers.

Here we rejoin the basic notion behind the "animism" common to most, if not all, indigenous peoples of the Amazon (Bird-David 1999; Descola 1996, 2013; Turner 2009). Kayapo animism is grounded in the idea that animals and other natural beings (animate and, in some cases, inanimate) possess spirit forms similar in character to those of humans, although different in specific functions and powers. These spirit forms consist of schemas of transformational processes that are oriented toward basic purposes like growth, reproduction, self-defense, and subsistence. Animism, as a general idea of the mental or spiritual life of animals and perhaps other beings, is based on the extension of the assumption that this spiritual property of form is shared to some extent by all animate (and some inanimate) beings. The energies and powers inherent in these processes comprise a generic notion of power possessed in varying measure by all beings, a sort of generalized demiurgic force. This is analogous, in some respects, to Marett's recension of Codrington's *mana*, but differs from it in that the Kayapo concept is oriented toward the life process of the creatures, plants, or other beings that employ it.

The life of an animate being, in this view, is the product of the union of the form (or spirit) and content (or bodily substance), which together constitute the body of the being in question. The spirit of the entity *is* its form transformed into a pattern of activity. The spirit requires the substance and energy of the material entity, its physical body, to exist and develop. Reciprocally, the material aspect of the entity, its substance and activity, depends on its spirit form to guide and orient its formation and relations with other entities.

This synthetic unity of form and content comprises the life process of the body, which has both subjective and objective aspects. It is not a fixed property but a quantitatively variable, unstable, dynamic relation that is susceptible to disruption and eventual dissolution. Such dissolution can be partial and temporary, as in illness, shock induced by extreme fright, or *aybanh* trances, or it can be permanent, as in the death of the person or being. Death is the permanent separation of spirit form from body substance, the dissolution of the synthetic unity of spirit and body that was the basis of the life process of the entity.

BODILY FORM AS SPIRIT AND AGENT: EMBODIMENT AS POWER

The objective forms of bodies, including the natural or, in the case of humans, socially modified configurations of their skin, hair, and other features, are not merely inert forms or semiotic categories but schemas of activity. Schemas are patterns of intentional or goal-directed activities, including physical growth and, for humans, social relations as well, such as marriage and recruitment to social groups (Turner 1994).

For the Kayapo, in sum, bodiliness includes not only the physical and cultural aspects of the body, but also extends beyond the body as a singular object to its relations with other bodies. It further includes processes of formation and disintegration, objectification and deobjectification, and the construction of subjectivity and of intersubjective relations. In all these respects, bodiliness is an active principle that consists essentially of activities and transformations rather than practico-inert categories or classifications. These active processes of bodiliness, as I have suggested above, comprise not only the life but also the death of bodies, embodied beings, and persons. In these dynamic aspects of bodiliness, form and content behave not merely as descriptive categories but as material forces of embodiment and disembodiment.

Bodiliness, in sum, comprises the tensions and mutual catalysis of these forces as together they constitute the embodied being. The forces, however, eventually weaken and are unable permanently to sustain the synthetic unity they produce, which ultimately disintegrates. What begins as a process of objectification of the person thus leads to its deobjectification as the unity of spirit and flesh disintegrates. This inexorable linear destiny, however, may be transcended by the ultimate power of embodiment: reproduction. In this context, reproduction as a total social fact refers not merely to biological renewal but to the replication of the form of the life cycle in all its natural and social features: the emergence of form from content, the integration of spirit and body, the replication of their transient unity in individual and social life, and their final separation.

DEATH AND MORTUARY POETICS

For the Kayapo, neither spirit nor physical body can exist independently for long without the other. The separation of spirit and body therefore results in the decomposition and disappearance of each separated part. The *karon* or spirit form continues to exist as a ghost for a time after the death of the body, but it gradually loses its human character, becoming an animal-like being in the forest and eventually dissolving completely (in keening for the dead, the spirit of the deceased is said to have "become an animal"). The material content of the body ("in, flesh; 'i, bones; and *kamrô*, blood) undergoes a parallel process of dissolution, losing the articulation of its parts as they become separately transformed by decomposition. The formation and development of living bodies and persons, a process of objectification of their material and social identities, is thus ultimately balanced by a complementary process of deobjectification.

This process of deobjectification is itself embodied by Kayapo mortuary practices, above all, by burial and the construction of the grave. After death, the corpse is painted and decorated, then carried to the burying ground outside the village. A circular hole is dug, large enough to accommodate the corpse in a flexed position. After the body is placed in the grave, the hole is roofed with logs that, in turn, are covered by mats and the dirt excavated from the grave pit, forming a conical tumulus on top of the mats. The deceased's possessions are broken and either thrown in the grave with the corpse or left on the tumulus. No living person can keep or use any of the deceased's possessions, which would serve as "paths" that the spirit could follow back to living users to kill them so they could join the spirit and keep it company in the haunts of the ghosts out in the forest. After a finite period of time, the ghost itself evaporates into nothing. The grave and tumulus keep pace with this dissolution. The mats placed over the log roof of the grave rot, and the earth from the tumulus filters through into the grave pit. Eventually, the grave is filled and the tumulus disappears; the grave is left level with the ground and disappears.

The grave tumulus starts its existence as the embodiment and sign of death: not of death as a static condition but as a transformational process in reverse, not constructive but destructive. The corpse in the grave is a content losing its form, and the grave tumulus is a form losing its content: they finally come together in a new unity of mutual disintegration of form and content—the death of death, as it were. In thus framing death as the disintegration of human form and content, however, the concrete poetics of the construction and demise of the tumulus manage to exemplify the uniquely human power that distinguishes humanity from animals and other beings. Kayapo think that a number of other beings—some animals, some birds, some fish—act socially, according to shared programs or recipes for transformative behavior. Some have ceremonies in which they give themselves names; some have families in which they reproduce and raise their young; some follow regular underwater fish paths along river bottoms to different kinds of places for spawning, resting, feeding, and holding ceremonies. In these respects, they are like humans, who also organize their behavior according to shared schemas of similar types of transformative activity. Only humans, however, apply transformative schemas to their own first-order schemas. They use fire to make fire; they employ the schemas of individual ceremonial processes to reintegrate relatives separated by the dispersion of old families and formation of new ones; and they construct the grave tumulus and allow it to disintegrate as an embodiment of the disintegration of a dead human body. Animals, birds, fish trees, and even the sun and moon do not do such things; as the Kayapo see it, only humans do.

CONCLUSION: HUMANS, ANIMALS, AND CULTURAL KNOWLEDGE

There is a long tradition in social anthropology of debate over the question of whether a cultural conception of the world is a projection of the structure of the members' own social system, or whether, on the contrary, their knowledge of the external, nonhuman world is taken as the model of their conception of their human society and themselves. The latest manifestation of this issue has been the revival of interest in animism and the development of what has been called "perspectivism," primarily in France and Brazil. According to some contemporary anthropologists, notably Descola (1994, 1996, 2013), animism is a form of knowledge or a set of ideas about the world based on projecting conceptions of human social relations or cultural traits onto animals and their supposed consciousness of themselves. "Perspectivism," an approach led by Viveiros de Castro (1998, 2004, 2005), has contributed the idea that members of indigenous Amazonian cultures think that animals see themselves as humans under the skin, as it were, and that each species, from its own perspective, considers all other species, including humans, to be natural beings. The essential idea appears to be that the distinction between animals and humans, culture and nature, so fundamental to Western civilization since Descartes or perhaps Aristotle, is, from the indigenous Amazonian perspective, fundamentally misguided. Rather, animals, as the leading exemplars of what have been viewed from the Western cultural perspective as the natural world, actually identify themselves as human, cultural beings.

I have elsewhere (Turner 2009b; see "The crisis of late structuralism," this volume) given reasons for considering these ideas to be based on erroneous interpretations of ethnographic evidence, as well as of Western philosophical and anthropological theories. Here I want to return to the question of the nature of indigenous Amazonian perspectives on the world, specifically the relation of humans to animals and other "natural" entities, on the basis of the Kayapo data I have discussed in this paper. I have suggested that the Kayapo do have a kind of animism, which identifies common features of human subjective identity and bodiliness, and those of animal and other "natural" beings. Nevertheless, this commonality constitutes only a partial overlap, as in a Venn diagram, between humanity and nonhuman beings, and the overlap is different for each species of animals and other natural entities. Partial overlap does not mean identity: on the contrary, I have argued that the Kayapo have developed quite a sophisticated notion of the essential differences between themselves, as humans, and animals. In other words, they have a complex, reflexive idea about the nature of specifically human consciousness, social practices, and perspective on the world. I have tried to define the essence of this conception in this presentation.

By way of summary, I wish to emphasize the particular features and power of the contents of the overlapping area in the Venn diagram, which comprise the Kayapo conception of the universal features of consciousness and existence shared by all beings; the fundamental role of transformational processes as the principal constituents of species and cultural consciousness; and the centrality of the dialectical interplay of form (as an active agency or spirit) and content (as substance, energy, strength, and sensory capacity). That these generic features are shared by all beings does not imply that they originally developed in one species (such as humanity) and were projected onto others, in what Marxists might describe as an alienated or fetishized mistaking of human subjective perspectives for natural features. Rather, they serve as a set of general ideas—or, perhaps better in this context, what Marett described as "preanimist" dispositions—which serve the Kayapo as the counterpart of a general scientific theory of the nature of the world.

Cosmology, objectification, and animism in indigenous Amazonia[1]

COSMOLOGY AS A THEORETICAL SUBJECT

Anthropologists use the term "cosmology" to refer to a culture's conception of reality in the broadest and most inclusive sense. In this sense, reality is conceived as a universe or totality with a form that is recapitulated in its parts, down to the level of its minimal units. A "cosmos," in other words, is a universe in which whole and parts are internally related as macrocosm and microcosm. Since the units of the universe obviously differ widely in scale, this implies that the structure of the cosmos must consist of a number of levels, each related to its internal units using the same macrocosm–microcosm pattern. Each entity or relation in such a structure will be a unit of the higher-level form that encompasses it and will, in turn, constitute an encompassing totality in relation to its internal parts. Each level and unit within the system may serve as the position of a subject and thus as a point of perspective on the rest of the cosmic system. Cosmologies may therefore be defined, at a first approximation, as hierarchically stratified, multiperspectival totalities, composed of parts with forms that replicate the formal properties of the cosmos as a whole.

The cosmic reality ordered in this way is dynamic: it is not a synchronic order analogous to a semiotic field of signification or a taxonomic classification but

---

1.   Originally presented to the first meeting of the Nordic Network for Amerindian Studies, Copenhagen, Denmark, November 9, 2008.

a system that consists of a continuous process of producing its own structure. From the cosmological principle of the formal identity of whole and part, it follows that the minimal units of cosmic structure must consist not of synchronic categories or semiotic signs but of diachronic patterns of activity in real space-time. These are patterns are continuously created and have both a material and an ideal form: in a word, they are schemas. Schemas are objective forms of activities that are also subjective forms of consciousness of those activities; as such, the units of a cosmology can be described as schemas. Indigenous cosmologies, like that of the Kayapo of central Brazil, commonly articulate this property of cosmological units as the idea that forms are not only the objective aspect of things but also their subjective *spirits*. As Piaget (1932) argued, the objective–subjective nature of schemas serves to guide the replication of the schemas in and through performance, which is borne out in Kayapo practices, as I shall explain.

Pre-Copernican cosmologies in general tend to represent human society, or the sector of the cosmos it occupies, as the focus or central point of the cosmic order, including its categories of space and time (or, more accurately, "space-time") and the nonhuman beings, entities, and processes it contains (Douglas 1966). This human sociocentrism has a series of conceptual consequences that manifest themselves as common features of indigenous cosmological systems. One such feature is the extrapolation of the conception of cosmic order from the forms of human social order. A second consequence is the tendency to fuse ontological and epistemological categories; the same schemas, such as notions of time, space, agency, causality, and classifications of things, tend to serve as ontological concepts of objective reality and as epistemological categories of conceptual and pragmatic perspectives on that reality. In sum, the same schemas serve as both the basic subjective and objective forms of culture and social consciousness. Indigenous cosmologies thus include what some anthropologists and philosophers have called a "world view," comprising subjects' cognitive and affective perspectives on the world (Kearney 1984).

Indigenous cosmologies thus envision the phenomena comprising objective reality, including what we might classify as natural and inanimate entities, through the epistemological filter of schemas of social activity. This perspective raises the question of whether and to what extent cosmology may be understood as a form of alienated consciousness—even perhaps a sort of fetishism. I shall return to this question in the conclusion of this paper.

As systems composed of forms of activity in real spacetime, cosmologies emerge not only in the schemas of everyday activities but also in the entire process of social existence, from its beginnings to the present and, in some cases, to its future as well. Concepts of the beginning of spacetime are often of great interest as representations of a society's ideas of its fundamental internal processes and relations with external entities and forces, including aspects of "nature" (not all of which, however, are conceived as external to society or "culture," as the case we will examine below demonstrates).

The approach I have outlined to cosmology as a totalizing conception of reality implies that it is concerned equally with the nature of its minimal units and with the system as a whole. A full analysis of a cosmological system must therefore seek to demonstrate the relevance of the overall structure of the system to the character of its parts. This hermeneutic perspective takes into account the ways that the form and character of the totality as a pattern of activity in spacetime is reproduced in the form and content of its parts. An essential consideration in this connection is clearly the specific meanings attached to the notions of structure, form, and content. Given the characteristics of the phenomenon under consideration, cosmology—namely, that it is an organized system of activities, that the forms of these activities are schemas, and that the contents of these schemas comprise transformational activities—it follows that the *structure* of such a system must consist of a way of coordinating the transformations so that they conserve some invariant relation among themselves. In other words, such transformations must remain within the boundaries of the system through the principle of conservation. A simple expression of such a principle is the reversibility of transformations, the ability to implement a transformation and then return to its starting point.

To the extent that a cosmology constitutes a structure, we may say that it consists of reversible schemas of transformational activity. The forms of these schemas, then, must contain the capacity for transformational activity and its reversibility in coordination with other schemas of the same system. As I have suggested, this capacity tends to be conceived in the indigenous cosmological systems I shall be discussing as the "spirit" of an entity or schema, considered in its capacity as a unit of the cosmic structure.

What I now propose is to try to put some ethnographic flesh on these abstract theoretical bones by investigating how these general propositions about the properties of cosmological systems may apply to the cosmology of the indigenous Amazonian people I know best, the Mebengokre Kayapo of central Brazil. Although my analysis will be grounded in a specific case, I believe it has general implications for the understanding of many indigenous Amazonian

and Amerindian systems. I recognize, however, that there are significant differences among the cosmological systems of these societies, which arise from their
differing social systems—just as the ideas set forth in this introduction would
predict. Our understanding of these systems of social consciousness must proceed in concert with analyses of the varying social systems in which they have
taken shape.

THE KAYAPO COSMOS

Following the general principles outlined in the introduction, I propose to approach the analysis of the Kayapo cosmological system through an account of
Kayapo schemas of the production, dissolution, and replication of the forms
of social things. The Kayapo, unlike many Amazonian peoples, do not have a
mythical account of the origin of the cosmos as a spatiotemporal continuum. It
does presuppose the existence of a timeless and unstructured space as the raw
material for the creation of spacetime, but, for that matter, so does the Biblical
myth of Genesis, which presupposes the existence of the ocean waters and the
spirit of God moving about over them. In the Kayapo myth, a primordial tapir
(a reasonable parallel to Jehovah) moves about over the land, gnawing down the
trees that held up the flat disc of the sky until its edges fell to earth, creating the
dome of the sky we see today. I shall return to this myth in a moment. First, let
me note that the Kayapo conception of the world can best be understood not by
starting from the myths of the creation of cosmic spacetime but from the actual
source and model of Kayapo cosmological ideas, namely, the Kayapo social universe as embodied by the village community and its surrounding region.

THE VILLAGE AS COSMOGRAM: THE TWO DIMENSIONS
OF SPACETIME

The Kayapo, like other central Brazilian peoples, are well known for their large,
geometrically laid-out villages (Figure 3.1). The Kayapo social community is
laid out as a cosmogram, such that their conception of the world as a circular
disc divided into concentric zones can be grasped from the spatial form of the
village itself. A circle of matriuxorilocal extended-family households surrounds
the open central plaza, which is the locus of communal social, political, and

Figure 3.1. Kayapo village as cosmogram. The men's house is in the center of the plaza, surrounding by extended-family houses; behind them is the *a-tuk* zone and an airstrip, beyond which is the forest.

ceremonial activities. In the middle of the plaza stands the men's house, called *ngà,* "center." It is also the midpoint or center of men's lives when, as boys, they move out of their natal houses, formally separating them from their boyhood relations to their fathers and mothers and enabling them to take up residence as bachelors in the *ngà.* Several years later, as youths, they move out of the center to their wife's house on the periphery of the village. This move occurs after the woman whom they have been courting becomes pregnant and gives birth, such that they become fathers in their own right. This move completes the spatial schema of male development.

Immediately beyond the circle of houses at the rim of the village is a ring, about two hundred meters wide, called *a-tuk,* the "black" or "dead" ground (Figure 3.2). This is a transitional zone between the social space of the village and the asocial domain of the savanna and forest beyond. Here are located the cemetery and various ritual seclusion sites used by those undergoing rites of passage, as well as middens of trash from the houses. It is also an area frequented by lovers pursuing extramarital affairs, often referred to as liaisons "behind the house" (*kikre bu'ã*). This zone is cross-cut by paths leading to water sources, swidden gardens, and sites of hunting, fishing and foraging activities in the

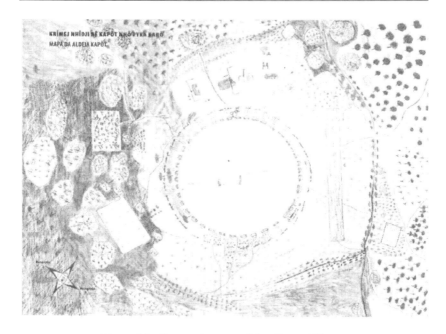

Figure 3.2. Kayapo drawing of the village of Kapôt.

forest and savanna. Thus, there are continual activities of coming and going that pass in both directions through this zone, the more important of them having the character of reversible transformations between the central village and the peripheral zone of nature beyond. In the conceptual scheme, the "natural" zone extends to the outer limits of spacetime.

Horizontal space is thus organized as a concentric series of zones. All of these zones constitute points or stages of reversible activities achieved through the processes of entering and leaving social space or, in other words, the processes of socialization and desocialization, detailed later. The concentric form of the world is thus not a purely spatial but a spatiotemporal form, a concentric dimension of social spacetime.

THE BEGINNING OF COSMIC SPACETIME: AN ORIGIN MYTH

Let us now return to the cosmic origin myth. As we have seen, the circular form of village space replicates in microcosm the macrocosmic form of cosmic spacetime, conceived as a circular, concentrically divided flat disc. The outer limits of this disc meet up with the dome of the sky, its edges resting directly on the earth around the circumference of the terrestrial disc. After the giant tapir gnawed through the trees that used to hold up the sky and the edges fell to earth, the cosmos then assumed the form of a dome resting on the earth. This direct contact of the celestial and terrestrial discs enabled the passage of the sun from one side of the dome to the other, where it then returns under the earth to its starting point to repeat the same journey the following day. The tapir's action thus brought about the diurnal movement of the sun from the point where it comes up from beneath the eastern edge of the terrestrial disc, follows its path along the dome of the sky to its highest point at midday, and descends to the point at its western edge, where it "hides itself" by going down under the earth again. The Kayapo liken this linear diurnal movement to the growth of a plant from "root" (*kratch*) to "tip" (*ênhôt*) (Figure 3.3). They call the place in the east where the sun rises the "root" of the sky (*kàykwa kratch*), and the point in the west where it sets the "tip" of the sky" or "the upper sky" (*kàykwa 'ênhôt*). These are the only Kayapo cardinal points: north and south are not lexically differentiated but are called merely "the edge of the sky" (*kàykwa nhirê*), referring to the points along the sun's path from east to west. The journey of the sun along its path across the middle of the celestial dome is thus conceived as creating a vertical dimension of spacetime, which is not concentric but, rather, linear and unidirectional, with a beginning and an end that is continually replicable.

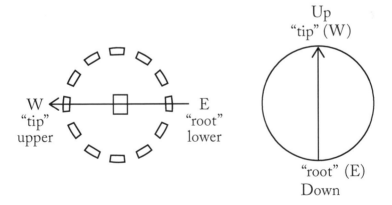

Figure 3.3. Kayapo society in spacetime: vertical space and linear time.

Notice that the diurnal journey itself is divided into two equal halves which reverse each other: the morning phase of the rise to the zenith, the midpoint of the journey (high noon), and the afternoon and evening phase of decline to the setting. However, the form of this journey does not yet contain within itself the element necessary for producing its own replication.

The tapir's creation of the dome of the sky by causing its edges to fall did not yet lead to the articulation of the terrestrial disc into the concentric zones that now constitute its reversible spatiotemporal structure (Figure 3.4). This concentric articulation of the horizontal dimension of cosmic spacetime only came into existence with the establishment of a differentiated human domain—the village. Being located directly beneath the midpoint of the sun's path at the exact center of the celestial dome, the village serves as the central point of reference in the horizontal and vertical dimensions. Likewise, the tapir's creative act did not fully activate the link it created between the horizontal and vertical dimensions of spacetime, a link that would allow the sun's journey along the linear, vertical dimension to become fully reversible and self-replicating. This active link is provided by the social schema in the movement of men as husbands and fathers from the central men's house to the end of their linear spatiotemporal life-paths as residents of their wives' houses. This move is only made possible by the men's consummation of their marriages by producing children, thus reproducing the father–son relationship that formed the starting point of their original journeys from their parents' houses to the men's house. This cycle produces the replication of that movement through the next generation, making the endpoint of one man's journey the starting point of a replication of that journey by their sons—a symbolic reversal. Linear movement in spacetime is thus made to produce its own reversal in a way that simultaneously brings about its formal replication.

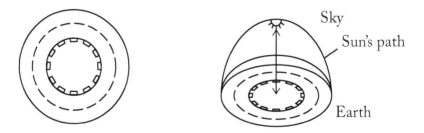

Figure 3.4. Kayapo society in spacetime; concentric space and cyclical time.

This cycle also brings the linear, vertical dimension into structural coordination with the concentric, horizontal dimension of spacetime. Such coordination imbues the map of concentric spatial zones emanating from the central men's house with a temporal, developmental dimension comprising consecutive stages of the life cycle. The developmental process also becomes reversible in the horizontal dimension, mapping both the formation and dissolution of human social identity. Socializing processes move from the periphery toward the center; desocializing processes move in the opposite direction. The two dimensions, vertical and horizontal, share a common boundary, and both are now made reversible through the temporal dimension.

THE CONCENTRIC ZONES OF SPACETIME AS HIERARCHICAL LEVELS OF NATURAL AND SOCIAL PROCESSES

The ring of houses on the outer edge of the village constitutes the boundary of the fully social and cultural space concentrated on the village plaza with its central men's house. The matriuxorilocal extended-family households comprising the segments of this circle are themselves internally organized in formally concentric terms. Monogamous nuclear family units form their central focus, surrounded by a penumbra of extended family relations composed of grandparents and grandchildren, cross-sex parental siblings, and affines (Figure 3.5). Although paternal aunts, paternal uncles, and adult maternal uncles are not residential members of the household, they continue to form part of the extended family for which the household serves as a focus. Because the nuclear families of procreation are created out of the sexual relationship between husband and wife, these units are considered to consist of relatively "natural" or animal-like links of biological procreation. Full social identity, embodied by names and ritual "valuables" (*nêkrêtch*), is conferred only by more peripheral extended family relations, such as grandparents, maternal uncles, and paternal aunts. This identity is bestowed in ritual ceremonies.

The household, in short, is a transformational structure, in which children, being the as-yet "natural" products of its minimal nuclear family units, receive socializing inputs of tokens of social identity (names and valuables) from peripheral extended family relations, their uncles, aunts, and grandparents. These inputs, combined with the linear process of the growth of the children, lead in turn to the dispersion of the nuclear families. The successive processes of formation and dispersion of nuclear families serve as points for the beginning and end of linear series of transformations that propel less socialized children

passage of time

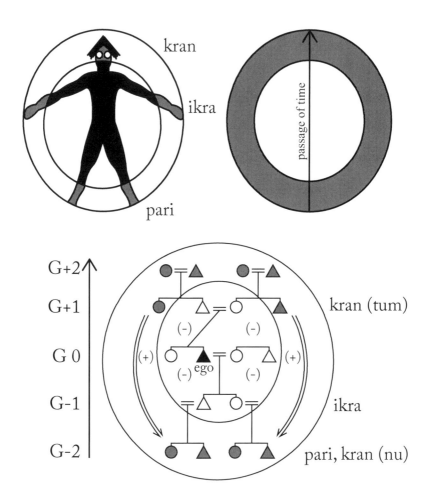

Figure 3.5. Homologies between the Kayapo social body and kindred. From ego's perspective, the inner zone is "natural" (black) and the outer zone is "social" (grey). The vertical axis indicates the passage of time in growth and generations.

into socialized adult persons, who then form new families of procreation in the households where they pass their maturity. As mature adults, parent-in-law, and household heads, they assume the statuses of name-givers, parents-in-law, and bestowers of ritual valuables, thus replicating the process of social reproduction.

As described above, a male Kayapo must move from his natal household to take up residence in the men's house, where he resides until he marries and can move on to his wife's and wife's mother's house after his wife gives birth to his first child. These moves coincide with successive promotions through the system of collective age grades as they are transformed from boys to bachelors to young husbands, fathers, and sons-in-law, and on to the higher statuses of fathers-in-law, grandfathers, and extended-family household heads. Women go through a similar series of transformations of family status and membership in the women's system of collective age associations; the major difference is that they remain resident in the households into which they were born (Turner 1979b). Both the women's and men's transformations in social age, family status, and collective group membership are effected by successive rites of passage of the person into progressively more fully socialized status identities.

THE CENTRAL PLAZA, MEN'S HOUSE, AND COMMUNAL CEREMONIAL SYSTEM AS A METATRANSFORMATIONAL ZONE

The complex series of communal ceremonies required for the transformations of personal status and family relations also serve as rituals of recruitment of male Kayapo to the men's age grades associated with the men's house and, for female Kayapo, to the women's associations, which are formally associated with the men's house as "wives of the men's house." It is these associations that carry out the communal ceremonies. These ceremonies take place primarily in the central plaza within the ring of houses, but they include reversible movements between the plaza and the transitional *a-tuk* zone beyond the houses.

The men's house thus serves as the focus of a cluster of collective male and female associations that replicates the form of the relations among the members of a household on the plaza periphery. These communal ceremonies of name-bestowing and initiation constitute the recruitment relations of the collective male and female age grades and ceremonial associations, which comprise the communal level of social structure. This means that the collective institutional structure of village society not only replicates the forms of extended family and household relations; it also pragmatically reproduces them through its activities, which in turn reproduce its own structure by continually re-recruiting new members to the communal associations.

What is involved here, however, is not a simple replication of forms. The collective associations and men's house represent a different order of scale from that of the family and household. This increment of scale and inclusiveness constitutes a higher structural level than that comprised by the interpersonal relations of an individual family. The men's house complex consists of generalized, uniformly replicable schemas that generate and encompass the pattern of extended-family household relations and which simultaneously constitute the social totality as embodied in the village as a whole. The movement of individuals through the stages of initiation also coordinates the reproduction of the structure of relations in the segmentary household units. In other words, this complex coordinates and replicates the component units.

The communal institutions and ceremonies identified with the central zone of social space thus constitute a metastructure composed of the same basic set of transformational schemas of family relations and personal identity but at a higher level. The communal institutions pragmatically serve to coordinate relations in each household unit. The circular space of the village and its immediately surrounding region thus create a microcosmic replication of the macrocosmic structure of spacetime as a pattern of reversible transformational processes, with the result that the segmentary units of the village replicate its structure in microcosm. The system of human social relations comprising the zone of social space thus assumes the form of a recursive hierarchy of transformational processes of cosmic spacetime (Turner 1979a, 1979b, 2003).

THE SOCIAL PERSON AND SOCIAL BODY AS MICROCOSMS

The cosmic structure is manifested not only in the forms of celestial and terrestrial spacetime and in the articulation of the segments of human social organization in the layout of villages but is similarly reiterated in the construction of social persons and bodies. In Kayapo society, the person is constructed through social appropriations of the physical body and its powers over the entire life cycle. It begins with birth and infancy, continuing through the development of muscular strength and coordination, the senses and understanding, sexuality and reproduction, and maturation and aging. The process ends with death and decomposition of the body in the grave and the temporary survival of the spirit as a ghost in the outermost zone of asocial, "natural" spacetime (Turner 1980, 1993).

All of these aspects and developmental transitions are marked and given social meaning by a series of rites of passage that confer communally recognized items and styles of bodily adornment. The development of these natural capacities is symbolically marked, channeled, and publicly communicated by standardized forms of decoration and adornment of the surface of the body. These serve as badges of identity that attest to the wearer's attainment of a specific category of social age, which, from the onset of adolescence, is accompanied by recruitment to a series of collective age grades and associations.

These forms of bodily adornment, in association with the aspects of bodiliness and social identity they represent, comprise a coherent semiotic system that divides the body into zones (Turner 1980, 1995). Such zones are analogous to those of cosmic and village spacetime and are mapped along the same two dimensions of cosmological structure. A vertical axis of irreversible linear development corresponds, in spatial terms, to the erect posture of the body and, in temporal terms, to the growth of the body from "root" or foot to "tip" or head. The body is also divided concentrically between a central inner space and a peripheral zone that interacts with external social space (see Figure 3.4, above). A brief summary of the patterns of everyday secular body painting and the contrasting system of ceremonial body decoration may suffice to bring out the main features of this complex code for the construction of social persons.

The Kayapo idea of the social development of the person emphasizes the progressive transformation of internal strength and energy, which are located in the central trunk of the body, into relations with the external social and natural world, effected through mobility and dexterity and focused in the feet and hands, and through the senses of sight, hearing, smelling and tasting, located in the head. These transformational processes are represented and channeled by the basic color scheme of body painting, which consists of black for the chest, abdomen, upper arms, and thighs, and red for the feet and lower legs, hands and lower arms, eyes, nose, and sometimes the mouth (Figures 3.6, 3.7). The word for black, *tuk*, which also means "death" and, as we saw, is applied to the transitional zone between the village and natural zone of the forest, is the appropriate color for the internal or central part of the body, the source of its strength and life energies. Such "natural" resources must be channeled in order

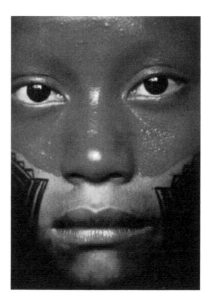

Figure 3.6. A child's face painting: the upper portion (outer zone) is painted red and the lower portion (inner zone) is painted black.

Figure 3.7. Mother and child with everyday body painting, coiffure, and ornaments worn along with Western dress. Child's eyes, mouth, and feet are painted red, while the inner zone is painted black.

to be transformed into socialized forms of activity and identity, through which the embodied person engages with external social space by way of the extremities of the body. Red (*kamrek*) is the appropriate color for the parts of the body that directly interact with external social space since it connotes vitality, life, and overt expression.

There is an important point to be made here about the relativity of structural perspectives. The individual body, with its blackened central area containing transformational processes and unsocialized "natural" powers, like the individual household with its central nuclear family units with their "natural" biological relations, appear to invert the form of the concentric spatiotemporal order of the higher levels of cosmic spacetime, those of the village and cosmos as a whole. In the cases of the body and the domestic household, the center comprises the "natural" zone, and the periphery consists of transformed, "socialized" relations and forms of activity. In the case of the village and the macrocosm, by contrast, the center is the zone of human sociality while the peripheral regions are the zones of decreasing sociality. The concentric form of the dimension is constant, but the structural values of its contrastive poles are inverted, because the direction of the transformational processes that mediate between its contrastive central and peripheral parts are reversed. This inversion results from the contrast between the subject's position and the spatiotemporal focus of sociality.

The subject changes perspective across spacetime. When the vantage point of the subject is his or her own individual body, or the nuclear family within an extended-family household, his or her perspective appears as a relatively peripheral, unsocialized element of the social totality constituted by village social space. When his or her perspective is centered in the village plaza or, even more focused, on the men's house, in contrast to the ring of houses or, even farther out, to the "black," peripheral, natural zone of forest and savanna, the center that forms his or her vantage point represents the zone of sociality, while the periphery represents the space of natural processes and desocializing transformations. This framework for viewing otherwise incompatible perspectives exemplifies the way that approaching cosmological and social structures as systems of transformational schemas can clarify and account for seemingly contradictory patterns and subjective perspectives. This allows us to understand these patterns and perspectives as integral parts of the internal structure of such systems, a view we would overlook if we considered only the level of external relations between systems as wholes.

CEREMONIAL COSTUME: FEATHERS, HOOVES, CLAWS, AND TEETH

For communal ceremonies, most of which are rites of passage of one sort or another, people adorn their bodies in ways that differ both in form and meaning from their normal secular forms of bodily presentation. They make prominent use of feathers for headdresses, feather capes, bunches of feathers fastened to their elbows, necklaces, and small breast plumage stuck over the whole central area of the body (the area normally painted black in the secular, quotidian style) (Figure 3.8). They also use noise-making belts and anklets of tapir hooves, and necklaces of jaguar claws or peccary teeth. In short, they try to present themselves as animals, or rather as hybrid animal–human beings, analogous to the ancestral human and animal forms of the mythical age before the differentiation of animals and human society. There is no space here to describe these costumes or the ceremonies themselves in the detail they deserve (but see a discussion of aspects of these rituals in Chapter Two, p.163–64). In general terms, however, it can be said that, in the adornment of their bodies for participation in the ritual transformation and reproduction of social relations, the Kayapo symbolically return to the undifferentiated mythical state in which animals and humans were much alike, before either developed into their present forms as socialized humans or fully natural animals. They then collectively enact the appropriation and transformation of their ancestral animal or avian powers into contemporary social and cultural form as a framework for the transformation of the relatively undeveloped social forms of the boy or girl initiands into new and more socially developed forms and identities (Turner 1991a).

These transformations typically entail choreographic formations and movements that combine concentric movements and linear sequences; for instance, dancers may repeatedly circle the central plaza while special rites are performed by selected officiants at its central point, or dancers may perform successive repetitions of a ceremony in a series of locations, beginning far out in the forest and moving inward to sites in the transitional *a-tuk* zone, the ring of houses, and finishing up in the central plaza of the village (Figure 3.9). The linear sequences of rites represent and inculcate irreversible transformations in the status and identity of the initiands, representing growth and the passage of time. The ceremonies themselves, in short, are organized as symbolic cosmograms that embody the complementary concentric and linear dimensions of spacetime that operate at all levels of cosmic structure; furthermore, the ceremonies move from a mythical

Figure 3.8. Man and boys with ceremonial body painting, ornaments, and white down covering central body and thighs. The upper part of their faces is painted with black jaguar spots, while their mouths are painted red.

time of equal coexistence with animals to the contemporary age of differentiation between human culture and animal nature. The socializing transformations that these rituals enact invariably involve transformations in bodily appearance in both those undergoing and those performing the ceremony. These bodily decorations and transformations themselves embody the same cosmic pattern.

Figure 3.9. Men's collective dancing encircling the central plaza, wearing feather headdresses to help the dancers "fly."

COSMOLOGICAL CONSCIOUSNESS IN THE AGE OF INTERETHNIC COEXISTENCE

The traditional cosmological vision continues to serve as the framework of Kayapo social consciousness in the contemporary era of interethnic relations with Brazil and the world system. The successful Kayapo efforts to defend and reclaim their original territory have enabled them to retain control of reserves covering close to 150,000 square kilometers, with 23 villages and a population of over 7,000 people. They have prevented occupation of their lands by members of the national population, such as ranchers, poachers, gold miners, and sports fishermen, and avoided extensive deforestation by loggers. Kayapo villages thus remain socially autonomous units surrounded by natural areas of forest and savanna. They continue to orient themselves and their communities according to the two cardinal points of the root and tip of the sky, with the men's house located directly beneath the apex of the sky dome and at the center of the plaza in the village conceived as a series of concentric zones of decreasing levels of socialization. The Kayapo have modified their traditional cosmological pattern in response to their contact with the national culture by relegating the location of technological and administrative functions involved in interaction with the Brazilians, such as airstrips, clinics, schools, pharmaceutical dispensaries, football fields, radio and electric generator shacks, and garages and parking areas for motor vehicles, to the "black" (*a-tuk*) transitional zone outside the ring of houses that defines the boundary of the village proper. This is indeed a zone of interethnic transformational processes that now mediate between the Kayapo community and national Brazilian society. Their location in the *a-tuk* zone is thus completely appropriate in traditional cosmological terms (see Figure 3.1, above).

This macrocosmic adjustment of spacetime at the village level has been coupled with a parallel adjustment in the treatment of the traditional pattern of bodily adornment. As described earlier, the surface of the body is a mediator between the Kayapo social person and the external environment. They continue to use body adornment to mediate their interaction with Brazilian society. Persons of both genders have supplemented their traditional repertoire of bodily decoration with token items of Brazilian clothing to cover the parts of their bodies that, by Brazilian standards of etiquette, must be concealed for normal social interaction to be possible. Men now tend to wear shorts and women one-piece dresses, but both sexes continue to wear body paint beneath their clothes and use traditional bodily ornaments, including Kayapo-style necklaces and bracelets, headdresses, and coiffure on the exposed parts of their bodies (Figures 3.7, 3.8, 3.9). Brazilian clothing thus constitutes a transformational zone around the central region of their Kayapo-decorated bodies, channeling their cultural agency into alien Brazilian social forms where appropriate, leaving their painted extremities and traditionally coiffed heads to protrude directly into external interaction space as themselves. During ritual events, they may even discard these outer Western vestments except for underwear. At both the level of the village and that of the individual body, therefore, an inner Kayapo core persists. The transitional zone now includes intercultural transformational elements—clothes and government services—that mediate between a Kayapo essence and a surrounding concentric zone of alien sociality.

These relatively minor changes in the traditional forms of bodily adornment may be only the beginnings of a more profound process of cultural change. Already there are signs that Kayapo body painting is becoming more and more dissociated from its roots in traditional notions of personhood and cosmological spacetime as new and unpredictable spatiotemporal zones beyond the village continue to proliferate and impinge on Kayapo society. The most flamboyant items of Kayapo ceremonial costume, particularly the magnificent feather capes that have a metaphorical role of enabling Kayapo ritual dancers to "fly" (the Kayapo term for dancing) are also being put to new and previously unimaginable uses in the contemporary global system (Figure 3.10).

Figure 3.10. Airplane adorned with Kayapo feather capes.

FORM AND CONTENT

I have thus far been attempting to present data to support my hypothesis that the structure and principal units of Kayapo cosmology consist of the schemas of the activities by which the Kayapo create their own forms as social persons and, in so doing, also create their social community and their world—in a word, their cosmos—which, in turn, produce and dissolve the constituent units of Kayapo society. From the data I have considered, I would now like to derive a second, more general hypothesis: Kayapo cosmology and, I suggest, many other Amerindian cosmological systems, are founded on the fundamental principle that the forms of things immanently contain the agency or power to produce themselves through the transformation of their own contents. In other words, the activities create the forms that structure the perpetuation of these activities. The forms of things are actually embodied processes of formation or the potential capacity for them. They contain the agency or force that drives the content of things to assume the specific characteristics and behavioral patterns proper to their species or kind. This proposition holds, in principle, for the cosmos as a whole and all its constituent units, including humans and their social groupings, animals and plants, and non-living beings such as celestial bodies like the sun and moon. It applies primarily to humans and higher animals, birds, and fish, but also to the forms of lower animals, plants, and major celestial bodies, which likewise undergo developmental processes and, in principle, partake of the same dynamic quality.

The spatiotemporal pattern of all such developmental processes has its own form, which is, as we have seen, the bidimensional pattern of linear and concentric dimensions. In this pattern, each entity can be viewed in turn as occupying a central position as an active subject, relegating the external others or circumstances to the encompassing periphery. The development of the specific forms of things, in other words, is an immanent property of those forms. This proposition exemplifies a fundamental principle of cosmological thought: the schematic pattern of the cosmos as a whole, considered as a self-replicating process, is reproduced in each of its constituent units. The self-generation of form is thus an essential aspect of cosmic spacetime, but it is simultaneously constrained to take certain material forms in relation to the rest of the system—the cosmos—in which they form a part. Forms, in other words, are not to be understood as mere envelopes without functional internal relations to their contents.

FORM, SPIRIT, AND "ANIMISM"

The cosmos, as conceived by indigenous Amazonians, is made up of beings or entities that are first engaged in processes of self-production as they assume specific objective forms. This is followed by processes of dissolution as these forms revert into relatively formless matter, on the one hand, and relatively evanescent, immaterial spiritual form, on the other. This process, whereby the relatively unformed content of a being or thing takes on its appropriate form, includes its habitus of affects and activities as well as its relations to other beings in the cosmic order of things. This transformation is the expression of a schematic process or an activity that is an immanent part of the thing itself. Such schemas, oriented toward the production of specific forms, serve as embodied intentions and thus constitute analogues, if not the conscious equivalents, of subjective purposes.

In this view, the guiding patterns of purposive activity create the objective physical form in question. The pattern of activity embodies the spiritual force or subjective agency of the entity, its essence. In the case of animate beings, the form is conceived to be the products or manifestations of a subjective power of intentional action. In particular, the Kayapo use the term *karon* to indicate the "image," "form," "shadow," as well as what we might call the "spirit," "soul," or "ghost" of a person or other entity. They consider humans as the exemplar of beings that possess *karon*, but they also believe that mammals, birds, fish, and many trees, vines, and other plants possess spirit forms and the subjective powers associated with them.

This is, I suggest, the basic notion behind the so-called "animism" common to most, if not all, indigenous peoples of the Amazon (Bird-David 1999; Descola 1996, 2005; Viveiros de Castro 1998, 2004). Their animism derives from what I have been describing here as the spiritual connotations of form. In terms of this conception, the form of an entity appears, from the perspective of the process by which it is produced, not only as the final product of the process but as its guiding principle and animating force. In these respects, the form of the entity acts as or, in pragmatic terms, *is* its spirit.

According to this view, the synthesis of form (spirit) and content (body) that constitutes living beings and even some inanimate ones like the sun and moon can be constructed and maintained only by means of exercising subjective agency. However, this synthesis is unstable and vulnerable to disruption and eventual dissolution as the subject loses its energy and power, either temporarily, as in illness or shock induced by extreme fright, or permanently, as in the death of the person or organism. Under extreme conditions, this spiritual force or formative aspect may become separated from the bodily or material content of the form, but it cannot exist independently for long without it. Death brings the permanent separation of spirit form from body content, thus dissolving the synthesis of form and content that is the basis of an organism's objective existence. The fission of the synthetic unity of spirit and body results in the further decomposition and ultimate disappearance of its separated parts. The *karon*, or spirit form, continues to live on after the death of the body as a ghost, but it gradually sheds its human character, becoming an animal-like being in the forest and eventually dissolving completely. Parallel to this, the material content (ˉin, the flesh or body) is transformed from a living body to rotting flesh and then to nothing more than white bones.

OBJECTIFICATION AND REVERSAL: LIFE, DEATH, AND THE DEATH OF DEATH

The essential concern of cosmology is with reality: not merely forms and spirits of things in the abstract but the process through which they become objective realities. Objectification is an intrinsically relational process. Things become objectified in relation to other things, and their forms embody the specific forms of these relations. In this relational sense, objectification is an essential aspect of the transformation of content into form. It is the aspect of the process that consists of its interaction with other entities, the way its formation is affected by and, in turn, affects those entities. Objectivity, in this form-mediated, relational sense, *is* reality, in cosmological terms. The objective form or external appearance of a being or thing is the mediating link between its content or inner essence, on the one hand, and, on the other, its objectified, realized relations to other beings or things in the world to which it belongs.

Just as the objective form of an entity constitutes a specific set of relations between itself and the system of which it is a part, this entity also embodies or implies a specific subject position or perspective in relation to the rest of the system, together with the power to interact with it. As this implies, the forms of activity that constitute the ontological process of objectification also serve as the epistemological categories that define the perspective of the objectified person or being toward the world.

Objectification, as a combined ideal and material activity, thus necessarily involves *subjectification,* or the construction of subjectivity. The identity of epistemological and ontological categories, and of objective and subjective perspectives, are logical corollaries of the egocentric and sociocentric structure of Kayapo cosmology. In this respect, human society is the center and perspectival vantage point on the cosmos; correlatively, the social person is constructed as a microcosmic replica of this central social zone of spacetime.

As the transformational process through which the constituent units of the cosmos take on objective reality and simultaneously become integrated into the cosmological structure, objectification must necessarily follow the fundamental structural constraint of reversibility. In Kayapo belief and practice, therefore, the activities of *objectification,* through which entities and relations in the human life-world are produced (objectified) as material and ideal realities, must inevitably be reversed by the processes of *deobjectification,* occurring through the destruction and dissolution of the objectified forms of the cultural identities and material being of social bodies and persons. Mortuary practices, focused in the transitional *a-tuk* zone outside of the social space of the village defined by the circle of houses, provide the paradigmatic case.

Kayapo graves enact this process of formal dissolution by deobjectifying themselves. Graves are dug as circular pits in which the corpse is placed in a flexed position. The pit is then roofed over with logs and mats (Figure 3.11). The earth from the pit is then heaped on the mats, creating a rounded tumulus. Many of the deceased's possessions are broken, their forms thus deliberately destroyed to share in the dissolution of the social and physical form of their owner, and thrown into the grave or on top of the grave mound. Wives and female relatives strike their heads with machetes, symbolically damaging their own forms in sympathetic identification with the deceased. Both male and female relatives cut off their hair, and tufts of the shorn hair of mourning relatives are fastened to poles stuck in the ground beside the mound or thrown directly onto it, along with leaf headbands used by the performers of the death dance if the deceased possessed name(s) belonging to the class of "beautiful" names (see "Beauty and the beast," this volume).

Figure 3.11. Mats being placed over logs covering the hole where a deceased person is buried.

For a few months following the burial, the close relatives of the deceased may visit the grave site, removing any weeds that spring up on or beside the tumulus

Figure 3.12. Family visiting a cemetery to remove weeds from a relative's grave mound. Headbands are attached to poles next to graves of people who received "beautiful" names.

(Figure 3.12). With time, however, the mats on which the tumulus rests decompose, and the earth from the tumulus filters down between the logs into the grave pit. Eventually the tumulus vanishes, the logs rot, and the grave becomes level with the surrounding earth, objectively sharing its owner's dissolution. The grave is not only the objective aspect of death, the material form of the end and dissolution of personal existence, but it also enacts the process of its own deobjectification—the death, as it were, of death. As such, it becomes the instrument through which the dissolution of death is turned against death itself, dissolving and deobjectifying its own social form, so far as the relations of the dead person are concerned. As this process is going on in the cemetery, the spirit form of the deceased separates itself from the decomposing body in the grave and the attributes that made it a social entity. It wanders into the forest, becoming an animal-like being, a white ghost that survives for a while in the company of others, dancing and singing in the village of ghosts, until its form also finally dissolves into nothing.

For the Kayapo, in sum, the existence of things, including people, consists of correlated processes of objectification and deobjectification that characterize not only the life but also the death of things and persons. It is crucial to recognize that, in both processes, form and content behave not merely as descriptive categories but as active principles, that is, the material forces or powers that drive the developmental processes of which the cosmos on all its levels consists. As powers, they complement and reinforce each other in processes of objectification but are unable permanently to sustain their synthetic unity, which weakens and ultimately disintegrates. Such episodes of deobjectification may be temporary, as in illness or shamanic activities, or terminal, as in death.

NATURE, ANIMALS, AND THE MYTHICAL FOUNDATIONS OF HUMAN CULTURE

The Kayapo think of their own bodies as hybrid combinations of natural animal qualities and acquired attributes of social identity. The former are exemplified by the internal physical processes located in the central trunk of the body that become transformed and directed into socially formed activities of various kinds. The natural animal faculties and powers of human bodies, as well as the wild faunal and floral resources of the surrounding forest and rivers, are sources of the life energy and sensory faculties that the social world needs in order to sustain itself. By constantly appropriating these natural resources and assimilating them, society transforms itself and thus ensures its reproduction. "Nature," in other words, is an integral component of social bodies and thus of social persons. Natural forces and aspects of being (things that exist in and of themselves independently of human social activity) thus constitute essential components of social spacetime and "culture" as well as the peripheral zones of forest and savanna.

In considering the way Kayapo cosmology sets the terms of both the conceptual and the pragmatic relations between "nature," as a category of beings that produce their own forms of objective and subjective being, and "culture," as the forms of consciousness and pragmatic activity produced by human society, it must be remembered that the structure of human society itself incorporates fundamental "natural" forms of spacetime, agency, and powers inherent in the animal content of human bodiliness and reproductivity. Human culture is thus conceived more as an incremental development of these natural elements, a "super-nature," as it were, than as a qualitatively distinct order of existence opposed to "nature," as if they were mutually external elements of a binary contrast with an excluded middle.

As beings with a specific form and spirit identity shared with other members of their species, humans and animals stand in a common spiritual relation to the world. All are similarly occupied with the form-giving, spirit-directed process of objectifying themselves, a process having a generic form and content of functional activities (i.e., hunting, foraging, eating, drinking, finding shelter, mating, and reproducing). This process is essentially identical for all embodied spirit beings, regardless of the particular differences in the content of the activities entailed by their specific differences of form.

Amazonian peoples express this identity by saying that animals are people too, a "person" being defined as any spirit being in the sense just defined. Humans do not, in this view, have a monopoly on personhood, any more than they do form or spirit. Beings of different species can thus identify their concretely different activities within the shared perspective of their common engagement in the fulfillment of the needs of sustaining their spirit forms. An anteater lunching on an ant hill and a human lunching on a sandwich can thus regard themselves as engaged in the same functional activity, lunching. The human might express this sense of equivalence metaphorically by saying that the anteater is eating his sandwich, and the anteater might express the same perception by thinking of the human as licking up his ants. In the Kayapo cosmological perspective, there is no basis for privileging the human's over the anteater's way of expressing the functional identity of their activities.

In a similar vein, the Kayapo think of other species as having their own forms of such human artifacts or activities as houses, songs, ceremonies, and even, for some purposes (such as shamanic communication), language, although the actual forms taken by these activities are very different from their human equivalents. The essential principle is the animist belief in panspiritism as the grounds for the essential identity of humans and animals. The belief in such a generic identity of spirit, however, does not imply that the Kayapo make no distinction between animal nature and human culture or that they imagine that animals identify themselves as modern, cultural humans like themselves.

There is a widespread Amazonian myth, which the Kayapo also possess, that describes an original Edenic state in which the ancestral forms of animals identified themselves with humans and shared human ways, as they were then. According to the myth, animals could speak and understand human language and shared certain rudimentary "cultural" forms with humans, such as bows and arrows or cooking fire, whereas humans had not yet developed the distinctive forms of contemporary human culture and society. Humans, however, did not completely identify themselves as animals, and they played a number of mean-spirited tricks on the naïvely trusting animals, which ultimately led to the breakup of the primordial solidarity among the species.

In interpreting this myth, it is important to recognize that the protohumans and protoanimals described by the myth are not represented as identical with contemporary forms of either humans or animals. The point of the myth is precisely to explain how humans became fully human and thus different both from their ancestral mythical prototypes and from animals. They did so by developing fully human culture, which, conversely, led animals to lose the quasi-human qualities they originally possessed, such as language and fire, so that they became like the nonhuman-like animals the Kayapo know today. The essential point of these myths, in other words, is not to assert a primal identity between humans and animals (or culture and nature) that somehow persists to the present day; rather, they explain why the original identity of ancestral humans and animals was destroyed by the humans' development of culture and consequent differentiation from animals and, most importantly, how the possession of culture makes contemporary humans different from their mythical ancestors.

This fundamental point is succinctly made in the myths that tell of the differentiation of humans from animals and the origin of human culture. The most well known of these is the story of the origin of cooking fire and how it was appropriated by humans (see Chapter One). It tells how, before humans possessed fire, it existed in nature, first as the sun in the sky and then as a jatoba tree set ablaze by lightning, which a jaguar couple with human-like attributes used to cook the meat of game killed by the male jaguar with his bow and arrow. The jaguars had only found the fire ignited by the lightning; they could not make fire themselves nor add other pieces of wood to their single burning log to make a human fire. Nor, significantly, could they reproduce their own kind: they had no offspring of their own, and there were no other jaguar houses, no jaguar village, only the single hut of the one jaguar couple. Only when the jaguars adopted a human boy and nurtured him so that he grew into a man, thus replicating the status of adult male hunter of which the male jaguar had served as his model, did it become possible for the young man to break off a bit of the fire, thus, for the first time, replicating the form of a unique prototype by using fire to make fire (see "The fire of the jaguar," this volume).

This deed created the essentially cultural form of classification, where the form of the prototype that is replicated becomes the general definition of the class, and the replicated instances become members of the class. The young man then returned with his instance of fire to the human village. There he explained to the adult men and women of the village the use of fire and how it could be made to reproduce itself without the limitations of the single fire of the jaguar. He led the men back to the jaguar's hut and all the men together brought the fire log back to their village, where they set it down by the men's house in the center of the village plaza. Then all the women came from their houses around the periphery of the plaza and took pieces of the burning log back to light cooking fires of their own, which they proceeded to nourish and rekindle with more pieces of wood.

This was the moment that human culture was born. The essential component was not simply cooking—a single transformational process, which itself is a natural phenomenon that the jaguars were able to use, albeit in a restricted, subhuman manner, with only a single fire consisting of a single log. The key move was the reflexive step of using the fire to produce itself: in other words, using the transformational process to transform itself into an open-ended, infinite series of uniform replications of itself. This difference is precisely the meaning of the cosmological contrast between the concentric zone of spacetime comprising the ring of households surrounding the village plaza and the central zone occupied by the men's house.

In sum, the structure of transformations embodied in the articulation of cosmological spacetime and, in microcosm, in the layout of the village, is identical to that laid out in the fire myth's narrative of the differentiation of human culture from animal nature. The cosmological frame of this mythical process helps to clarify not only the differences but the continuities between animal and human nature. Animals, like humans, develop their own forms—and thus their own spirits—through their own growth processes. Humans have no monopoly on "spirit," and many of their characteristic ways of behaving—their species-specific "habitus"—are functionally analogous to animal behaviors. The Kayapo are acutely aware of these commonalities between their own ways of acting and feeling and those of animals, but they are also cognizant of their differences. They readily think of animals with their mates and offspring in their dens as living in their own "houses" with their own "families," but they do not imagine that animals have their own men's houses.

COSMOLOGY AS IDEOLOGY

I have sought to show that the Kayapo vision of the order of the cosmos is no mere pattern of symbolic oppositions or synchronic semiotic structure but, rather, the schematic form of the process of producing and reproducing the social world, including the actors and groups of which it is composed. As a (re-) productive process that is itself its own ultimate product, its structure is embodied in the entities that produce it and are, in turn, produced by it. All levels of social organization, from the community as a whole to its individual members, are thus conceived as formed through the same process, which is, in turn, conceived as instantiating the encompassing form of the natural universe. This form itself is therefore seen as self-existing prior to any particular instance of human social activity and its collective framework of social organization (created, in fact, by a mythical tapir before the appearance of humans), even as it constitutes the encompassing framework of that organization.

Kayapo cosmology, in these terms, appears to constitute an alienated form of social consciousness (Turner 2002). The essence of the fetishistic inversion of consciousness is that the existence and structure of society are seen as a "natural" (cosmic) pattern rather than as being produced as a result of its own productive activity. As social consciousness, this results in a view of society as an ahistorical form, a natural part of the cosmological order, rather than a product of the activity of human agents. Social activity is thus understood as limited to the reproduction of a received pattern that was not socially created.

At first glance, Kayapo myth and ritual appear to represent striking examples of such inversions of social consciousness. Ceremonial performance implicitly involves a shift of subjective perspective from the everyday perspective of contemporary humans in secular social contexts to the perspectives of monstrous quasi-human, quasi-animal beings, such as those of the mythical past, in order to reenact the drama of the creation of fully human society and personal identities, such as their own. This shift is explicitly represented in the forms of ceremonial bodily adornment, described earlier, and also in the animal- or bird-like movements of the dancers and the lyrics of the songs they sing to accompany them, which describe the actions, habits, and feelings of animals or birds but are frequently framed in the grammatical first person.

We may note here, in passing, that this ceremonial perspective corresponds more or less closely to Viveiros de Castro's idea of the perspective of humans and animals in contemporary social time. He conceives of this perspective as directly continuing from the view of one another they held in mythical times, when the relative undifferentiation of humans and animals took the form of both groups thinking of animals as "humans," meaning modern-style, fully cultural humans (Viveiros de Castro 1998, 2004). I have given my reasons for disagreeing with this characterization elsewhere (2009b; see "Beauty and the beast," this volume). Here, however, I want to emphasize my basic disagreement with "perspectivism," which is that it conceives perspectives as singular and fixed, located only at the level of external relations between species or systems (such as human society in general and animals in general) rather than as integral parts of the internal processes of systems, shifting and transforming with changes in the context of subject positions. The whole point of Kayapo ceremonial activity, as I have described, is precisely the dramatization of a shift in perspective from one of relative identity between protohumans and protoanimals to differentiation between their respective contemporary descendants, fully socialized humans in contrast to dehumanized animals.

The Kayapo, at any rate, *are* fully conscious of constructing themselves and their society through their ritual dramas of socialization. The aim of the ceremonies is to reenact, through a process with actual contemporary effect, the transformation from protosocial, still animal-like identities or subject positions to the identities and perspective of fully socialized contemporary humans. They perform the ceremonies that recreate the forms of social relations and personal identity, doing so by taking the alienated forms of animals or primal undifferentiated animal and human beings. Nevertheless, they do this of their own will in collective social actions under their own control for purposes and values that they consciously choose. Moreover, their conception of the cosmic forms of their ritual and secular actions alike are logically articulated as general notions of reversible structures of linear and concentrically organized schemas. Whatever their mythical derivations, the schemas serve them as generic ontological concepts and epistemological categories applicable to phenomena in the physical world as well as to sociological forms in contexts where they are framed as self-conscious subjective activities and perspectives.

Here we arrive at a fundamental paradox of Kayapo and other Amazonian indigenous peoples' cosmology considered as a form of social consciousness. On the one hand, the Kayapo collectively organize themselves to reproduce the forms of their social order, transform their social identities and the membership of their social groupings, and thus assume the unalienated role of producers of themselves and their social world. On the other hand, they assume the character of asocial, quasi-natural monsters, dancing around the village plaza covered with feathers, leaves from the forest, and animal claws, hooves, and teeth. Why do they do so to reenact the drama of their own transformation and that of society as a whole from raw natural content to a self-cooking social form?

One possible answer is that they have not been able to conceive of the development of contemporary social and cultural forms of humanity as the historical products of social human beings like themselves. They may therefore attribute their creation to quasi-human, partly animal-like beings, like those they impersonate in their rituals in order to appropriate and socialize their creative powers. As frequently seen in cosmological systems, the Kayapo displace their creative powers outside of themselves.

The projection of the structure of society as the structure of the natural cosmos implies the naturalization of that structure, but the continual reproduction of that creation (that is, overt control) by collective social action in the great communal ceremonies implies a socialization of consciousness of the human capacity to produce the forms of society and those of the individual social actors who perform the ceremonies. This appears to present the paradox of an unalienated reproduction of an alienated structure. Are other Amerindian cosmologies, and perhaps those of other peoples, founded upon variants of this same paradox? If so, perhaps we can learn from them to temper our own concepts of alienation and fetishism and to recognize, as did Marx himself at certain points, that formations of social consciousness may be complex mixtures of alienated and unalienated forms of praxis and consciousness, the two coexisting for many purposes in noncontradictory ways and varying widely in the relative degrees to which either dominates in determined contexts.

The crisis of late structuralism: Perspectivism and animism
Rethinking culture, nature, spirit, and bodiliness[1]

THE PASSING OF LÉVI-STRAUSS

The death of Claude Lévi-Strauss in November 2009 was an event that called for due commemoration of a brilliant anthropological career. It was also an occasion that called upon his epigones and critics among Amazonian anthropologists, as well as the many thinkers from other lines of intellectual and cultural work who were inspired and influenced by his ideas, to contemplate the nature

1. This was first published in 2009 in *Tipití: Journal of the Society for the Anthropology of Lowland South America* 7 (1). Many of the ideas in this paper were presented in lectures at the Federal University of Paraná in Curitiba, Brazil ("Humanidade, forma e objetivação na consciência social Kayapó," presented to the Graduate Program in Social Anthropology on October 17, 2007), and at the University of Copenhagen, Denmark ("Perspective on perspectivism," delivered to the Department of Anthropology on November 13, 2008). I benefited greatly from the discussion of these lectures by students and colleagues. I am particularly indebted to Dr. Morton Pedersen of the Department of Anthropology at the University of Copenhagen for his comments after my lecture in Copenhagen, his writings on Mongol perspectivism, and a seminar he presented to the Department of Anthropology at Cornell University several months earlier. Robin Wright made many valuable comments and provided me with numerous references during the writing of this paper. Laura Rival provided pertinent critical comments and bibliographic references. Hanne Veber and Sören Hvalkov contributed valuable personal ethnographic data on the Asheninka.

of his contribution and the extent to which it remains a vital force that continues to influence theoretical work in the social and cultural disciplines.

The excitement stimulated by the earlier works of Lévi-Strauss derived from three original theoretical contributions. Firstly, the new theoretical and methodological approach represented by his synthetic concept of "structure," fully presented for the first time in *The elementary structures of kinship* (1969a [1949]), combined the mathematical idea of a group of transformations constrained by one or more invariant principles (not previously applied in anthropology, although used at least a century earlier in economics by Marx, among others), the semiotic notions of classification developed by Saussure in his concepts of the sign and the field of signification, the componential phonology of the Prague School linguists Troubetzkoy and Jakobson, psychological associationism, gestalt ideas of pattern perception, and anthropological notions of comparative typologies of kinship systems and cultural systems of categories. It was a bold and creative synthesis drawn from disparate sources, many of which were unfamiliar to the anthropologists of the day.

Secondly, Lévi-Strauss offered a powerful new idea of the ultimate object of anthropological analysis, the "fundamental structures of the human mind," which he conceived as the invariant constraints governing the groups of transformations comprising his structural models, rendered accessible by the methodological application of his new concept of structure. These were invariably conceived as psychological or social psychological principles like reciprocity or the distinction between nature and culture. They constituted sign posts on the way to Lévi-Strauss' ultimate goal of reducing culture to psychology and psychology to the natural processes of perception and unconscious association that produce the categories of cognition and classification. The end of this analytical trajectory, as Lévi- Strauss conceived it, was the revelation of nature as both the ultimate transcendental subject and the source of the cognitive features of objective reality. These ideas comprised Lévi-Strauss' idea of anthropology's way of answering the big question that was its reason for being, to wit, "what is the nature of humanity"? He was perhaps the last major anthropologist to make the quest for an answer to that question the focus of his career.

Thirdly, Lévi-Strauss can be said to have discovered a new subject matter for anthropological analysis: the apparently arbitrary and meaningless details of indigenous myths, cosmologies, and systems of knowledge, which he recognized could be analyzed as the code of logical oppositions and identities that constituted the cognitive structures of culture.

The three-fold analytical program based on these three fundamental theoretical innovations exercised great influence on anthropology and related fields,
even among many who remained skeptical of Lévi-Strauss' own analytical practice and his ultimate theoretical goals. It took time for critical thinkers to digest
the ideas and clarify their problematic aspects both in theory and in application.
Among the many criticisms that have been leveled at the structuralist edifice,
three stand out for their relevance to this paper. Firstly, there is a fundamental
flaw in Lévi-Strauss' application of his theoretical model of structure, which can
be summed up as applying the right model to the wrong level of the data. Lévi-
Strauss followed the conventional conceptions of contemporary semiotics and
kinship studies in conceiving the formal organization of individual kinship systems or myths as synchronic tableaux of relations or feature contrasts, leaving no
room for internal transformations, such as those of mythical plots or developmental cycles of families. He was therefore obliged to try to apply his structural
model of groups of transformations bounded by invariant constraints to sets of
multiple myths or kinship systems, each considered as a unitary "transform" or
"variant" of a master structure (embodied by the invariant principle or principles
that supposedly comprise the boundary condition of the group) that cannot be
located or defined within any member of the group—nor, as it has turned out,
anywhere else. Neither Lévi-Strauss nor any other avowed structuralist has ever
succeeded, to my knowledge, in producing a single analysis of the structure of
any "group of variants" of any cultural construct or kinship system that actually
meets the formal requirements of "invariance" specified by Lévi-Strauss. This
does not mean that the model itself is unviable or inapplicable, only that it has
not been applied where it should have been, to wit, the internal transformations comprising the developmental processes or plots of the individual systems
in question (kinship systems or mythical narratives), which do form "groups"
of transformations constrained to remain within invariant limits by the overriding requirement of reproducing the system of relations or schematic pattern of symbolic actions in question. If this were done first, the results of these
analyses might then be compared at a second level as a "group" of analogous
cases, but what one would be comparing would be quite different from the synchronic "variants" that comprise structuralist analyses. A fatal consequence of
the synchronizing of the internal patterns of relations comprising the "variants"
or "transforms" of structuralist analyses is the flattening of their constituent
elements into inert, disarticulated relational or sign-elements deprived of many
of the intentional and dynamic (transformative) meanings they have in their

original systemic context. This is a point with equal relevance to structuralism and some of its more recent offspring.

The other two main points of Lévi-Strauss' original structuralist synthesis are also adversely affected by the unviability of his approach to structural analysis. His inability to apply his structural model to the structure of individual systems or "transforms" meant that he was never able to define invariant constraints coordinating any "group" of transforms as "fundamental structures" with the precision demanded by his group-theoretic definition of structure. His characterization of his procedure for analyzing "groups" of myths in the "Overture" to *The raw and the cooked* (1969b) as analogous to a growing crystal, which is clearly structured at its center but fuzzy and ill-defined at its periphery, metaphorically evokes his failure to find the structure of any such group—which means, given his definition of structure as the invariant law of the group, his failure to find the structure of any myth. The massive outpouring of unstructured analyses of mythical patterns and transformations comprising the four volumes of *Mythologiques*, stimulating as they are, represent, by Lévi-Strauss' own theoretical standards, the failure of his structuralist quest for fundamental structures (Lévi-Strauss 1966b).[2]

When he moved on from kinship structures to myth and systems of knowledge as his principal subjects, Lévi-Strauss' attempts to translate the significata of the semiotic elements of myths and cosmological systems were likewise hobbled by his inability to recognize the significance of the fact that such individual elements are regularly transformed in the course of the myth or social process in question—transformations that apply to their signification as well as to features of their form or relations with other elements. In the Gê and Bororo myths of the origin of cooking fire that constitute the initial subject of *The raw and the cooked* (Lévi-Strauss 1969b), for example, the fire makes its first appearance as the distant sun in the sky, which men use to warm meat that they must cut into small pieces and set out on rocks to catch its rays, then descends to earth as the burning end of a log in the house of the jaguars, who use it to roast big pieces of meat, and finally ends up being carried by men to their village, where it is broken up and used to light other cooking fires (Lévi-Strauss [1964]: 35–79).

---

2.   For a fuller discussion of the limitations of structuralism, including its failure to produce viable structural analyses consistent with Lévi-Strauss's own definition of structure, becoming, in effect, a form of poststructuralism *avant l'heure*, see Turner 1990.

Each of these transformations of the fire carries a different signification, and this series of transformations conveys a cumulative meaning that is the point of the myth. Lévi-Strauss analyzes the fire only as the sign of the operation of cooking, a function it exercised in the precultural house of the jaguars, missing completely the significance of its use at the end of the myth as a general means of making other fires, the essential step to full human culture.

In approaching a critique of the development of structuralism or the ideas of its more recent theoretical epigones, it is essential to bear in mind that none of them have developed as purely academic anthropological projects. Rather, they and their authors have all, to varying degrees, led double lives as public intellectuals engaged in supra-academic controversies of their times. Since its beginnings shortly after World War II, structuralism was framed by its advocates as much as a critique of modern Western philosophical and social thought, in particular existentialism, Marxism, hermeneutics, and structural-functional social anthropology, as an anthropological approach concerned with the kinship systems and myths of indigenous Australian and Amerindian cultures. The brilliant career of Lévi-Strauss exemplifies this double focus of the structuralist project, with its combination of anthropological interest in the more remote and exotic cultures of aboriginal Australia and the Amazon and its borrowings from currently modish scientific theories of structural linguistics and semiology, Merleau-Ponty's work on the psychology of perception, and what Lévi-Strauss called the new "mathematics of man," the "qualitative math" of set theory, cybernetics, and information technology that became popular following World War II (Lévi-Strauss 1955).

The success of structuralism as an intellectual movement owed much to this double focus, with its seductive methodological implications that the "fundamental structures" of human mental operations, manifested in their purest and simplest forms in the cultural productions of the most "primitive" (i.e., by implication, the most "natural") human cultures, bore a family resemblance to the new methods of structural analysis in linguistics and group theory, thus lending their scientific cachet to structuralist anthropology. This complex intellectual heritage helps us to understand one of the more problematic aspects of structuralism and its more recent offshoots from an anthropological perspective, namely, its tendency to reify general conceptual categories such as "nature" and "culture" and to treat them on the same footing as ethnographic evidence for indigenous ideas about what can be defined in terms of these categories as "natural" or "cultural" phenomena. One consequence of this is a tendency to treat entities or relations that can be attributed to one category or the other as internally homo-geneous, rather than as complex amalgams of both. This tendency is accentuated by a theoretical reliance on Saussurean semiology, in particular its concepts of the sign, the field of signification, and the distinction of *langue* and *parole* as models for cultural classifications and cosmologies, which push analyses in an idealist direction toward the abstraction of epistemological and classificatory categories from forms of material activity and social relations.

As an anthropologist working with Gê-speaking people of central Brazil, who have played a central role in the formation of Lévi-Strauss' ideas about Amazonian social structure and mythology, I have inevitably found myself car-rying on my ethnographic and theoretical work in a personal and conceptual dialogue with Lévi-Strauss: conceptual, because his writings pointed me toward problems and ideas that became central to my own work; and personal, because, like many fellow Amazonianists, I found him to be a lively and interested in-terlocutor, invariably receptive and generous with his time when I would call on him when in Paris. I began my work with the Kayapo in 1962, when the influence of Lévi-Strauss was at its height and "structuralism" had become a focus of intense interest and controversy, not only in France but increasingly in Anglophone, Hispanic, and Lusophone anthropological and cultural circles. Since the end of the '60s, I have witnessed (and to a small degree participated in) the decline of its intellectual eminence, which was hastened, if not caused, by the events of May 1968 in Paris.

MAY 1968 AS ANTISTRUCTURALIST REVOLT

The waning of the influence of structuralism as a theoretical approach within anthropology, as well as in literary and cultural studies more generally, which began after 1968, was gradual and never total. While Lévi-Strauss continued to teach and produce published works at an amazing rate, he nevertheless became an increasingly isolated figure without direct intellectual heirs. Structuralism, however, has enjoyed a prolonged half-life in various ostensibly "poststructural-ist" and "deconstructionist" recensions, which have continued some of struc-turalism's most fundamental tenets in different terms. Chief among these was Lévi-Strauss' failure to produce "structural" analyses that satisfied his own cri-teria for structure, thus making him, in effect, a pioneer of poststructuralism *avant l'heure*.

The students and workers of May '68 did not adorn their barricades with banners calling for the defense of *langue*, but with the demand to *prendre la parole*. They had not sought to defend existing structures but to deconstruct them. They were not concerned with the contemplation of objectified patterns of unconscious thought but with subjective action that might change and create new forms of consciousness as well as materially transform existing social relations. Parisian philosophers reacted to what they perceived as the 1968 crisis of structuralism as a perspective founded upon a contemplative, Saussurean notion of structure by repudiating the aspects of Lévi-Strauss' thought that appeared most out of keeping with the new ideological climate, which had been germinating in the universities, factories, and other social contexts before it burst into the open in the demonstrations of May '68.

That the epigones of the structuralist hegemony managed to conserve key aspects of Lévi-Strauss' theoretical synthesis and to recycle them as components of the new ostensibly antistructuralist positions they developed is an impressive tribute to the hold that structuralism had acquired over the French cultural imagination. An even more telling tribute is how many, in their haste to redefine themselves as poststructuralists, energetically asserted, against the evidence of their own previous writings, that of course they had never been structuralists. The post-1968 succession of hybrid theoretical formations that followed did not so much overtly confront and overcome the theoretical and analytical problems of structuralism as readapt them in new forms that would appear to make virtues of its theoretical vices. It is this post-1968 succession of hybrid theoretical formations, juxtaposed with the continued outpouring of new but theoretically repetitive work by Lévi-Strauss himself, that I refer to as the crisis of late structuralism.

The most notable among the hybrid positions to emerge in the immediate aftermath of the events of 1968 came from philosophers and public intellectuals rather than from anthropologists. They included Derrida's heterodox interpretation of Saussure's theory of the sign, which Lévi-Strauss had employed as the basis of his concept of structures of sign elements, as the basis of decentered antistructures (Derrida 1967). Derrida managed this by reinterpreting Saussure's notion of the arbitrariness of the signifier–signified relation as an existential gulf of *différance* of the supposed original unity of signifier and signified. The original model for Derrida's notion of *différance* may be sought in Lévi-Strauss' notion of the incest tabu as a requirement that men should give away their consanguineal female relations as sexual partners in reciprocal affinal exchanges with other men, thus deferring the primal unity of familial relations, rather than follow their supposed natural preference to retain them in incestuous (presocial) unity.

A different tack was taken by Foucault's inversion of Lévi-Strauss' use of Saussure's concept of *langue* as the model of his conception of structure (which Foucault himself had employed in his pre-1968 structuralist period. In a clear break with Lévi-Strauss, Foucault offered a transvaluation of Saussure's fundamental distinction of *langue* and *parole* that artfully co-opted the rhetoric of the movement of 1968, substituting for *langue* as the foundational category of his "poststructuralist" system the complementary Saussurean category of *parole*, reworked and rebaptized as *discours* (Foucault 1968). Foucault's conception of discourse, however, departed from Saussure's concept of *parole* in its denial of any role for the subject as speaker. Instead, he continued to conceive it in the approved austere Lévi-Straussian fashion as subjectless, like *langue*, in effect, a kind of activated form of *langue*, now understood as a structuring demiurge of "power", imposing subjective identities on social persons to enable them to serve the needs of power, which turn out to be the requirements of social structure. Althusser produced an analogous theory of the subject as an "interpellation" of society as a corollary of his "structuralist Marxist" theory of ideology (Althusser 1971).

These avowedly anti- or post-Lévi-Straussian theoretical positions were actually formulated as continuations of essential aspects of the theoretical framework of Lévi-Straussian structuralism by other means, above all, the concept of the subject as an epiphenomenon of impersonal, unconscious linguistic or ideological structures, and the consequent irrelevance or illusoriness of subjective consciousness, agency, and material activity.

THE CRISIS OF LATE STRUCTURALISM: ANIMISM AND PERSPECTIVISM AS SUCCESSORS

Anthropologists were also influenced by the social and ideological upheaval of the late 1960s and the new emphases on social action and subjective agency that followed from them, but they also responded to distinct influences arising from their discipline's concerns with the interaction of human subjects with the natural environment and the social meanings and cultural treatments of the human body. All of these concerns informed the reactions within the discipline to the twin crises of Lévi-Straussian structuralism: the failure of his own project of structural analysis to reveal the structures he sought, and the rejection of structuralism as a quietist, theoretical dead-end incapable of dealing with the realities of the contemporary social and cultural inequities of French society, in particular, its class structure and educational system, but also, in the cases we shall consider here, to the poststructuralist and deconstructionist reactions of Foucault, Derrida, and others.

Among anthropologists deeply engaged with, and influenced by, Lévi-Strauss' theoretical framework, the two most important critical tendencies that have emerged have been the revival of theoretical and ethnographic work on animism by Descola, Bird-David, and others (Bird-David 1999; Descola 1994, 1996, 2005; Descola and Viveiros de Castro 2009), and the development of perspectivism as an approach to indigenous Amazonian and, more broadly, Amerindian cosmological notions by Eduardo Viveiros de Castro, his students, and his associates (Viveiros de Castro 1996, 1998, 2004, 2005, 2011). In both cases, the theorists who initially developed these positions either began as Lévi-Straussian structuralists (the case of Viveiros de Castro, a Francophone Brazilian closely involved with Lévi-Strauss and French anthropology) or, as in the case of Descola (a student of Godelier with ecological and Marxist leanings), formulated their ideas in a critical dialogue with his vision. Both of these approaches began by challenging Lévi-Strauss' central conception of the relation of nature and culture, and of its role as the frame of his vision of anthropology as "entropology," the reduction of culture to the status of an epiphenomenon of nature. Lévi-Strauss conceived the reduction of culture to nature as operating through the medium of the determination of subjective consciousness by an objective "Kantian" unconscious constituted by the neurological apparatus of perception and the gestalt-like patterns of association it transmitted to the conscious mind.

Perspectivism proceeded by turning Lévi-Strauss' reductionist proposition inside out through an equally radical but opposite reduction of nature to culture, achieved through the elevation of subjective perspective over objective associationism as the determining constituent of the "spiritual" identities of all creatures, animals and humans alike. The foundational claim of perspectivism is that indigenous Amazonians believe that animals, as the archetypal "natural" creatures, subjectively identify themselves as humans, the archetypal cultural beings. Animism arrived at an analogous claim for the universality of the spiritual identity, presumed to be essentially human and thus cultural, of humans and all natural entities (including animals, plants, and some inanimate beings such as celestial bodies) by way of Descola's ethnographic documentation of the social relations between human and nonhuman beings among the Achuar, resulting in a pragmatic blurring of the boundary between the natural and cultural domains through a spiritual and material infiltration of each domain by beings from the other category.

Both animism and perspectivism thus take as their point of departure a reconception of the relation of nature and culture through an exploration of indigenous conceptions of the common subjectivity of cultural and natural beings, while diverging on a series of philosophical and theoretical points. Both tendencies have moved away from basic aspects of Lévi-Strauss' thought, as well as from each other, but both have continued in different ways to work within the framework of Lévi-Strauss' master concept of the categorical opposition of nature and culture as the basic concern of Amazonian and, more broadly, Amerindian cosmologies, despite their otherwise heterodox reformulations of its terms. Both sides have presented their positions in rhetorically provocative articles clearly intended to invite critical engagement. I offer the following remarks in the spirit of a collegial response to this invitation, from the perspective of yet another former fellow traveler of the structuralist project.

NATURE AND CULTURE: THE WOLVERINE AND THE PANSY

The attraction of structuralism for both anthropologists and humanist intellectuals in its earlier years seemed only to be intensified by its rejection of foundational concepts and concerns of conventional philosophical, textual, and anthropological analysis: consciousness, meaning, production, history, form (as distinct from "structure"), the subject (including perspective, intentionality, agency, Freudian psychodynamics, and affect), and all aspects of language falling within the Saussurean category of speech or discourse (from syntax, deixis, object reference, and discourse forms, such as narrative, to the social pragmatics of speech in context), to select a few headings from a longer list. Another factor contributing to the curious prestige of structuralist analyses was their preoccupation with the exotic and apparently arbitrary, unmotivated details of indigenous myths, rituals, and cosmologies involving unfamiliar animals, plants, and natural forms, which it was the great achievement of Lévi-Strauss to bring within the purview of a theoretical vision able to recognize their significance.

Lévi-Strauss' concern with these particulars was integral to his conception of the great theme of Amerindian myths as well as that of structuralist anthropology: the relation of nature and culture. Lévi-Strauss conceived of this relation on two levels. On the one hand, he interpreted the Amerindian myths recounting the differentiation of humanity and culture from a state of nature once shared on more or less equal terms with animals as expressions of the natural mental processes of perception and association through which he believed cultural forms are constructed. On the other hand, he sought to understand how the sensuous forms and properties of natural entities, such as flowers or animal species, are unconsciously appropriated by the perceptual apparatus and related to one another by cognitive psychological processes of association to form cultural structures like classification and representation. Lévi-Strauss thus always conceived of the process of constructing basic cultural structures to be psychological and unconscious rather than an aspect of intentional (conscious, subjective) social interaction, and conceived the product of the process, the structures or structural variants themselves, as abstract synchronic patterns rather than as including the transformational operations through which they were produced. Cultural structures, in other words, may be conceived as practico-inert transforms of a more inclusive set of related structural "variants," but not as themselves transformational processes.

The synthesis at which he arrived, set out in *The savage mind* (in French, *La pensée sauvage*, a pun meaning both "natural thought" and "wild pansy") was concisely evoked by the visual layout of the book's cover, which shows a picture of a wild pansy below the French title on the front and a wolverine, celebrated in the text for its intelligence, on the back cover (Lévi-Strauss 1966b). The book as an object thus constitutes a "sensuous gestalt" (the term comes from Merleau-Ponty, to whom the book is dedicated), encoding the message of the book that the human mind, in its natural state, is constituted by the relation between the sensuous forms of the natural world (the pansy) and the natural mental faculties of perception and association (the wolverine). Culture and the ideational content of subjective consciousness are represented by the pages of text encompassed by the two covers. Structural analysis, as Lévi-Strauss conceived it, thus became a sort of ironic reductionism or, to use his term, "entropology," revealing how human cultures in their very attempts to construct representations of their differentiation from nature ironically succeed only in producing constructs that reveal in their form and content the true character of culture as an epiphenomenon of nature. The outcome of the structuralist analysis of human cultural forms is therefore the reduction of humans and their cultures to their true status as products of nature's interaction with itself, employing humans as the unwitting medium of the process.

For Lévi-Strauss, the important point was the natural quality of the faculties and substantive contents of human mentation and culture, but in emphasizing this he was also obliged to recognize the logical implication that these natural sensory and cognitive faculties could not be conceived as exclusively human but must be understood as qualities of mind and intelligence shared with other natural beings, which is why the wolverine found its way onto the back cover of *La pensée sauvage*. In this way, Lévi-Strauss' structuralism opened the possibility of a more radical theoretical exploration of the sharing of mind or spirit by humans with animals and other natural entities.

The major obstacle to this opening appeared to be the limitations of the major constituents of structuralist theory itself, associationist psychology, the approach to structure as synchronic pattern abstracted from the transformational processes of its production, and, above all, the straitjacket of Saussurean semiotics, with its fixation on *langue* to the exclusion of *parole*, signification to the exclusion of reference and meaning, and abstract objectivity to the exclusion of subjective consciousness, intention, and agency. As these limitations became increasingly evident to later generations of *structuralistes* receptive to new anthropological interests in subjectivity, agency, and the integration of human culture in ecological systems, the ascetic grandeur of Lévi-Strauss' structuralist vision came to be seen more and more as the product of an ironic limitation all its own: the theoretical and methodological inadequacy of his use of his own concept of structure. New ethnographic work carried out in the light of new interests in cultural modes of subjective consciousness, constructions of bodiliness, and interactions with the environment led to attempts to formulate more holistic approaches to the relation of culture and society with animals, plants, and the natural environment. It must be emphasized, at the same time, that much of this new work took inspiration from Lévi-Strauss' ideas of the natural sources of mind and culture, following out the implications of his suggestions that the structures and contents of mind and intelligence are not specifically human possessions but are shared with natural beings. Descola's revision of animism, with its emphasis on relations with plants as well as animals and other natural entities, was in the forefront of this new cultural ecology.

Lévi-Strauss conceived the nature–culture relation ambiguously as both external and internal: externally as a boundary between human culture and the

world of nature beyond the village; and internally as the psychological divide between the mental processes of perception and association, and the consciousness
of the cultural subject. Across this psychological frontier, the former confront
the latter as objective extensions of the external natural world they mediate for
the latter. The forms of this mediation, in Lévi-Strauss' conception, are thus not
only themselves continuations of the objective natural environment but serve
as the transcendental categories of consciousness and subjectivity. Subjectivity
and meaning, in this perspective, become epiphenomena of the objective forms
and processes of nature. At the theoretical level, this may be taken to imply a
reduction of culture to nature. This, as we have seen, was Lévi-Strauss' view,
embodied by the wolverine on the cover of *La pensée sauvage*—the exemplar
of Lévi-Strauss' conception of the naturalness of the mental processes that also
constitute the foundation of human culture and consciousness.

The wolverine itself, however, is not a cultural subject, despite its raw intelligence. Lévi-Strauss' naturalistic epistemological idealism implicitly raises
but does not answer the difficult question of the existence of subjectivity—the
product, if not the source, of natural intelligence and perception in humans as
"natural" beings. If human culture and subjective consciousness are asserted to
rest upon a foundation of natural psychological processes and gestalt-like patterns composed of sensory features of the objects of perception, are we to infer
that the possession of such natural mental faculties and the ubiquity of sensory
gestalten in the natural objective world imply the existence of superstructures of
subjective consciousness, intentionality, and even cultural identity on the part of
all beings thus endowed? A positive answer to this question may take two main
forms, one emphasizing the subjective aspect of mind as self-identity, the other
the objective, material consequences of subjective identity for relations with
other beings (especially humans). Either way, the structuralist concept of the
relation of nature and culture as mutually external, contrastive domains becomes
unsustainable. The attempt to reformulate this fundamental relationship in the
context of an answer to the question of the nature of the mentality of natural
beings has thus become the focus of the crisis of late structuralism.

The first way of dealing with the question is to recognize that if animals,
plants, heavenly bodies, and spirits are conceived to have subjective consciousness, then the paradoxical indication, given the orthodox structuralist interpretation of the binary opposition between nature and culture, through which subjective consciousness is relegated to the domain of culture, is that they may share
the conscious identity of human (cultural) subjects. The radical implication is

that what orthodox structuralists had considered the domain of nature is really a psychological and epistemological colony of the domain of culture: natural beings have, in short, become cultural beings, at least as far as they themselves are concerned. This conclusion, reached by impeccable structuralist logic, nevertheless clearly stands in contradiction to the orthodox structuralist conception of the nature–culture relation as a privative opposition of natural/objective and cultural/subjective domains. In so doing, it offers a way (however bizarre) to move beyond it.

The second way of dealing with the same question proceeds from the realization that if natural beings are conceived as possessing not only "wild" intelligence and qualities of mind (i.e., *la pensée sauvage*) but also subjective identities that include personhood and culture, such that humans might form social relations with the natural beings with whom they share a common mentality, subjectivity, and spirit, then the material and social boundary between cultural and natural domains itself disappears or at least becomes porous. The resulting inclusion of animals, plants, and other natural entities in the human social and cultural domain now becomes not merely an issue of ideal categories or cultural classification but also and equally of material social relations and activities. We thus arrive by a different route at another contradiction of the orthodox structuralist conception of the nature–culture relation as a privative opposition of objective nature to subjective culture. This points to the possibility of a second way of answering the question and thus a different escape route from the late structuralist impasse. This is the way that Descola calls the "domestication" of nature.

The former answer is the way followed by perspectivism; the latter is the way followed by the revival of animism. These, in sum, are the paths out of the impasse of Lévi-Straussian structuralism that have been followed by his more restive intellectual followers: in the former case, by Eduardo Viveiros de Castro (from now on, EVC) and those he has inspired; in the latter, by Philippe Descola and others who have shared his ideas. In neither case do we see a complete break with structuralism. The concern with the nature–culture relationship remains central to both but is transformed in different ways that involve consequential departures from the received Lévi-Straussian canon. The framing of cultural analysis in terms of the nature–culture relationship remains, but in each case the meaning of its terms has been transformed in ways that open up new lines of theoretical and ethnographic inquiry, while much of the Saussurean and formal structuralist theory responsible for the late structuralist crisis is tacitly jettisoned. A critical understanding of the sources of the crisis, however, provides a useful basis for understanding the common features and differences of the new animism and perspectivism as the two principal theoretical offspring of structuralism and how it is that both have converged upon the issues of body and "spirit."

ANIMISM: NATURE AS UNIVERSAL PAN-SPIRITISM

The revival of anthropological interest in animism, Tylor's conception of the original form of religion, is primarily due to the work of Philippe Descola. Tylor's concept was based on the idea that natural objects and beings, both animate and inanimate, possess spirits, conceived as consisting of mental faculties, affects, and subjective consciousness, although not necessarily human-like personalities. Descola had noticed in his fieldwork that the Achuar formed adoptive relations of kinship with natural beings, including both plants and animals, considering them to have subjectivity, intelligence, affect, and communicative abilities. Although humans participate in this pan-spiritism, spirit is not itself conceived as an intrinsically human or cultural entity but, rather, as an innate product of natural powers possessed by all species, including humans, animals, plants, and spirits of the dead. Subjectivity and mentality as constituted by these powers are believed to be universal natural attributes of all beings; although they may be amenable to social and cultural relationships with humans, they are not products of human culture. Rather, it is the possession of these powers by natural entities independently of human culture that makes possible communication with them by humans and the adoption of some of them by humans as members of human society, thus constituting them, in Descola's terms, as elements of *la nature domestique* (Descola 1994 [1986]). The universality of spirit does not imply universal homogeneity, in the sense that all species of beings possess identical spirits, any more than the universality of bodiliness implies that the bodies of all species are the same. Rather, the heterogeneous bodily forms of different species of beings correspond to distinctive spiritual forms, in many cases represented by "master" spirit beings that embody the differential attributes of their species-being. "Nature" thus comprises a world of objective differences of bodily form associated with distinctive spirit forms, for which the generic subjective faculties of spirit serve as a universal common denominator.

This is my interpretation of the ethnographic evidence, which differs in one critical respect from Descola's. He considers spirit to be an essentially human quality, so that the sharing of spirit by animals and plants comes down to a sharing of humanity. In his interpretation, it is this common humanity that makes possible the formation by humans of kinship relations with animals and plants. This does not seem to me to be a logically necessary conclusion that would be valid for all instances of animism in Amazonia, but Descola offers ethnographic evidence for it from his own Achuar research data and some other Amazonian societies.

It is clear in any case that animism, as Descola conceives it, has no place for the nature–culture distinction conceived in structuralist fashion as a privative opposition between the domains of human culture and nature. Rather, Descola's ethnographically based account of the interactions of (Achuar) humans and nonhuman beings of various kinds, many of whom enter into shared social relations, has the effect of transforming the nature–culture relation from a binary opposition of logically distinct, mutually exclusive *categories* presumed to correspond to discrete classes of beings to a social relationship (or not) between discrete natural and cultural *beings*. This creates a shifting and permeable boundary between the natural, nonsocial world and a social domain understood to include both cultural humans and natural beings, where the latter are understood to be endowed with human spirit identities. Culture, in its fully developed form, thus remains conceived as a distinctive characteristic of human society, but that society, in Descola's heterodox formulation, does not form a bounded cultural unit, since it may include relations with noncultural but spiritually human natural beings. This still leaves unanswered the questions of the source, form, and content of this common spirit. These are issues that may be clarified by a further consideration of the relations of bodiliness, subjective identities, and perspectives, which properly belongs to a critical discussion of perspectivism.

PERSPECTIVISM: NATURE AS ANTHROPOCENTRIC PANCULTURALISM

Taking its inspiration at least as much from structuralism's critical dialogue with modernist humanism as from anthropological interpretations of Amazonian cultures, perspectivism has shaped itself through a radical polemic against tenets of modernist Western thought from Descartes to Lévi-Strauss as well as all received schools of cultural anthropology. EVC presents perspectivist ideas as features of Amazonian indigenous thought, but he develops his propositions not so much through ethnographically based description and analysis of Amazonian cultures as through a philosophical dialogue between ideal-typical formulations of Western modernist ideas and correspondingly general representations of purportedly common Amazonian cultural ideas. This rhetorical approach serves a methodological purpose and has theoretical effects. The representation of Western modernist ideas employed in the cultural comparison as an integral, homogeneous system of highly abstract ideal-type concepts rhetorically serves to authorize the perspectivist representation of Amazonian ideas as an equally homogeneous system of abstract concepts comparable in generality and corresponding in thematic content and philosophical concerns to the Western system with which they are compared—in short, a philosophical system not dissimilar from modern Western speculative idealism. The result is the misrepresentation and mistranslation of the form, content, and meaning of the ideal categories and social meanings of many Amazonian cultural systems, not to mention some of the Western ideas drawn upon for comparison. There is furthermore a failure to recognize fundamental features of the construction and meaning of specific categories and propositions that differentiate the Amazonian categories in question from the modernist ideas with which they are compared. I agree with Lévi-Strauss as well as Viveiros de Castro and other perspectivists that there are important common ideas shared by many Amazonian systems (such as animism), but I also think that there is equally good ethnographic evidence for significant differences among the cultural constructions of different Amazonian societies, such as those societies possessing large, effectively endogamous villages with stratified systems of social groupings, like the Gê and Bororo, and those with dispersed hamlets that are effectively exogamous and unstratified, like many Tupian, Cariban, Shuar, Achuar, and some smaller Arawakan groups, with the Tukanoan and Arawakan societies of the northwest Amazon appearing to combine features of both.

These conceptual and structural differences among Amazonian societies, not to mention the differences among conflicting Western modernist philosophical and ideological positions, which receive equally short shrift, have important implications for some of the theoretical points at issue. This is not merely a matter of thematic content, but of the form and construction of what are presented as corresponding or opposing categories in these comparisons. The supposed Amazonian notions presented as counterparts of the modern Western notions of "nature" and "culture," and the related categories of "humanity," "spirit," "habitus," and "form," are prime examples of this problem. I shall return to these points in a moment. The existence of such significant variations within both cultural systems points to the inadequacy of a purely idealist approach that is unable to account for them. This is not the place for a critique of the representations of modern Western thought that serve as contrastive frames for perspectivist formulations of Amazonian concepts. For present purposes, it will be better to go directly to the ethnographic and theoretical basis of perspectivist propositions about Amazonian ideas.

ANIMALS ARE HUMAN?

The most radical and distinctive perspectivist claim for the uniqueness of Amazonian cosmologies and epistemological perspectives as contrasted with Western ideas (including received structuralist anthropological ideas about Amazonian cultures) is that Amazonians do not, after all, conceive of nature, as represented by animals, and culture as mutually distinct and contrastive categories, in the manner of Lévi-Straussian structuralism. Rather, animals, as the supposed embodiments of nature, subjectively identify themselves as humans and thus as cultural beings. Culture and humanity are not limited to humanity, but extend to encompass nature as well (at least animal nature: the extent to which plants and inanimate entities, so prominent in Tylor's concept of animism, are included in EVC's conception of cultural identity remains unclear). Subjectively speaking, animals are really human, albeit with different outward forms, which EVC dismisses as mere "envelopes" without significant connections to the subjective identity of the essential being within. Similarly, the material forms of activities are dissociated from their essential mental content, from the perspective of the animals that perform them. Animals thus supposedly see themselves as engaging in the same cultural activities as humans, even as the objective forms of their activities appear to humans as animalistic and uncultured. For example, jaguars, as they guzzle the blood of their victims, conceive themselves to be sipping fermented manioc beer, a typical cultural activity of some (though by no means all) human Amazonian societies.

EVC derives this challenging revision of received structuralist and modernist ideas from his reinterpretation of Amazonian myths and related ideas from a number of Amazonian peoples. The myths in question relate that, before the development of human culture in its contemporary form, humans and animals coexisted on relatively undifferentiated terms, sharing language and, on the animals' side, the prototypes of cultural implements, such as cooking fire, bows and arrows, dwelling houses, ways of hunting, collecting, and preparing food, and the spinning of cotton string. Animals and humans could assume each other's forms, converse, and even in some cases marry. Each species nevertheless had its own characteristic bodily form, essentially that which it has today, and humans were marginally cleverer than the animals (and meaner—they sometimes lied to the animals or played tricks on them). According to EVC, animals identified themselves with humans and came to think of their behavior as cultural, continuing to do so until the present day.

This last part of EVC's interpretation, however, is not supported by the actual texts of the variants of the myth with which I am familiar.[3] According to these Gê and Bororo variants, ancestral humans did not yet possess culture in the mythical era when they and the animals coexisted. Rather, as I have mentioned, it was the animals rather than the ancestral humans who initially possessed prototypes of key cultural products. Humans had to steal or otherwise acquire these before they could learn to produce them and thus create culture in the full, contemporary sense. The human development of culture and the acts that led to it disrupted the Edenic coexistence of the ancestral humans and animals, resulting in the loss by the animals of the protocultural possessions and skills they once had. Animals thus became fully differentiated from humans as completely natural beings, and humans correspondingly became fully differentiated from them as contemporary cultural humans.

EVC's interpretation of this myth (he seems to include the Gê and Bororo myths, which Lévi-Strauss [1969b] takes as the point of departure of *The raw and the cooked*, among the "Amazonian myths" to which he refers) provides much of the foundation for the theoretical edifice of perspectivism. It proceeds from the assumption that the ancestral humans of the myth, those who cohabited as equals with the animals, were identical for all relevant purposes with contemporary humans: that is, they were already cultural beings. This assumption is essential to his thesis that the animals of the mythical era, in identifying with their contemporaries, the ancestral humans, thereby identified themselves as beings with culture in the contemporary sense. EVC further interprets the myth as

---

3.   See, for example, the following myths reproduced in Wilbert (1978), listed by number and page: 57 (160), 58 (164), 59 (166), 62 (177), 63 (181), 64 (184), 65 (190), 66 (191), 90 (242), 93 (247), 94 (248), 96 (251), 99 (257), 104 (263), 105 (265), 106 (266), 107 (266), 108 (268) 109 (269), 111 (274), 112 (276), 113 (279), 114 (285).

evidence that contemporary Amerindians believe that the descendants of the animals have continued to identity as human, cultural beings down to the present.

The main features of the mythical narrative (or at least the Gê and Bororo
variants), however, contradict these assumptions. In them, both the humans and
the animals of the mythical era are described as being more like each other than
is the case of contemporary humans and animals. The myth tells how the contemporary forms of each became differentiated through a process in which the
ancestral humans transformed themselves into modern humans through their
invention of culture, while the ancestral forms of the animals became less like
humans, losing their protocultural possessions and thereby became totally natural beings like modern animals, completely lacking cultural traits. The perspectivist interpretation of the myth, in short, gets it exactly wrong, at least as far as this
set of myths is concerned. The whole point of these myths is not how animals
became and continue to be identified with humans, thus subverting the contrast
between nature and culture, but how animals and humans became fully differentiated from each other, thus giving rise to the contemporary differentiation of
nature and culture. Rather than recount how the mythical community of humans
and animals resulted in a lasting identification of the latter with the former, the
myths tell the opposite story of how the mutual differentiation of the species,
along with their respective subjective identities and perspectives, actually came
about as a corollary result of the one-sided possession of culture by humans.

The perspectivist interpretation not only misconstrues the overt message of
the Gê variants of the myth, but also rests upon other inferences that find no
support in the mythical narrative. These inferences do not logically follow and
appear to proceed from an unexamined anthropocentrism. To begin with, the
myth's account of the original state of relative undifferentiation between humans and animals does not include any explicit assertion that the animals subjectively identified themselves with humans. What the myths say is that animal
and human identities, and thus also, in perspectivist terms, their perspectives,
were relatively undifferentiated. Both possessed language and some other protocultural traits, but they both also possessed animal traits, such as devouring their
meat raw. That the ancestral animals adopted some quasi-human traits no more
implies that they thereby identified with the proto-humans than that the ancestral humans, by eating their meat raw, thereby identified themselves as animals.

The implicit anthropocentrism of the perspectivist formulation appears
more starkly in other propositions of perspectivist theory, such as those dealing with the "spirituality" of animals and their participation in social relations

with humans. EVC assumes these aspects of animal character and behavior must be the result of the animals' identification with humans, on the grounds that "spirit" and the capacity for social relations are intrinsically human attributes. Neither Amerindian cultures in general, Amazonian cultures in particular, nor the myths in question, however, offer any support for this anthropocentric assumption. On the contrary, indigenous Amazonian myths, cosmology, and ritual practice provide ample evidence for the opposite assumption, to wit, that all entities, not only animals but plants and even some inanimate objects, possess spirits in their own right. It follows that they may have the capacity, if not necessarily the propensity, to enter into social relations with humans, but this does not make them identify as humans. In this respect, the ethnographic evidence is consistent with a nonanthropocentric version of animism rather than an anthropocentric perspectivism.

THE NATURE OF CULTURE AND THE RELATION OF CULTURE TO NATURE

These critical reservations about perspectivism's self-presentation as a revolutionary transformation of orthodox structuralist and modernist conceptions of the nature–culture contrast and its claim to have identified the basic principle of Amazonian cosmologies serve to bring into sharper focus the continuities of perspectivism and structuralism in other essential respects. Perspectivism actually retains the orthodox structuralist conception of the relation of nature and culture as a privative binary opposition of mutually exclusive classificatory categories defined through the contrastive presence or absence of traits: thus, culture is defined by the possession of distinctive features like language, cooking fire, manioc beer, and so on, while nature, as the opposing category, is defined by the absence of these features. Closer attention to the ethnographic details of the myths on which both structuralist and perspectivist notions of these categories are based, however, reveals that this way of thinking misunderstands indigenous conceptions of the nature of culture as well as the domain or condition of nature. Most importantly, it misunderstands the ubiquity and role of mediations between the two, such as those constituted by the prototypes of cultural items possessed by the ancestral animals in the myths).

The myths do not represent the transition from the relatively undifferentiated coexistence of humans and animals to fully developed human culture and noncultural animality as a simple process of the loss or acquisition of traits. They emphasize the importance of the possession of the protocultural possessions of the animals (the cooking fire, bow and arrows, manioc beer, etc.) as a crucial transitional stage between the two. The essence of fully developed culture, as contrasted to the half-way house of the animals' prototypes, is described, rather, as the ability to *produce* these things, and most importantly, what this ability further implies: *the reflexive ability to produce the process of producing them as a generalized and infinitely replicable form of activity.*

What is involved here is not merely classification or even a simple cognitive or perceptual process of objectification, but a reflexive process of metaobjectification in an abstracted and generalized form, that is, the process of objectification itself. This clearly requires a different level of cognitive operations from those involved in the simple possession and use of individual objects, even ones that may constitute prototypes of cultural artifacts. This is the difference, for example, between the one-piece cooking fire possessed by the jaguars in the Gê myths of the origin of cooking fire and the specimen piece of that fire used to light other cooking fires at the climactic end of the myth (Turner 1985: 87–96). The ancestral animals in the myths possess objects like cooking fire or beer or bows and arrows, but these are represented only as singular possessions, as if they were, as far as their animal owners are concerned, self-existing or self-objectifying things or found objects that the animals appropriated but never made. The animals are nowhere described as having the cultural ability or power to produce or copy such things. When humans acquire them from the animals by whatever means, the animals simply lose them. They cannot make others to replace them, because they cannot produce production.

Culture comes fully into existence when the ancestral humans not only come into possession of these objects but become able to objectify and replicate the processes of objectification (in pragmatic terms, production) by which they are produced: how to use fire to make fire, how to ferment manioc to make manioc beer, or how to transform the surface forms of their bodies with painting or ornaments to produce or regulate in culturally standardized ways the internal bodily processes of transformation that give rise to aspects of social personhood.

The products of such a process, whether material artifacts or conceptual objects of knowledge, cannot be understood as simple, internally homogeneous classes in a semiotic order of signification or ethnoscientific taxonomy, but as complex schemas composed of heterogeneous elements and levels of features, comprising transformational steps in a process of mediating relatively natural to relatively cultural forms (for example, from the appropriation of "natural" entities, such as fire or game animals, to the use of the fire to cook the flesh of the animals, and on to the use of the fire to cook itself, that is, to make fire). The cooked meat, as a representative cultural product, can be opposed in good structuralist fashion to raw meat as an instance of the binary contrast of culture to nature, but what has made it a cultural artifact is the transformative operations condensed within it, not merely the cooking but the lighting of the cooking fire. Culture is thus not opposed to nature as a simple, mutually exclusive binary contrast of semantic features but, rather, consists of a complex, reflexive, transformative relation to it. This process both contains and overlies its basic natural components as a series of incremental levels in a hierarchy of transformational operations (schemas) of increasing generative (productive) power. Cultural things, in other words, are compounds of natural content (the meat, the physical body of the social person) and the transformative activities through which it is objectified (that is, transformed into) cultural forms. Culture, understood in these terms, neither excludes nor suppresses natural contents or qualities but, rather, retains and reproduces them through the employment of more abstract and generalized metaforms of the processes and powers that produce them.

The emphasis of my discussion of the meaning of myths on the role of the serial transformations of symbolic elements like the cooking fire may recall the critique of Lévi-Strauss' one-dimensional, synchronic conception of the signification of the semiological elements of myth offered in the introduction to this paper. An integral part of that critique was the recognition that the "fundamental structures" of culture and the mind that Lévi-Strauss hoped to reveal through the structural analysis of "groups" of myths should properly be sought at the level of the invariant principles governing the internal transformations that comprise the structures of individual myths or kinship systems. These transformations, of course, are not limited to the individual symbolic or semiotic elements of cultural constructs such as myths, but may involve more complex constructs such as tropes (Turner 1991a, 2006b) or episodes of mythical narratives (Turner 1985). In the case at hand, I suggest that the progressive transformations of the cooking fire as the central theme of the mythical allegory of the emergence of culture from nature conform to the principle that the efficacy of transformational activities (such as cooking) varies directly with the power of those activities to produce (and thus transform) themselves. Production, considered as a self-objectifying and self-transformative activity, is thus the essence of culture and its differentiation from nature.

This relatively sophisticated conception of the relation of nature and culture as a transformational process rather than a synchronic, practico-inert semiological contrast is clearly formulated in the Gê and Bororo myths, but is rendered invisible by structuralist analysis. Lévi-Strauss' (1969b) analysis in *The raw and the cooked* uses the conceptual filter of Saussurean semiotics, which blocks recognition of the cultural significance of the activities by which the objects and categories in question are produced. This is a fundamental point of disagreement between the Amazonian myths, as interpreted here, and perspectivism, given EVC's assertion that production is not a transformational process, leaving only exchange as a truly transformational activity capable of inducing the transformation of perspectives. On this critical point, EVC shows himself an orthodox structuralist, following Lévi-Strauss' (1969a) lead in *The elementary structures of kinship* and other early writings on kinship. In these writings, Lévi-Strauss uses exchange theory, grounded in the "fundamental structure" of reciprocity, as the basis of his analysis of kinship, begging the question of how to account for the existence of the exchangers (the groups of men who supposedly gave rise to human culture by exchanging women, not to mention the men and women themselves). In sum, the transformations of productive activity, which include exchange as one of their mediating moments, are, according to the myths of at least one numerous and important group of indigenous Amazonian peoples, the principle mediators of the relation of nature to culture and directly construct the pragmatic and conceptual structures of culture itself. Perspectivism's failure to theorize the role of productive transformations in cultural structures is a major lacuna in its conception of perspectives. It leads to its failure to recognize the reflexive operations of objectification and metaobjectification, which the myths represent as the distinctive properties of culture for what they are: the most powerful and important perspectives of all.

"MULTINATURALISM": DIFFERENT WORLDS OR DIFFERENT PERSPECTIVES?

Perspectivism's focus on Amazonian concepts of the self (for perspectivism this essentially means the epistemological subject rather than the agent of praxis) constitutes a salutary departure from structuralism's one-sided objectivist theoretical perspective and its disinterest in the role of subjective perspectives in the formation of cultural and semiotic representations, including cosmologies.

The one-sided subjectivism of perspectivism would seem to qualify it as a form of relativism: if different subjects see the world differently, it might be because they have different subjective points of view or different ways of seeing the world. EVC, however, rejects this view of perspectivism as relativism, on the grounds that Amazonians (and indeed, at several points in his argument, all Amerindians) think that although animals, from their identical perspectives as humans, see the world *in the same way*, they arrive at different ideas of it because *they see different worlds* (this is what he calls "multinaturalism").

To understand what is at issue here, one must start by asking what the differences are among the "worlds" that the animals supposedly see. The answer given by EVC is the animal identity of the different species of animals, as seen by animal subjects of each species, which identify themselves to themselves as humans. Every species is seen by every other as an animal but sees itself as a human (i.e., cultural) being. For every species, therefore, the boundary between nature and culture is differently drawn. Each species thus sees a different "nature" than all the others. One may ask in what way this differs from the conventional "naturalist" idea that each species of animal recognizes its own kind and sees all other species as different kinds of animal from itself. The answer is that the only difference appears to be the assumption that each animal continues to identify itself as a human and thus a citizen in good standing of the domain of culture, in contrast to all the other animals. We may note in passing that this seems to leave the form of the conceptual opposition of nature and culture intact as far as its logical structure is concerned. Only its content is treated as variable ("multiple") and this only by virtue of the psychological principle of the egocentricity of animal perspectives. The form of the worlds seen by all species remains the same.

An additional problematic consequence of EVC's idea of multinaturalism is that having committed himself to the thesis that all animals see themselves as humans, it becomes necessary for him to maintain that the visible bodies of the different species (animals can of course see their own bodies or parts of them, as well as those of other animals) have nothing to do with their inner subjective identities as humans. As he writes:

> Manifest bodily form of each species is an "envelope" (a "clothing") that conceals an internal humanoid form... this internal form is the soul or spirit of the animal: an intentionality or subjectivity formally identical to human consciousness. (Viveiros de Castro 2004: 465)

Inner subjective identities, however, are invisible to other animals (and humans). Animals of different species therefore must see one another as animals rather than as they see themselves (with their minds' eyes) as humans. But on what basis do they "see" the animal natures of these other species? The manifest form of the physical body has already been ruled out as a mere "clothing" irrelevant to essential species identity. How, then, to find a way of recognizing the significance of physical bodiliness to the perspectival animal identities of other animal species? EVC deals with this question as follows:

> Animals perceive differences among species of animals not on the basis of physiological differences—Amerindians recognize a basic uniformity of bodies—but rather [of] affects, in the old sense of dispositions or capacities that render the body of each species unique... the body is in this sense an assemblage of affects or ways of being that constitute a habitus... and the body is the origin of perspectives. (Viveiros de Castro 2004: 475)

I don't understand what EVC means by his claim that "Amerindians recognize a basic uniformity of bodies" (not so in any relevant sense, in my limited experience), nor what relevance the assertion that "*animals* do not perceive physiological differences among species" is meant to have to his claim about how "Amerindians" see the world (my italics). I do, however, have some other questions about EVC's use of the concept of habitus and its place in his complex argument for the relevance of bodily form to subjective identity, spirit, and perspective.

As a distinctive mode of affective orientation and behavioral disposition toward the world, the habitus constitutes a pragmatic form of perspective on it. In so many words, it constitutes part of an animal's differential perspective on the world and thus the "different world" it sees. In sum, the habitus must be the aspect of the *body* that is the "origin" of perspectives and, as such, conditions the specific "nature" seen by the species. This is quite apart from its putative inner subjective identity as human, which is supposedly unrelated to its bodily form, although in other connections that is the aspect of animal being that EVC claims is the basis of its perspective (indeed, the basis of "perspectivism" as a theory).

The concept of habitus is critical for EVC because it does not purport to point inward to the subjective identity of the animal, but outward to its behavior and interaction with the world. EVC defines the concept as affective rather than cognitive (in contrast to other theorists like Mauss or Bourdieu, who employed the concept to denote both cognitive and affective modes of subjective perspective) and as composed of the specifically bestial behaviors of the species. Thus, by virtue of this idiosyncratic definition, it becomes identified as the "natural" aspect of species identity in contrast to the cognitive, cultural human aspect comprising its inner subjectivity. In effect, the reformulation of the concept of habitus becomes the indispensable basis for the reimportation of the structuralist opposition of nature and culture as the frame of EVC's concept of animal identity, in a way that leaves the cultural (spiritual, human) component intact and insulated from the natural (bodily, bestial) aspect of the creature. The fundamental principle at issue here is the mutual dissociation and irrelevance of external bodily (natural, affective) form and internal spiritual (cultural, cognitive) content.

It is no doubt in order to highlight the distinctive role of habitus in this respect that EVC asserts that "Amerindians recognize a basic uniformity of bodies," which, if taken literally, would mean that they do not perceive or cognitively "recognize" bodily differences among animals, which, if true, would indeed seem to leave affective habitus as the animals' only visibly differentiable property. Apart from the question of what evidence could possibly be found for such an assertion, the attempt to restrict the meaning of habitus to affective dispositions seems untenable; as soon as a cognitive dimension is admitted, the use of the concept in EVC's argument becomes contradictory. As a specific mode of material activity, the habitus of a species must obviously take into account the physical shape, size, and capacities of the species' physical bodily form. It must thus constitute the framework not only of an integral subjective (affective and cognitive) perspective on the world for the animal in question but also of the objective identity of each species as it is perceived by other species. It therefore appears to stand in contradiction to the putative conceptual "uniformity" of their bodies as well as to the dissociation of bodily features and appearance as mere "clothing" from aspects of the character (affective disposition, typical modes of behavior, etc.), if not the inner spiritual identity of the species.

MULTINATURALISM AS "TYPE" AND "BOMB"

"Multinaturalism," as I have suggested above, rests squarely upon the foundation of the familiar structuralist contrast between a general and, at the most abstract level, unitary category of culture and an equally generic, abstractly unitary category of nature. Both categories can be, and routinely are, employed at less abstract and general levels to apply to the varieties of specific cultures and natural species, giving rise to multiculturalism and multinaturalism, respectively. These are simply analogous moves within a taxonomic hierarchy consisting of different levels of generality and more or less ample provision for differing subjective perspectives, not whole opposing philosophies, as EVC argues. In the same way, "naturalism" and "multinaturalism," which EVC represents as contradictory theoretical perspectives, the former being that of outmoded, preperspectivist modernism and the latter the perspectivist view that is now supplanting it, are more accurately if simply understood as tags for foci on different levels of the same conceptual hierarchy. "Naturalism" does not imply a denial of differences among species any more than "multinaturalism" entails a rejection of common natural (biological) animal properties shared to varying degrees by all of them. It differs from "multinaturalism" in taking seriously the positive relationships between bodily features, habitus, and the inner character and perspectives of natural creatures, but in this, I believe, it is closer to the thinking of most, if not all, Amazonian Indians than perspectivist "multinaturalism."

"Multinaturalism," in any case, does not logically supplant the nature–culture distinction shared by most varieties of modernism, including structuralism and anthropology, which EVC collectively terms "naturalism," as he claims. Rather, multinaturalism continues to presuppose it as the common form of the contrast between the habituses of all the different animal species and the human (cultural) identity that constitutes their "formal subjectivity." For EVC, as I have described in the preceding section, the psychic and bodily structure of each species constitutes a logically identical microcosm of the privative contrast between spiritual, human, cultural identity and a bodily, bestial, affective, natural perspective. Thus, the binary nature–culture opposition that had supposedly been shattered and transcended by the concept of multinaturalism returns as the formal framework of a potentially infinite number of cases, like the many little brooms that arise from the shattered broomstick in Disney's film of "The Sorcerer's Apprentice" in "Fantasia."

This metaphorical interpretation of the implications of multinaturalism for the human and natural sciences may be contrasted with EVC's claim (as reported by Bruno Latour in his deliriously enthusiastic account of the public *disputatio* between EVC and Descola held in Paris in January 2009) that perspectivism and multinaturalism constitute:

[A] bomb with the potential to explode the whole implicit philosophy so dominant in most ethnographers' interpretation of their material… [Multinaturalism is] a much more troublesome concept [than perspectivism]… Whereas hard and soft scientists alike agree on the notion that there is only one nature but many cultures, Viveiros wants to push Amazonian thought… to try to see what the whole world would look like if all its inhabitants had the same culture but many different natures. (Latour 2009: 2; cf. Descola and Viveiros de Castro 2009)

This, according to Latour, is the essence of EVC's conception of "the Amerindian struggle against Western philosophy," spearheaded by the concepts of perspectivism and multinaturalism, which he accuses Descola of trying to reduce to "just another curio in the vast cabinet of curiosities that he [Descola] is seeking to build" (Latour 2009: 2). "'Pushing' Amazonian thought" into propositions patently alien to it (Amazonian peoples are keenly aware of, and interested in, the differences among their own cultures, let alone those of the nonindigenous peoples with whom they have come into contact, and they would be the first to find the idea of a monocultural world absurd) may be a fascinating speculative exercise for nonindigenous intellectuals, but it has left anthropology far behind to take a place all its own as a "curio in the vast cabinet of curiosities" of perspectivist philosophy.

THE BODY AS THE "ORIGIN OF PERSPECTIVES": BUT WHAT BODY (-IES)?

These difficulties at least have the merit of focusing attention on the centrality of the idea of the body as the "origin of perspectives." This idea of the relation of bodiliness and perspectives actually contains several issues of critical importance to the anthropology of Amazonian cultures. The first is that of precisely what is meant by "the body": the physical body, to be sure, but there is also a social body, which is something else again. The physical body itself is a complex entity that is not at all moments of its existence an individual entity. It originates as a union between two physical bodies of opposite sexes, is born as cultureless, being more animal than human, acquires cultural personhood, then dies and is transformed into a spirit, which becomes an animal-like being again who terrifies his or her surviving relatives by seeking to kill them so they can join him or her in the spirit world (this, at any rate, is the Kayapo idea). In short, the body, even as a physical entity, is not an abstract object with a fixed, culturally human perspective, but a process comprising a series of transformations, each of which entails a transformation of perspectives, not all of which are cultural: in the Kayapo view, at least, we start and finish as animals.

As noted, however, there is also a social body. This is a polymorphous, androgynous entity, defined as a conjunction of relations among all the relevant social types of bodily identities constructed of contrastive values on shared dimensions like gender and social age, which formulate the signification of each bodily type through their contrastive relations to the other types that form part of the same system (e.g., bachelor youth, married woman, elder man and/or woman). The relationally defined identities of social bodiliness define the perspectival relations of each embodied person to other bodily identities that form part of the same system. It is this system of contrastive values as a whole, comprising every socially marked stage of bodily development of both genders, from before birth to after death, that constitutes the external relational form of the social body (Turner 1995).

There is also, however, an internal composition of the social body, made up of the bodily senses, powers, and processes that together comprise the socially relevant content of the externally related gendered and generational categories of bodily form. In some Amazonian societies, different senses, for example, are considered not only as having varying importance but also as the channels of different modes of knowledge. As Santos-Granero has noted, the Kayapo associate hearing, -*mari*, with knowing, but it is a specific kind of knowing, passive understanding as contrasted with the active knowledge of how to do things, which is more associated with sight, -*omun* (cf. Santos-Granero 2006: 72; Turner 1980, 1995). Vocalization (speech and singing), though not a sensory faculty, is associated with the system of senses and modes of knowledge, since speech is the channel of the knowledge that must be internalized through the auditory channel. Smell is not much emphasized by the Kayapo, but, as Santos-Granero reports, it is a culturally emphasized source of knowledge among the Yanesha, who, however, consider hearing the most important sense, followed by seeing, with smell in third place; C. Crocker reports that among the Bororo smell is the faculty used to perceive the presence of a class of spirits (the *bope*), the dead, and the giant water spirits who take part in mortuary and initiation rites (Santos-Granero 2006: 72, 73, 77; Crocker 1985). The point for present purposes is that, for the Kayapo and many other Amazonian peoples, these differentiated sensory modes of knowledge are also integrally identified with distinct categories and aspects of social identity that are culturally marked by specific forms of bodily adornment (ear plugs, lip plugs, body painting in different age- and gender-related styles, etc.) (Turner 1980, 1995). The same can be said for stages of physical growth, the development of sexuality and reproductive powers, and, for a man, whether or not he has acquired power by killing an enemy.

Taken together, all of these internal bodily powers, sensory forms of knowledge, and stages of growth, culturally marked by modifications of the surface of the body, collectively constitute a template or filter for the channeling, regulation, and selective suppression of internal bodily powers, energies, sensory capacities, and modes of knowledge as well as the contents of the external relational categories, identities, and perspectives that I have called the social body (Turner 1980, 1995). It is this system of external and internal articulations of the social body, as articulated by the culturally stylized decoration of the form of the body's surface (skin, coiffure, items of costume and adornment), that in indigenous Amazonian societies shapes and defines the social meaning of the physical body to its social and natural environment. It is this complex entity, composed of the physiological body as mediated by the social body, then, that is "the origin of perspectives." Rather than identify this point of origin with the physical body in opposition to the social identity and cultural subjectivity of the person, which seems to be EVC's point, I would argue the contrary, which is that the synthetic social and physical body is the origin of perspectives precisely because it *is* the formal (culturally defined) subjective identity of the person.

A second major issue has already been mentioned in passing, which is the mutable nature of perspectives considered as moments of transformational social and natural processes (as distinct from their abstract ideal character as attributes of semiotic or cultural classification). EVC appears to conceive of perspectives as fixed aspects of species identities, which are essentially like synchronic signifieds in Saussurean fields of signification abstracted from discourse, social uses, and processes. For perspectivism, the class as an ideal identity thus becomes the subject position that functions as the real "origin of perspectives" (as I have pointed out above, this does seem awkward for EVC's contention that animals' subjective identity as humans is unconnected with their bodies, which are supposedly the origin of all perspectives). There is thus for perspectivists only one, fixed perspective per species-class, or even per superclass of species (e.g., all species of animals, who collectively have the identities and thus the perspectives of humans, if only on themselves). Against this I would argue that perspectives, rooted as they are in the synthetic social and physical body, are for that reason also integrally connected with the social relations of that body to other social and physical (cultural and natural) bodies. These compound entities and relations go through developmental processes and therefore undergo regular transformations at several levels.

For individuals, there are the developmental transformations of social age and status that comprise the life cycle. In turn, these are bound up with the transformations of family relations and role identities that constitute the developmental cycles of the family and domestic group, which produce *sui generis* transformations of subjective perspectives of the members of these social units.

These transformations remain within the generic class of human social relations and perspectives as contrasted to natural (animal, plant, etc.) ones. One can thus speak of hierarchies of perspectives, comprising the overall common perspective of members of the class as they go through successive transformations of their species or class identities. I have referred to collectively standardized transformations, such as those that constitute the normative patterns of the life cycle or family cycle, but, as Rosengren (2009) and also Pedersen (2007) have emphasized, there are idiosyncratic individual identities and perspectives that also go through transformations below the level of any collective social pattern. These may coexist with the collective institutional patterns I have described or they may not, as in the cases discussed by Rosengren.

Some transformations may produce changes in the generic human or animal subjective or spirit identities of an individual. For the Kayapo, as I have noted above, the human life cycle does not end with death but continues through a transformative period of separation of the spirit from the decomposing body, after which the disembodied spirit loses its human identity and becomes "transformed into an animal," in the metaphorical language of Kayapo keening for the dead. At this point, therefore, the basic species identity itself and the human perspective that goes with it are lost, and the ghostly spirit assumes the perspective and identity of an animal. It should be emphasized that such perspectival inversions and transformations are not the result of "predation" or the "cannibal cogito," as adduced by perspectivist theory to account for ambiguous instances of the juxtaposition of contradictory aspects or elements, as Wright has pointed out in an analogous context (Wright 2009: 151–152).

FORM AND CONTENT, BODY AND "SOCIAL SKIN," SCHEMA AND SPIRIT

The third major issue associated with bodiliness is the complex matter of the relation of external bodily form to inner subjective identity, a common concern of Amazonian cosmologies and concepts of subjectivity alike. It can be argued (and has been so argued by EVC) that, for many Amazonian peoples, the physiological body is considered a mere "envelope" of the spirit or subjective consciousness: external physical form, in so many words, does not determine inner subjective content. In speaking of bodily form and its relation to subjective identity, spirit, or perspective, however, it is essential to distinguish between the form of the physical body as a property of the species and the metaform of the social body constructed by adornment and modifications such as coiffure, painting, and clothing, which together constitute what I have called a "social skin" (Turner 1980).

As a general ethnographic point, the universal practice of Amazonian cultures in altering the external form of the body through changes in adornment, painting, coiffure, dress, and scarification, which mark and help bring about transformations in the social identity and subjective perspective of persons, is inconsistent with assertions that the Amerindian peoples of Amazonia regard bodily form as modified by this "social skin" merely as an external "envelope" unrelated to the inner material and spiritual content of subjective identity and/or personhood. The critical point is that the deliberate adornment of the surface of the body is for Amazonians a means of defining and regulating the identity and social relations of the person. The significance of this practice arises from the idea that subjectivity or spirit is, to an important degree, the product of a person's social relations. More precisely, it is the product of an interaction between the inner powers and senses of the body, along with the modes of knowledge and capacities for growth and activity they make possible, and the external world of social relations and activities. The natural form of the unadorned body is a *tabula rasa* across which the interchange between the internal content of bodily powers and senses and the external social world that is mediated by the metasurface of the "social skin" takes place. In this sense, the physical body considered as surface form could be called an "envelope" that does not determine the inner character of the spirit or subject, while cultural forms of bodily decoration take over the role of imposing definite perspectival form on both the inner subjective identity and external objects of interaction of the embodied person.

ANIMISM AS A NATURAL SPIRITUAL PERSPECTIVE OF ALL ENTITIES

Many, if not all, Amazonian cosmological systems are founded on the principle that the forms of things immanently contain the agency or power to produce themselves through the transformation of their own contents. The forms of things, in other words, are actually embodied processes of formation, or the potential capacity and templates for them. They contain the agency or force that impels the content of things to assume the specific characteristics and behavioral patterns proper to their species or kind. This proposition holds, in principle, for the cosmos as a whole and all its constituent units, including humans and their social groupings, animals and plants, and spirits of the dead and nonliving beings, such as celestial bodies like the sun and moon. In practice, it applies primarily to humans and higher animals, birds, and fish, but it also holds in principle for the forms of lower animals, plants, and major celestial bodies. It is intuitively most directly applicable to beings that undergo developmental processes and thus most obviously partake of the dynamic quality of formation.

The forms of things, in this view, are the guiding patterns of purposive activity that cause their objective physical contents to take on the form in question. In this sense, they embody the spiritual force or subjective agency of the entity, that which makes it what it is. In the case of animate beings, their objective forms are thus conceived to be the products or manifestations of a subjective power of intentional action. An example of this is the Kayapo term *karon*, which is used equally to mean "image," "form," "shadow," or the spirit, soul, or ghost of a person or other entity. Although humans are thought of as the spirit-possessing beings par excellence, mammals, birds, fish, and many trees, vines and other plants are also thought to possess spirit forms and associated subjective powers.

Here we rejoin the basic notion behind the "animism" common to most, if not all, indigenous peoples of the Amazon (Bird-David 1999; Descola 1996, 2005). Animism, in other words, is grounded in the idea that spirit is essentially the guiding principle, animating force, and intentional goal of the bodily process by which it is produced. The synthesis of form (or spirit) and content (or body) that constitutes a natural entity—a living being or inanimate natural entity like celestial bodies—can only be created and maintained by the exercise of the agency or power immanent in the form in question. The spirit of the entity is the form considered as an image or pattern that needs material content to exist. It is this need that becomes the force holding the form and content of the entity together. This unity is variable in strength, unstable, and susceptible to disruption and eventual dissolution as the subject loses its energy and power. Such dissolution can be either temporary, as in illness or shock induced by extreme fright, or permanent, as in the death of the person or organism. The spiritual force or formative aspect of the entity may thus, under extreme conditions, become separated from the bodily or material content of its form, but neither spirit nor body can exist independently for long without the other. Death brings the permanent separation of spirit form from body content and thus dissolves the synthesis of form and content that is the basis of the objective existence of the organism. The fission of the synthetic unity of spirit and body results in the further decomposition and ultimate disappearance of its separated parts. The *karon* or spirit form continues to live on after the death of the body as a ghost, but gradually loses its human character, becoming an animal-like being in the forest and eventually dissolving completely. The material content (‾*in*, flesh or body) undergoes a parallel transformational process from living body to mass of dead (*tuk*, "black," "dead," or "in transformation") rotting flesh, finishing as a disarticulated jumble of white bones.

BODILINESS, SPIRIT, AND THE HUMAN DIMENSION OF ANIMISM

The Kayapo think of their own bodies as hybrid combinations of natural animal qualities of form and content, supplemented by acquired formal attributes of social identity. The former are exemplified by internal physical processes located primarily in the central trunk of the body, such as growth, digestion, sexuality, and reproduction. These natural energies and powers become transformed and directed into socially patterned activities of various kinds that are associated with transformations of bodily form, including the natural processes of growth, aging, and puberty, and the cultural modifications of the surface of the body such as painting, hair-styling, and the wearing of ornaments. These modifica-tions of surface form serve as a two-way filter that gives specific social meaning to relations between the embodied person and external beings with which he or she interacts.

"Nature," in other words, is an integral component of human social bod-ies and thus of social persons. Natural forces and aspects of being (things that exist of themselves, independently of human social activity) thus constitute es-sential components of central sites of social spacetime and "culture," as well as the peripheral natural zones of forest and savanna. The structure of human society, in sum, like human beings as individual embodied persons, incorporates fundamental "natural" forms of spacetime, agency, and powers, including those inherent in the animal content of human bodiliness and reproductivity. Human beings, moreover, undergo transformations to and from animal forms of being and identity in the course of their life and death cycles: fetuses in the womb and newborn babies are thought of as animal-like beings with special affinities and vulnerabilities to influences from animals and ghosts. The latter are likewise considered to lose their identities as humans and to end their existence as animal forms (they are addressed as having transformed themselves into animals in mortuary chanting and keening). Human culture is thus conceived more as an incremental transformation of these natural elements, a "super-nature," as it were, than as a qualitatively distinct order of existence contrasted to "nature" in a mutually exclusive binary contrast with an excluded middle. The essence of this cultural increment is the application of natural transformational processes (such as fire) to themselves (as in the use of fire to make fire), thus generalizing and replicating what in nature remain relatively isolated processes.

As beings with specific forms and spirit identities shared with the other members of their species, humans and animals are similarly occupied with the form-giving, spirit-directed processes of growing, aging, and dying, producing and reproducing, and objectifying and deobjectifying themselves. The generic forms and contents of these processes consist of functional activities (i.e., hunting, foraging, eating, drinking, finding shelter, mating, and reproducing), which are essentially identical for all embodied spirit beings regardless of the particular differences in their forms and contents. Beings of different species can thus identify their concretely different activities on the basis of their functional equivalence from the perspective of their common engagement in sustaining their bodies and spirit forms. Plants also engage in analogous processes, but, in many Amazonian cases, they are not conceived to do so as individual organisms but, rather, as instances of collective entities, which embody the spirit of their species.

An anteater lunching on an ant hill and a human lunching on a sandwich can thus regard themselves as engaged in the same functional activity, lunching. The human might express this sense of equivalence metaphorically by saying that the anteater is eating his sandwich, and the anteater might express the same perception by thinking of the human as licking up his ants. In terms of their shared perspective as form-guided, content-sustaining entities, there is no basis for privileging the human's over the anteater's way of expressing the functional identity of their activities.

In a similar vein, the Kayapo think of other species as having their own forms of such human artifacts or activities as houses, songs, and ceremonies, and even, for some purposes (such as shamanic communication), language, although they clearly recognize that the actual forms taken by these activities are very different from their human equivalents. The belief in a generic identity of spirit and the consequent equivalence of functionally identical activities does not imply that either humans or animals make no distinctions between the specific differences in the forms of animal and human spirits or activities, or that they imagine that animals identify themselves as humans "under the skin." It does mean, however, that all living beings and some nonliving ones are engaged in processes of forming, sustaining, and eventually losing their synthetic unities of form and content. The intentional orientation, form of consciousness, and energetic force that drive these processes constitute what we, like the indigenous peoples of Amazonia, call their spirits.

CONCLUSIONS

Structuralism as a theoretical and ethnographic quest has passed through successive stages of construction, expansion, and dissolution. Like its subject matter, the myths, kinship systems, bodies, and persons of the indigenous societies of the Amazon and, more broadly, the Americas, it can be seen to have developed through a series of transformations, each affording distinct perspectives but all constrained to remain within the invariant limitations of its own theoretical shortcomings. Chief among these was its failure to grasp the proper application of its eponymous concept, structure, to its own research data and thus to realize its potential as an anthropological project. Its failures, however, have been instructive. Like a giant star that has burned up its internal sources of energy, in its terminal implosion it has been sending out dazzling flares rich with material for new planetary systems. These new systems, the dissident successor movements it has inspired, above all, perspectivism and the new work on animism, have raised new issues of importance to the field and stimulated fresh discussion, of which the present paper is but one of many examples.

At the beginning of the paper, I suggested that the basic problem of structuralism was that it started with the right idea but applied it to the wrong level of the data. My critiques of perspectivism and, to a lesser extent, animism have taken the form of suggestions of how the original structuralist notion of structure (the group of transformations constrained by invariant principles of conservation) could be applied to the data in question in a way that would strengthen the theoretical formulations of perspectivism and animism. For example, in the case of the body and its avatar, the subject, I argued that the perspectivist notion of the body as the origin of perspectives, where both the body and its associated perspective are conceived as singular, unchanging entities, should be substituted by a conception of both bodies and perspectives understood as sequences of multiple transformations (thus potentially constituting groups of transformations bounded by one or more principles of conservation, as called for in the structuralist model). I further suggested, as a qualification of different aspects of both perspectivist and animist ideas, that the perspectives and bodily conditions of humans transform themselves from "natural" (the condition of embryos and infants) to "cultural" and ultimately back to "natural" with the onset of the dissolution of human form in aging, death, and postmortem ghostly existence. Extending my dialogue with animism, I urged that conceiving the body in appropriate structuralist terms as such to be a series of transformations opens a perspective on bodiliness as a process of interaction of the physical body, social body, and person, stimulated and guided by relations with other embodied actors filtered and regulated by formal treatments of their bodily surfaces ("social skins"). This process of producing subjective perspective and objectified bodily form, drawing upon the natural bodily content of senses and powers, goes through a series of stages, but it ultimately enters a terminal stage of deobjectification as the natural content of bodily powers weakens to the point where it cannot sustain its integration within the frame of personal identity and social form. The dissolution of form and content continues through the physical dissolution of death and the separate disintegration of spirit and body.

For the Kayapo and other indigenous Amazonian peoples with whom I am somewhat familiar, this dialectical process of production and dissolution, objectification and deobjectification, and embodiment and ultimate disembodiment of subjective intention and identity, manifested and articulated through the integration and disintegration of form and content, is the essence of the material and spiritual existence of the animate and inanimate beings that constitute their life world. It is in no way unique to cultural humans but is, rather, common to all natural entities. It can be understood as a broadly "animist" perspective, but this view gives no justification for the anthropocentric bias of some animist discussions of "spirit" as an essentially human attribute. This is also an important point for perspectivism: the mere possession of a spirit or subjectivity does not in and of itself indicate that an animal or plant therefore identifies itself as human (as it would if spirit and subjectivity were intrinsically human qualities). It is true that some, though certainly not all, Amazonian cultures consider at least some animals to identify themselves subjectively as humans in some respects, but this should not be understood as following necessarily from their possession of their own spirits. There are many cases of beliefs that animals and plants (or their collective species spirits, the "masters" of the game or plant species, etc.) possess spirits that owe nothing to human contacts or culture.

I have argued that closer attention to the detailed structure of indigenous conceptions, both of natural beings and human embodied persons, is essential to avoid the distortions inherent in attempts to treat all Amazonian (or even all Amerindian) cultures as a single, homogeneous philosophical system. Dismissing the importance of divergent or even contradictory formulations of the same points on the part of societies of different types precludes the most useful anthropological method for understanding the social and cultural basis for such agreements as do exist. The critique of structuralist, animist, and perspectivist theories I have offered in this paper has served as the context for reformulating the concept of structure as a series or group of transformations internal to the developmental process of entities, ranging from individual symbols or tropes to bodies and spiritual identities. I have attempted to show that this way of conceiving structure can serve to integrate Marxian concepts of productive praxis as well as interpretationist and semiotic approaches with the valuable contributions of Lévi-Straussian structuralism and its more recent epigones. Most importantly, I have sought to suggest how the hybrid, post-poststructuralist theoretical amalgam I have outlined may contribute to understanding some of the features of Amazonian cultures that have been brought to light through the ethnographic and theoretical work so powerfully stimulated by the debates of late structuralism.

Bibliography

Althusser, Louis. 1971. "Lenin and philosophy." In *Lenin and philosophy and other* essays, translated by Ben Brewster, 23–70. Paris and London: Monthly Review Press.

Banner, Horace. 1957. "Mitos dos índios Kayapó. *Revista de Antropologia* (São Paulo) n.s. 5: 37–66.

Bateson, Gregory. 1972. *Steps to an ecology of mind: Collected essays in anthropology, psychiatry, evolution, and epistemology*. San Francisco: Chandler.

Bird-David, Nurit. 1999. "'Animism' revisited: Personhood, environment, and relational epistemology." Special issue: "Culture—A second chance?" *Current Anthropology* 40 (S1): S67–S91. http://www.jstor.org/stable/10.1086/200061

Crocker, Jon Christopher. 1985. *Vital Souls: Bororo cosmology, natural symbolism, and shamanism*. Tucson: University of Arizona Press.

Cowell, Adrian. 1961. *The heart of the forest*. London: Headway.

Derrida, Jacques. 1976 [1967]. *Of grammatology*. Translated by Gayatri Chakravorty Spivak. Baltimore: Johns Hopkins University Press.

Descola, Philippe. 1994 [1986]. *In the society of nature: A native ecology in Amazonia*. Translated by Nora Scott. Cambridge: Cambridge University Press.

———. 1996. "Constructing natures: Symbolic ecology and social practice." In *Nature and society: Anthropological perspectives*, edited by Philippe Descola and Gísli Pálsson, 82–102. London, New York: Routledge.

———. 2013 [2005]. *Beyond nature and culture*. Translated by Janet Lloyd. Chicago: University of Chicago Press.

Descola, Philippe, and Eduardo Viveiros de Castro. 2009. "Perspectivism and animism: Debate between Philippe Descola (Collége de France) and Eduardo Viveiros de Castro (Museu National de Rio de Janeiro)," January 30, 2009. Paris: Maison Suger, Institute of Advanced Studies.

Douglas, Mary. 1966. *Purity and danger: An analysis of concepts of pollution and taboo.* New York, Praeger.

Geertz, Clifford. 1973. "Religion as a cultural system." in *The interpretation of culture*, 87–125. New York: Basic Books.

Hugh-Jones, Stephen. 1996. "Shamans, prophets, priests and pastors." In *Shamanism, history and the state*, edited by Nicholas Thomas and Caroline Humphrey, 32–75. Ann Arbor: University of Michigan Press.

Jakobson, Roman, and Morris Halle. 1971. *Fundamentals of Language*, second rev. ed. The Hague: Mouton.

Kearney, Michael. 1984. *World view*. Novato, CA: Chandler & Sharp.

Latour, Bruno. 2009. "Perspectivism: 'Type' or 'bomb'?" *Anthropology Today* 25 (2): 1–2. doi: 10.1111/j.1467-8322.2009.00652.x

Lea, Vanessa. 1992. "Mebengokre (Kayapo) onomastics: A facet of houses as total social facts in central Brazil." *Man* (n.s.) 27 (1): 129–153. http://www.jstor.org/stable/2803598

Lévi-Strauss, Claude. 1955. "Les Mathematiques de l'Homme." *Bulletin International des Sciences Sociales* 4 (4): 643–653.

———. 1963 [1958]. *Structural anthropology.* Translated by Claire Jacobson and Brooke Grundfest Schoepf. New York: Basic Books.

———. 1966a [1965]. "The culinary triangle." Translated by Peter Brooks. *Partisan Review* 33 (4): 586–596. http://www.bu.edu/partisanreview/books/PR1966V33N4/HTML/files/assets/basic-html/index.html#586

———. 1966 [1962]. *The savage mind.* Translated by George Weidenfeld and Nicolson Ltd. Chicago: University of Chicago Press.

———. 1969a [1949]. *The elementary structures of kinship.* Edited by Rodney Needham, translated by James Harle Bell, John Richard von Sturmer, and Rodney Needham. Boston: Beacon Press.

———. 1969b [1964]. *The raw and the cooked: Mythologiques*, vol. 1. Translated by John and Doreen Weightman. New York: Harper Row.

———. 1973 [1966]. *From honey to ashes: Mythologiques*, vol. 2. Translated by John and Doreen Weightman. New York: Harper Row

———. 1979 [1968]. *The origin of table manners: Mythologiques*, vol. 3. Translated by John and Doreen Weightman. New York: Harper Row.

———. 1981 [1971]. *The naked man: Mythologiques*, vol. 4. Translated by John and Doreen Weightman. New York: Harper Row.

Makarius, Raoul, and Laura Lévi-Makarius. 1968. "Des jaguars et des hommes." In *L'Homme et la Societé* 7: 215–236.

Metreaux, Alfred. 1967. *Religions et magies indiennes d'Amérique du Sud*. Edited by Simone Dreyfus. Paris: Gallimard.

Neisser, Ulrich. 1976. *Cognition and reality*. San Francisco: Freeman.

Nimuendajú, Curt. "Myth of the origin of fire among the Kayapó." Unpublished manuscript.

Pedersen, Morten Axel. 2007. "Multiplicity without myth: Theorizing Darhad perspectivism." *Inner Asia* 9: 311–328. doi: 10.1163/146481707793646485

Piaget, Jean. 1932 [1923]. *The language and thought of the child*, second ed. Translated by Marjorie Gabain and Ruth Gabain. London: Routledge & Kegan Paul.

———. 1970a [1968]. *Structuralism*. Translated and edited by Chaninah Maschler. New York: Basic Books.

———. 1970b [1970]. *Genetic epistemology*. Translated by Eleanor Buckworth. New York & London: Columbia University Press.

Rosengren, Dan. 2009. "Matsigenka corporeality, a nonbiological reality: On notions of consciousness and the constitution of identity." *Tipití: Journal of the Society for the Anthropology of Lowland South America* 4 (1–2): 81–102. http://digitalcommons.trinity.edu/tipiti/vol4/iss1/5/

Santos-Granero, Fernando. 2009. "Sensual vitalities: Noncorporeal modes of sensing and knowing in native Amazonia." *Tipití: Journal of the Society for the Anthropology of Lowland South America* 4 (1–2): 57–80. http://digitalcommons.trinity.edu/tipiti/vol4/iss1/4/

Turner, Terence S. 1965. "Social structure and political organization among the northern Kayapo." Doctoral dissertation, Harvard University.

———. 1969. "Oedipus: Time and structure in narrative form." In *Forms of Symbolic Action*, edited by Robert F. Spencer, 26–68. Seattle: University of Washington Press.

———. 1977. "Transformation, transcendence, and hierarchy: A reformulation of Van Gennep's model of the structure of rites de passage." In *Secular Ritual*, edited by Sally Falk Moore and Barbara G. Myerhoff, 53–70. Assen, Amsterdam: Van Gorcum.

————. 1979a. "The Ge and Bororo societies as dialectical systems: A general model." In *Dialectical societies*, edited by David Maybury-Lewis, 147–178. Cambridge, MA: Harvard University Press.

————. 1979b. Kinship, household and community structure among the northern Kayapo. In *Dialectical societies* edited by David Maybury-Lewis, 179–217. Cambridge, MA: Harvard University Press.

————. 1980. The social skin. In *Not work alone: A cross-cultural view of activities superfluous to survival*, edited by Jeremy Cherfas and Roger Lewin, 111–140. London: Temple Smith. Reprinted 2012 in *HAU Journal of Ethnographic Theory* 2 (2): 1–19. doi: http://dx.doi.org/10.14318/hau2.2.026

————. 1985. "Animal symbolism, totemism, and the structure of myth." In *Natural Mythologies: Animal symbols and metaphors in South America*, edited by Gary Urton, 49–106. Salt Lake City: University of Utah Press.

————. 1990. "On structure and entropy: Theoretical pastiche and the contradictions of 'structuralism.'" *Current Anthropology* 31 (5): 563–568. https://doi.org/10.1086/203902

————. 1991a. "We are parrots, twins are birds: Play of tropes as operational structure." *Beyond metaphor: The theory of tropes in anthropology*, edited by James Fernandez, 121–158. Stanford: Stanford University Press.

————. 1991b. "Representing, resisting, rethinking: Historical transformations of Kayapo culture and anthropological consciousness." In *Colonial situations: Essays on the contextualization of ethnographic knowledge*, edited by George W. Stocking, Jr., 285–313. Madison: University of Wisconsin Press.

————. 1992. "Defiant images: The Kayapo appropriation of video." *Anthropology Today* 8 (6): 5–16. http://www.jstor.org/stable/2783265

————. 1994. "Bodies and antibodies: Flesh and fetish in contemporary social theory." In *Embodiment and experience: The existential ground of culture and self*, edited by Thomas Csordas, 27–47. Cambridge: Cambridge University Press.

————. 1995. "Social body and embodied subject: The production of bodies, actors and society among the Kayapo." *Cultural Anthropology* 10 (2): 143–170. doi: 10.1525/can.1995.10.2.02a00010

————. 1997a. "Social complexity and recursive hierarchy in indigenous South American societies." In "Structure, knowledge, and representation in the Andes: Studies presented to R. T. Zuidema on the occasion of his seventieth birthday." *Journal of the Steward Anthropological Society* 24 (1–2): 37–60.

———. 2002. "The sacred as alienated social consciousness: Ritual and cosmology among the Kayapo." In *Indigenous religions and cultures of Central and South America*, edited by Lawrence Sullivan, 278–298. New York: Continuum.

———. 2003. "The beautiful and the common: Gender and social hierarchy among the Kayapo." *Tipiti: Journal of the Society for the Anthropology of Lowland South America* 1 (1): 11–26.

———. 2006a. "Selected bibliography of Terence S. Turner." Special Issue: "For a Critique of Pure Culture: In Honour of Terry Turner." *Critique of Anthropology* 26 (1): 131–134. doi: https://doi.org/10.1177/0308275X06062498

———. 2006b. "Tropos, marcos de referencia y poderes." *Antropologia Social* (Madrid) 15: 305–315. https://revistas.ucm.es/index.php/RASO/article/viewFile/RASO0606110305A/9292

———. 2009a. "Valuables, value and commodities among the Kayapo of central Brazil." In *The occult life of things: Native Amazonian theories of materiality and personhood*, edited by Fernando Santos-Granero 152–169. Tucson: University of Arizona Press.

———. 2009b. "The crisis of late structuralism. Perspectivism and animism: Rethinking culture, nature, spirit, and bodiliness." *Tipiti: Journal of the Society for the Anthropology of Lowland South America* 7 (1): 1–41. http://digitalcommons.trinity.edu/tipiti/vol7/iss1/1

———. 2012. "Schemas of kinship relations and the construction of social categories among the Mebêngôkrê Kayapó." In *Crow-Omaha: New light on a classic problem of kinship analysis*, edited by Thomas R. Trautmann and Peter M. Whiteley, 223–239. Tucson: University of Arizona.

———. 2017. "Beauty and the beast: The fearful symmetry of the jaguar and other natural beings in Kayapo ritual and myth." *HAU: Journal of Ethnographic Theory* 7 (2): 51-70. https://doi.org/10.14318/hau7.2.008

Viveiros de Castro, Eduardo B. 1996. "Images of nature and society in Amazonian ethnology." *Annual Review of Anthropology* 25: 179–200. https://doi.org/10.1146/annurev.anthro.25.1.179

———. 1998. "Cosmological deixis and Amerindian perspectivism." *Journal of the Royal Anthropological Institute* (n.s.) 4 (3): 469–488. http://www.jstor.org/stable/3034157

————. 2004. "Exchanging perspectives: The transformation of objects into subjects in Amerindian ontologies." *Common Knowledge* 10 (3): 463–464. doi: 10.1215/0961754X-10-3-463

————. 2005. "Perspectivism and multinaturalism in indigenous America." In *The land within: Indigenous territory and the perception of environment*, edited by Alexandre Surrallés and Pedro García Hierro, 36–73. Copenhagen: International Work Group for Indigenous Affairs (IWGIA).

————. 2011. *The inconstancy of the Indian soul: The encounter of Catholics and cannibals in 16th-century Brazil.* Translated by Gregory Duff Morton. Chicago: Prickly Paradigm Press.

Wilbert, Johannes, ed. 1978. *Folk literature of the Gê Indians*, vol. 1. UCLA Latin American Studies Publications 44. Los Angeles: University of California Press.

Wilbert, Johannes, and Karin Simoneau, eds. 1984. *Folk literature of the Gê Indians*, vol. 2. UCLA Latin American Studies Publications 58. Los Angeles: UCLA Latin American Studies Center Publications.

Wright, Robin. 2009. "The fruit of knowledge and the bodies of the gods: Religious meanings of plants among the Baniwa." *Journal for the Study of Religion, Nature and Culture* 3 (1): 126–153. doi: 10.1558/jsrnc.v3i1.126

Index

HAU Books is committed to publishing the most distinguished texts in classic and advanced anthropological theory. The titles aim to situate ethnography as the prime heuristic of anthropology, and return it to the forefront of conceptual developments in the discipline. HAU Books is sponsored by some of the world's most distinguished anthropology departments and research institutions, and releases its titles in both print editions and open-access formats.

www.haubooks.com